Cambridge Lower Secondary
Computing

LEARNER'S BOOK 8

Victoria Ellis & Sarah Lawrey

CAMBRIDGE
UNIVERSITY PRESS

Shaftesbury Road, Cambridge CB2 8EA, United Kingdom

One Liberty Plaza, 20th Floor, New York, NY 10006, USA

477 Williamstown Road, Port Melbourne, VIC 3207, Australia

314–321, 3rd Floor, Plot 3, Splendor Forum, Jasola District Centre, New Delhi – 110025, India

103 Penang Road, #05–06/07, Visioncrest Commercial, Singapore 238467

Cambridge University Press is part of the University of Cambridge.

It furthers the University's mission by disseminating knowledge in the pursuit of education, learning and research at the highest international levels of excellence.

www.cambridge.org
Information on this title: www.cambridge.org/9781009309295

© Cambridge University Press & Assessment 2023

This publication is in copyright. Subject to statutory exception and to the provisions of relevant collective licensing agreements, no reproduction of any part may take place without the written permission of Cambridge University Press.

20 19 18 17 16 15 14 13 12 11 10 9

Printed in Poland by Opolgraf

A catalogue record for this publication is available from the British Library

ISBN 978-1-009-30929-5 Paperback with Digital Access (1 Year)
ISBN 978-1-009-32067-3 Digital Learner's Book (1 Year)
ISBN 978-1-009-32058-0 eBook

Additional resources for this publication at www.cambridge.org/go

Cambridge University Press has no responsibility for the persistence or accuracy of URLs for external or third-party internet websites referred to in this publication, and does not guarantee that any content on such websites is, or will remain, accurate or appropriate. Information regarding prices, travel timetables, and other factual information given in this work is correct at the time of first printing but Cambridge University Press does not guarantee the accuracy of such information thereafter.

....

NOTICE TO TEACHERS IN THE UK
It is illegal to reproduce any part of this work in material form (including photocopying and electronic storage) except under the following circumstances:
(i) where you are abiding by a licence granted to your school or institution by the Copyright Licensing Agency;
(ii) where no such licence exists, or where you wish to exceed the terms of a licence, and you have gained the written permission of Cambridge University Press;
(iii) where you are allowed to reproduce without permission under the provisions of Chapter 3 of the Copyright, Designs and Patents Act 1988, which covers, for example, the reproduction of short passages within certain types of educational anthology and reproduction for the purposes of setting examination questions.
....

Endorsement statement

Endorsement indicates that a resource has passed Cambridge International's rigorous quality-assurance process and is suitable to support the delivery of a Cambridge International curriculum framework. However, endorsed resources are not the only suitable materials available to support teaching and learning, and are not essential to be used to achieve the qualification. Resource lists found on the Cambridge International website will include this resource and other endorsed resources.

Any example answers to questions taken from past question papers, practice questions, accompanying marks and mark schemes included in this resource have been written by the authors and are for guidance only. They do not replicate examination papers. In examinations the way marks are awarded may be different. Any references to assessment and/or assessment preparation are the publisher's interpretation of the curriculum framework requirements. Examiners will not use endorsed resources as a source of material for any assessment set by Cambridge International.

While the publishers have made every attempt to ensure that advice on the qualification and its assessment is accurate, the official curriculum framework, specimen assessment materials and any associated assessment guidance materials produced by the awarding body are the only authoritative source of information and should always be referred to for definitive guidance. Cambridge International recommends that teachers consider using a range of teaching and learning resources based on their own professional judgement of their students' needs.

Cambridge International has not paid for the production of this resource, nor does Cambridge International receive any royalties from its sale. For more information about the endorsement process, please visit www.cambridgeinternational.org/endorsed-resources

Cambridge International copyright material in this publication is reproduced under licence and remains the intellectual property of Cambridge Assessment International Education.

Third-party websites and resources referred to in this publication have not been endorsed by Cambridge Assessment International Education.

> Introduction

Welcome to Stage 8 of Cambridge Lower Secondary Computing!

Computers and technology play an important role in our lives and our futures. Technology is all around us, and learning about it will help you to understand the world you live in.

In this book, you will:

- develop your text-based programming skills, using rules and test data
- build on your computational thinking skills, testing and improving algorithms, and using pseudocode
- evaluate data and ways we store data
- learn all about how we can keep data safe and secure
- discover how augmented reality is used in all parts of life
- find out how machines can learn
- and much more!

Throughout this book, you will have lots of opportunities to work with a partner or a group. Sharing your ideas with other people helps you to learn more about how people use computers and technology. You can always learn new skills from working with others – just like a computer scientist!

Some of the activities will be done away from a computer. These activities will develop your computing knowledge, and activities on the computer will develop your computing skills. You will have lots of opportunities to develop your programming skills using physical objects like boxes and paper, which will help you to understand ideas and concepts. There is also a project for you to complete at the end of each unit. These give you the chance to be creative and will help you to develop your understanding.

We hope that you enjoy learning more about computers and the world around you.

Victoria Ellis and Sarah Lawrey

Contents

Page	Unit
6–8	How to use this book
9–196	1 Computational thinking and programming 1.1 Pseudocode 1.2 Selection in pseudocode 1.3 Searching algorithms 1.4 Conditional statements in text-based programming 1.5 Data in text-based programs 1.6 Library programs 1.7 Software development 1.8 Physical computing
197–229	2 Managing data 2.1 Modelling 2.2 Data and databases
230–254	3 Networks and digital communication 3.1 Types of network 3.2 Data transmission and security
255–299	4 Computer systems 4.1 Computer architectures 4.2 Types of software 4.3 Data representation 4.4 Logic gates and truth tables 4.5 Augmented reality and AI
300–305	Glossary
306	Acknowledgements

Note for teachers: Throughout the resource there is a symbol to indicate where additional digital only content is required. This content can be accessed through the Digital Learner's Book on Cambridge GO. It can be launched either from the Media tab or directly from the page.

The symbol that denotes additional digital content is:

Source files can also be downloaded from the Source files tab on Cambridge GO. In addition, this tab contains a teacher guidance document which supports the delivery of digital activities and programming tasks in this Learner's Book.

How to use this book

This book contains lots of different features that will help your learning. These are explained below.

This list sets out what you will learn in each topic. You can use these points to identify the important topics for the lesson.

> **In this topic you will:**
> - understand that pseudocode is used when designing programs
> - understand the rules that are, and are not, associated with pseudocode
> - understand the purpose of pseudocode
> - read and follow algorithms that use pseudocode.

This contains questions or activities to help find out what you know already about this topic.

> **Getting started**
>
> **What do you already know?**
> - You know that the circuits in a computer contain lots of logic gates. A logic gate is a tiny piece of hardware that uses Boolean operators to control the flow of electricity in a computer.
> - You understand the role of the NOT, AND and OR logic gates. You also know the symbol for each of these logic gates.

Important words are highlighted in the text when they first appear in the book. You will find an explanation of the meaning of these words in the text. You will also find definitions of all these words in the Glossary at the back of this book.

> **Key words**
> field
> format
> null
> primary key
> purpose
> record
> validation
> wizard

You will have the opportunity to practise and develop the new skills and knowledge that you learn in each topic. Activities will involve answering questions or completing tasks by using a computer. Some activities don't require a computer. These are called unplugged activities, and they help you to understand important ideas about computing.

> **Unplugged activity 1.2**
>
> **You will need:** a pen and paper, scissors
>
> Take a look at this pseudocode algorithm.
>
> ```
> value1 ← 10
> value2 ← value1 + 2
> value1 ← 100
> value1 ← value1 - value2
> value3 ← value1 * 2
> value4 ← value3 / 4
> ```
>
> There are four variables in the program. Divide some paper into four separate pieces, either by cutting it into four pieces

6

How to use this book

Activity 3.2

You will need: a desktop computer, laptop or tablet with software to create a diagram or flowchart

Create a diagram or a flowchart to show how an echo check looks for errors in data after it has been transmitted.

Self-assessment

Compare your diagram to the list of steps for an echo check here in the book. Have you included all the steps? Does your diagram clearly show how an echo check works? What have you done to make sure it is easy for another person to follow your diagram?

Self-assessment questions help you think about your work and how you learn.

Programming task 1.2: Investigate

You will need: a pen and paper

Read the following algorithm and identify its purpose.

```
INPUT total
INPUT cost1
total ← total + cost1
INPUT cost2
total ← total + cost2
INPUT cost3
total ← total + cost3
```

These tasks help you to practise what you have learnt in a topic.
Programming tasks are in Unit 1

Peer assessment

Work with a partner and compare your outputs. Were they the same? If they were different, work through the algorithm together to identify which is the correct answer and where the error was made.

Peer assessment questions help you to evaluate the work of your peers.

Practical task 2.5

You will need: a desktop computer, laptop or tablet with access to Source file 2.2_book_reviews.accdb

You are going to set two more validation rules for the database. These are a length check and a range check. You need to be in 'Design View' again to do this.

Descriptions of length check and range check validation rules are in Table 2.2.

Length check

A person is not likely to have a name that is more than 25 characters long. This means that a sensible length check to put for the name fields would be 25.

Actually, database software automatically gives each field a length check. This is 255 characters. You can find this by looking for the field in the lower table labelled 'Field Size'. You will see that each one is set to 255.

Practical tasks are in Unit 2

When you see this icon, you are going to do a digital activity using a Source file or website link. This content can be found on Cambridge GO. Your teacher will help you to get started.

How to use this book

These questions help you to practise what you have just learnt.

Questions 1.9
1. What does decomposition mean?
2. How do you decompose a problem?
3. Why do we decompose problems?
4. Why do we decompose programs?

Important safety tips to remember when using a computer and going online.

Stay safe!
Make sure you check that web pages you visit are from a trusted source. If you do not know whether the source is safe, ask your teacher for help.

These tell you interesting facts connected to the topic.

Did you know?
At the time this book was written, there were over 137 000 Python libraries that people could import into their programs.

This contains questions that ask you to look back at what you have covered and encourages you to think about your learning.

How did you approach each programming task? For example, how did you design your solution? Would you approach it differently next time? How?

This list summarises the important material that you have learnt in the topic.

Summary checklist
- ☐ I can describe what a constant is in a program and explain why constants are used.
- ☐ I can write a program that uses a constant.
- ☐ I can describe the Boolean data type.
- ☐ I can identify data that should be stored as a Boolean data type.
- ☐ I can create a program that uses a Boolean data type.

These questions look back at some of the content you learnt in each unit. If you can answer these, you are ready to move on to the next unit.

Check your progress
1. Give one similarity between RAM and ROM. [1]
2. Give one difference between RAM and ROM. [1]
3. Describe the main role of an operating system. [1]
4. Give three tasks that an operating system does. [3]
5. a. State what a character set is. [1]
   b. Give an example of a character set. [1]

At the end of each unit, there is a project that you might carry out by yourself or with other learners. This will involve using some of the knowledge that you developed during the unit. Your project might involve creating or producing something, or you might solve a problem.

Project: Technology work placement

There is an online company that creates lots of courses about technology and computer science. They produce lots of learning resources to teach students. Zara has a work experience placement with this online company. Zara wants to make sure the resources are fun for learners, so she has decided to ask the users what they would like.

Zara has been asked to produce three resources for the website, and she has asked you to help. Based on the results of her user questionnaire, Zara would like to produce the following things.

Task 1 Infographic about RAM and ROM
Zara would like an infographic that will help learners understand the differences between RAM and ROM in

1 > Computational thinking and programming

> 1.1 Pseudocode

In this topic you will:

- understand that pseudocode is used when designing programs
- understand the rules that are, and are not, associated with pseudocode
- understand the purpose of pseudocode
- read and follow algorithms that use pseudocode.

Key words

arithmetic operator

assignment

concatenation

construct

high-level programming language

identifier

input

language independent

output

pseudocode

string

syntax

variable

variable declarations

Getting started

What do you already know?

- Algorithms are a series of steps that are followed to solve a problem.
- Algorithms can be represented in lots of ways.
- One way the steps of an algorithm can be represented is in a flowchart. You should already have followed and created flowcharts to design an algorithm. A flowchart uses different shaped boxes for different code and connects these boxes using data flows (arrows). Box shapes include those shown in Figure 1.1.

1 Computational thinking and programming

Continued

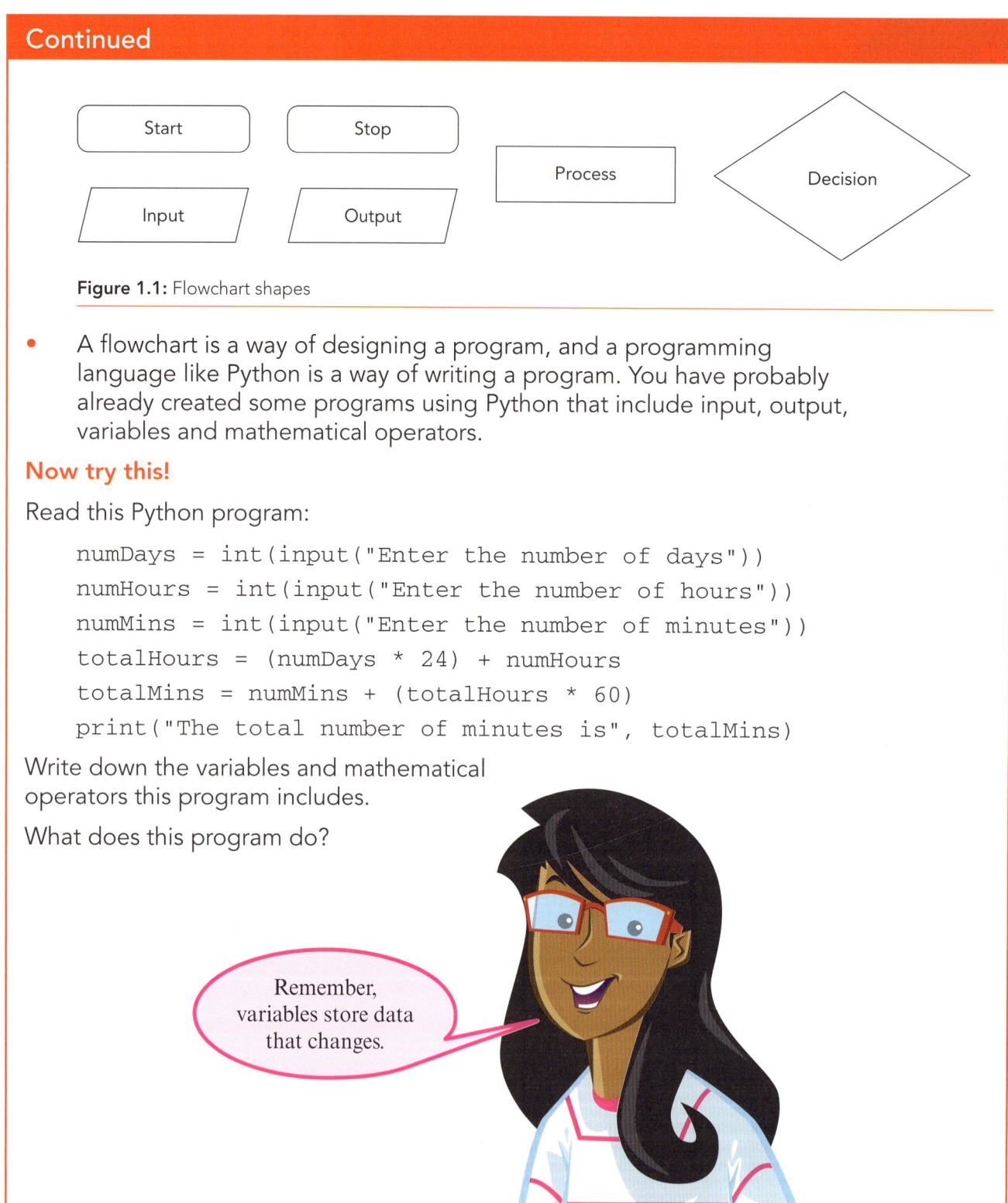

Figure 1.1: Flowchart shapes

- A flowchart is a way of designing a program, and a programming language like Python is a way of writing a program. You have probably already created some programs using Python that include input, output, variables and mathematical operators.

Now try this!

Read this Python program:

```
numDays = int(input("Enter the number of days"))
numHours = int(input("Enter the number of hours"))
numMins = int(input("Enter the number of minutes"))
totalHours = (numDays * 24) + numHours
totalMins = numMins + (totalHours * 60)
print("The total number of minutes is", totalMins)
```

Write down the variables and mathematical operators this program includes.

What does this program do?

> Remember, variables store data that changes.

1.1 Pseudocode

What is pseudocode?

Pseudocode is a tool that is used when designing programs.

Pseudocode is made up of two words: 'pseudo' and 'code'. Pseudo means 'not real', or 'not genuine'. Code is the programming statements you use when you write computer code. Pseudocode means 'not real program statements'. It might sound a bit odd that you need to learn something that is not real!

Figure 1.2 shows how pseudocode is halfway between a flowchart design, or a series of steps written in everyday English, and a **high-level programming language** program code. A high-level programming language is a programming language such as Python that helps human programmers communicate easily with computers.

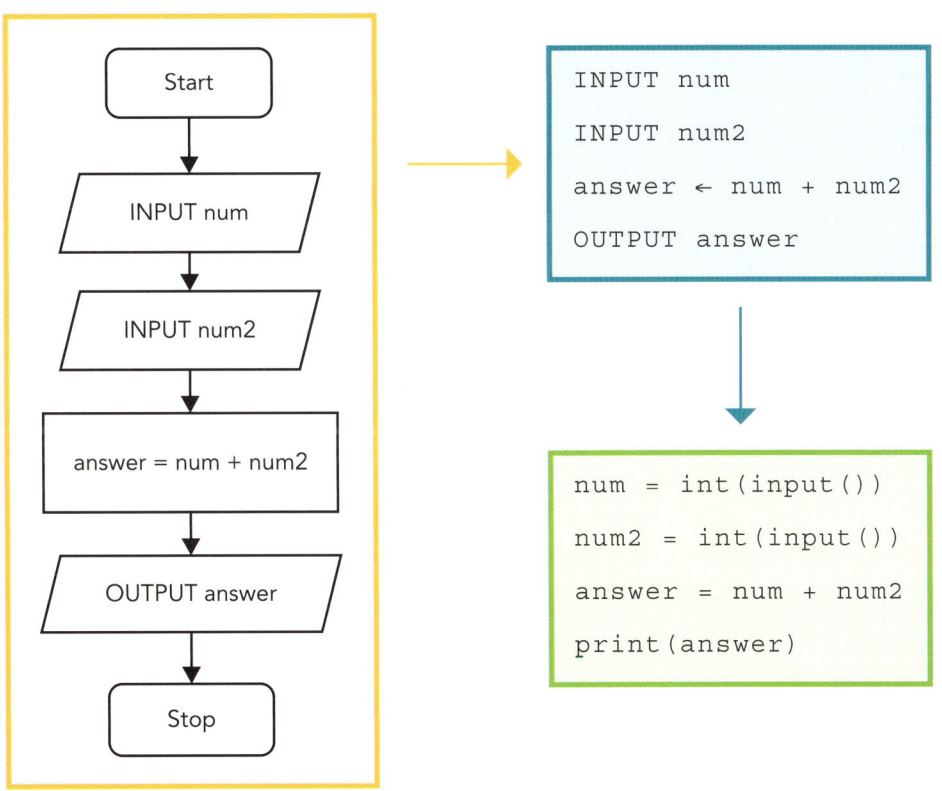

Figure 1.2: Flowchart to pseudocode to Python

Unlike in high-level programming languages, there is no set **syntax** in pseudocode (syntax is the arrangement of words and phrases in a sentence). However, pseudocode will follow the structure of a high-level language, so it will look like a program. Pseudocode uses **variable declarations**: statements that tell a program we need a **variable**.

1 Computational thinking and programming

A variable is a named location in memory that can store one item of data.

Pseudocode is used to design programs because anyone who can write in any high-level programming language can follow programs written in pseudocode. This is because pseudocode is written in everyday English, so everyone can understand it. The program can then be translated into a high-level programming language. You might be working with lots of other people to write a program and you need a common language to design it.

Pseudocode might be used instead of flowcharts because it is more similar to code, so it is easier for programmers to write and follow.

Figure 1.3: Programmers translating pseudocode into a high-level programming language

> ### Did you know?
>
> If pseudocode becomes formalised (given a syntax or mandatory format) and a program is written that can read and run the pseudocode, then it is no longer pseudocode. It is now actual code written in a programming language.
>
> Sometimes people claim that pseudocode has to be in a given format and always use specific symbols or words, or it is not pseudocode. However, this is not true. For example `Input`, `INPUT` and `input` can all be used. However, it is best to use the same formatting throughout one program, otherwise it could get confusing!

In Table 1.1, you can see an instruction in English (called a statement) for inputting a value, an example of the pseudocode and then the code in Python.

English statement	Pseudocode	Python
Take user's name as input	`INPUT name`	`name = input("Enter your name")`

Table 1.1: Statement in an English sentence, in pseudocode and in Python

1.1 Pseudocode

However, as we know, there are no formal rules to pseudocode. So, this line could be written in pseudocode in many ways, such as:

```
name = INPUT
name ← INPUT
INPUT "Enter your name", name
name = input("Enter your name")
READ name
name = Console.Read
```

These statements all have the following in common:

- They all have a command for getting **input**, for example `input` and `Console.Read`. Input is data the user enters.
- They all have a variable to store the data in, for example `name`.
- Sometimes we want the program to **output** some text that requests user input. To do this, we need to put the text in double quotation marks, as you can see in two of the lines of code. Output is data the computer sends out, in this case by displaying it on the screen.

The statements have the following differences:

- The commands are different.
- Some use assignment (=), some use an arrow (←) and some don't use either.
- Some output a message and others don't.

You might have noticed that one of these is actually Python code. You can write pseudocode in Python code, but without needing to worry about the syntax. For example, in Python, you need to make sure you include the required colon(:). In pseudocode, you do not.

These are all valid examples of pseudocode. Pseudocode is **language independent**. This means that any programmer, no matter what high-level programming language they use, should be able to read one of those statements and then create it in their chosen programming language. It is independent of the language.

However, pseudocode cannot just be any combination of words. It must include the same elements as high-level programming languages:

- Pseudocode has **command words** to perform tasks, as you will find out in Topic 1.2.
- It uses **selection statements** in the same way as high-level programming languages.
- It has the same **mathematical operator actions**, although sometimes different symbols can be used.

When and why do we use pseudocode?

Pseudocode is used when you are planning a program. You can use it instead of a flowchart, or you can use it together with a flowchart. It allows you to get an idea of how your program will work, the variables you will use and the calculations that you need. You can do all of this without having to worry about getting the syntax exact. It's a bit like writing a plan for an essay: you write down your main points, but you don't need to worry about spelling and grammar just yet!

Pseudocode also allows multiple people, who know different programming languages, to design and work on an algorithm together. Because it is a language-independent code, everyone on the project should be able to read and understand what everyone else has written.

Figure 1.4: Learners coding

1.1 Pseudocode

The aim is to design an algorithm using programming **constructs** that any programmer can write in any high-level programming language. Programming constructs are the main tools used when writing programs. The three main constructs are:

- sequence (the order statements run in)
- selection (checking a condition and running code when this condition is true or false)
- iteration (running code multiple times in a loop).

Rules

There are some rules that you need to follow when you are writing pseudocode. One example is using double quotation marks around **strings** (one or more characters that are treated as text), like we saw in the previous statements:

```
INPUT "Enter your name", name
name = input("Enter your name")
```

These rules will be explained as you work through this unit.

A pseudocode algorithm needs to have a clear start and end. This can be done in a range of ways, for example:

- writing START at the beginning and STOP at the end (or other similar words, for example BEGIN and END), like this:

    ```
    START
    OUTPUT "This line will run first"
    OUTPUT "This line will run last"
    STOP
    ```

- writing the pseudocode in a series of statements, one after the other, in order from top to bottom, like this:

    ```
    OUTPUT "This line will run first"
    OUTPUT "This line will run last"
    ```

In this unit, we will be using the second style, writing each statement on a new line without a start and stop. This will make it look similar to a program in a high-level programming language like Python.

There are some rules to follow when writing pseudocode!

1 Computational thinking and programming

Figure 1.5: Translating pseudocode to Python

Questions 1.1

1. What is pseudocode used for?
2. What is the difference between pseudocode and program code?
3. Which of the following is a valid example of pseudocode?
   There may be more than one answer.
   - A `number ← INPUT`
   - B `number = INPUT`
   - C `INPUT "Enter a number between 1 and 10", number`
   - D `number = input("Enter your name")`
4. Which of these is not a valid example of pseudocode?
   Explain your choice.
   - A `Output a message that tells the user to enter a word.`
   - B `OUTPUT "Enter a word"`
   - C `writeToScreen("Enter a word")`

Input

You have already seen some examples of input statements. Some programming languages use `input`, others use `read`, some use `readline` and others use `in`. These examples are all telling the program that the user needs to input a value. For this pseudocode, we will use the word `input`.

The key elements in an input statement are:

- a command word for input
- a variable to store the input in.

We will use the format:

    INPUT variable

where `variable` is the name of a variable. For example:

    INPUT colour
    INPUT name
    INPUT animal

If you miss out the **identifier**, then the value the user inputs will not be stored anywhere. An identifier is the name we give to a variable or a sub-routine.

The identifiers in these three examples are **colour**, **name** and **animal**.

Output

There are different forms of output. Some programming languages use `print`, some use `write`, others use `writeline` and some use `out`. The one thing in common is that they all output data. So, for this pseudocode we will use the word `output`.

The key elements in an output statement are:

- a command word for output
- the data to be output.

We will use the format:

    OUTPUT data

The data output follows the same rules as in high-level programming languages.

1 Computational thinking and programming

To output specific characters, the characters must be surrounded by double quotation marks. If these characters are not surrounded by double quotation marks, even in pseudocode, they will be seen as the identifier for a variable. Here is an example:

This algorithm states that the words "The sun has got his hat on" will be output:

```
OUTPUT "The sun has got his hat on"
```

Sometimes you might have text in different variables, or you might want to output the content of a variable with some extra words. To do this, you will need to join the text together. This is called **concatenation**. Here is an example:

This algorithm states that the contents of the seven variables The, sun, has, got, his, hat and on will be output:

```
OUTPUT The & sun & has & got & his &
hat & on
```

Concatenation is when two strings are joined together to make one string, for example the string "Foot" and the string "ball" could be concatenated to create "Football", as Figure 1.6 shows.

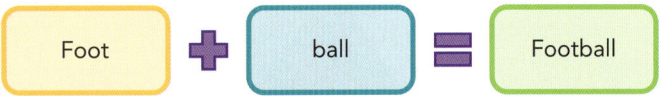

Figure 1.6: Concatenation of "Foot" and "ball" to make "Football"

There are multiple possible symbols that can be used as a concatenation symbol. Common examples include those shown in Table 1.2.

Operator	Symbol
comma	,
plus sign	+
ampersand*	&

*Remember that an ampersand stands for the word 'and'.

Table 1.2: Concatenation symbols

For this pseudocode we will use a comma (,), but either of the other two symbols could be used in the same place as the comma.

1.1 Pseudocode

Example: This algorithm will output the word `"Hello"` then the input data the user entered.

```
INPUT name
OUTPUT "Hello", name
```

If Arun enters "Arun", then the algorithm will output `"Hello Arun"`.

Unplugged activity 1.1

You will need: some coloured pens or highlighters and paper

Read this algorithm written in pseudocode and copy it onto your paper.

```
OUTPUT "What is your favourite animal?"
INPUT animal
OUTPUT "I like ", animal, " as well."
OUTPUT "What is your favourite song?"
INPUT song
OUTPUT "The song ", song, " is OK, but I think there are better songs!"
```

Complete these tasks by yourself.

1. Highlight or circle all of the input and output command words in the algorithm in one colour.
2. Highlight or circle all of the variable identifiers in another colour.

1 Computational thinking and programming

Continued

3   Highlight or circle all of the words that will be output (the words in double quotation marks) in a different colour.

4   Highlight or circle all of the concatenation symbols in a new colour.

Peer assessment

Now join with a partner and compare your answers for tasks 1 to 4.
Did you highlight or circle all of the examples for each task?
Discuss with your partner anything that you might have missed.

5   Extend the algorithm by writing pseudocode to:
   a   ask the user to input their favourite film
   b   take the input from the user and store it in a variable
   c   output a message telling them that you don't like the film they entered, including the film name they entered
   d   output a film that you prefer.

Activity 1.1

You will need: a desktop computer, laptop or tablet, a flowchart, a Python program

For this activity you will need a partner. You and your partner will each receive either a flowchart or a Python program from your teacher to use as your Source file for this activity. Without showing your Source file to your partner, write down each of the input and output statements in pseudocode.

When you have both completed this task, swap your pseudocode with your partner and use their pseudocode to recreate the Source file they received.

Peer assessment

Compare your and your partner's work with the original flowchart and Python program.

- Do both algorithms have the same number of inputs?
- Do both algorithms have the same number of outputs?
- Do the statements in each algorithm run in exactly the same order?
- Are the output messages exactly the same?

Figure 1.7: Peer assessment

20

1.1 Pseudocode

Variables and assignment

A variable is a named location in a computer's memory that can store one item of data. The data in the variable can change as the program executes. Each variable has an identifier, or a name. You have already seen variables used in the input and output section.

Storing data in a variable is called **assignment**.

Variables in pseudocode follow the same rules as in a high-level programming language. The left-hand side is the variable's identifier, then there is an assignment sign, then the right-hand side is the data that will be stored in the variable. In this example, the assignment sign is =.

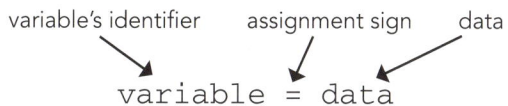

```
variable = data
```

In pseudocode, identifiers follow similar rules to the ones you learnt when selecting an identifier in Python. A variable identifier:

- must be one word without spaces
- cannot start with a number or symbol
- cannot be the same as a reserved key word (see the list given by Zara)
- should be unique, for example if you are using INPUT in your pseudocode, you cannot also name a variable INPUT
- must be in the same format within the same program, for example you should not use both input and INPUT.

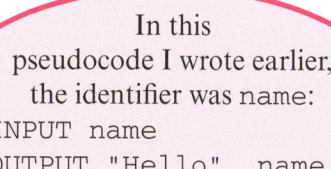

In this pseudocode I wrote earlier, the identifier was name:
INPUT name
OUTPUT "Hello", name

There are 31 reserved key words that have a specific function in Python. These words cannot be used as other variable names.

and as assert break class
continue def del elif else
except finally for from global
if import in is lambda nonlocal
not or pass print raise
return try while
with yield

1 Computational thinking and programming

In pseudocode, an equals sign = or an arrow ← can be used. In this pseudocode, we will use an arrow ←. This makes it clear that you mean 'assignment', because = is also used in comparisons when you are testing whether A = B.

Example: This algorithm will store the text `"Red"` in the variable `colour`, and the number 12 in the variable `age`.

```
colour ← "Red"
age ← 12
```

> **Did you know?**
>
> You can change a symbol midway through a pseudocode algorithm as long as it can be understood. You could use = in some places and ← in others.
>
> However, it is best to try and stay consistent!

Unplugged activity 1.2

You will need: a pen and paper, scissors

Take a look at this pseudocode algorithm.

```
value1 ← 10
value2 ← value1 + 2
value1 ← 100
value1 ← value1 - value2
value3 ← value1 * 2
value4 ← value3 / 4
```

There are four variables in the program. Divide some paper into four separate pieces, either by cutting it into four pieces or drawing lines to create four sections.

On each of the four pieces of paper or in each section, write the identifier of one of the variables. Each variable should be on its own piece of paper or in its own section.

Follow the algorithm by writing the values stored in each variable on the appropriate piece of paper or section. If a value is changed, cross out the previous value and write the new value.

Compare the final value in each variable with a partner. Do you have the same values? If they were different, repeat the process as a pair to identify the differences and find the correct answer.

Arithmetic operators

Arithmetic operators are symbols we use to perform mathematical calculations.

Some arithmetic operators you should be familiar with are shown in Table 1.3.

1.1 Pseudocode

Operator	Symbol
addition	+
subtraction	−
multiplication	*
division	/

Table 1.3: Arithmetic operators

*In maths, the symbols for multiplication and division are × and ÷. In computing, including in spreadsheets, the symbols are * and / .*

These symbols are usually the same in all high-level programming languages, including Python, so we will use these in pseudocode.

Arithmetic operators need a numeric value (a number or a variable containing a number) on both sides of the operator. Something needs to happen with the result from the calculation. For example, the result could be assigned to a variable or output in a message.

Example 1

This algorithm will add together two numbers, store them in a variable and output the result.

```
num ← 1
num2 ← 2
result ← num + num2
OUTPUT(result)
```

Example 2

You can also output the result without storing it in a variable:

```
num ← 1
num2 ← 2
OUTPUT(num + num2)
```

Programming task 1.1: Make, Investigate, Modify, Predict and Run

You will need: a pen and paper, a desktop computer, laptop or tablet with an IDE for Python

Make: Write a Python program to recreate the pseudocode algorithm shown in Example 1. You need to add two numbers together, store them in a variable and output the result.

Investigate: Compare your Python program to the pseudocode algorithm. Create a table with the pseudocode command in one column and the line of Python code in the other.

Modify: Change the data stored in `num` and `num2` in your Python program.

Predict: Write down your prediction for what the output will be.

Run: Test the program with these new values.

1 Computational thinking and programming

Programming task 1.2: Investigate

You will need: a pen and paper

Read the following algorithm and identify its purpose.

```
INPUT total
INPUT cost1
total ← total + cost1
INPUT cost2
total ← total + cost2
INPUT cost3
total ← total + cost3
OUTPUT "The total cost is ", total
```

Now answer the following questions:

1. How many variables are in the algorithm?
2. What are the identifiers of the variables?
3. Which arithmetic operator is, or operators are, being used?
4. How many times is the assignment symbol used?
5. What is the purpose of the comma (,) in the final statement?

Test the program with the following inputs, in the order given:

   10 20 10 25

Write down the output.

Peer assessment

Work with a partner and compare your outputs. Were they the same? If they were different, work through the algorithm together to identify which is the correct answer and where the error was made.

Following a pseudocode algorithm

To follow an algorithm written in pseudocode:

- find the start, which might be labelled as 'START', or could be the first line of pseudocode
- read the first statement and do what it tells you to do
- continue until you reach either a 'STOP' or the last statement.

1.1 Pseudocode

It is important that you read each line in order and do not try to jump ahead. Sometimes it helps to put a piece of paper over the algorithm and then move it down, revealing one statement at a time. Once you have done that action, move the paper down to reveal the next line of code.

Even if you think you can follow the algorithm without covering it up, it is good to practise doing this for algorithms that use more constructs later on.

Sometimes you might be able to follow an algorithm in your head. Sometimes you might need to write down what is happening. Sometimes you might need to talk through the algorithm with someone else. Whichever way you choose, make sure you read the algorithm one line at a time.

Questions 1.2

1. Give a suitable pseudocode command word to output a message.
2. Why is pseudocode called 'language independent'?
3. What are the two signs that can be used for assignment in pseudocode?
4. What are the names of the variables in this pseudocode program?

    ```
    first ← 1
    second ← 2
    third ← first + second
    ```

1 Computational thinking and programming

5 What is the value stored in `answer` after each pseudocode statement is run?

   a   answer ← 1 * 10
   b   answer ← (20 / 2) + 5
   c   answer ← 50 * 2 - 1
   d   answer ← 1 + 2 - 3

Summary checklist

☐ I can explain what pseudocode is.
☐ I can describe the rules that are, and are not, associated with pseudocode.
☐ I can read algorithms that use pseudocode.
☐ I can follow a pseudocode algorithm that uses input and output.
☐ I can follow a pseudocode algorithm that uses variables and assignment.
☐ I can follow a pseudocode algorithm that uses arithmetic operators.

1.2 Selection in pseudocode

In this topic you will:

- understand how selection is used in pseudocode
- learn how to follow a pseudocode algorithm that uses conditional statements
- understand the meaning of AND, OR and NOT in conditional statements
- identify the important characteristics of pseudocode
- learn how to follow a pseudocode algorithm that uses AND, OR and NOT in conditional statements.

Key words

Boolean
brackets
condition
conditional statement
ELSEIF statement
IF statement
indentation
precedence

Getting started

What do you already know?

- Pseudocode is a tool we can use to design algorithms that are not language specific. Pseudocode has rules to follow, but it does not have set words like programming languages do.

    An example of a pseudocode algorithm is:

    ```
    OUTPUT "Welcome to my program."
    OUTPUT "Enter your year of birth."
    INPUT year
    age = 2063 - year
    OUTPUT "In 2063 you will be", age, "years
            old."
    ```

1 Computational thinking and programming

> **Continued**
>
> - A flowchart is a way of representing an algorithm using symbols and data flows (arrows). You will have seen selection statements in flowcharts. Selection statements are conditions that give a true or false answer. If the condition is true, one set of statements runs, and if the condition is false, another set runs.
> - You will have used variables in flowcharts, pseudocode and programming. Variables are storage areas in memory that are given a name (identifier). You can store data in a variable. You can get data out of a variable and you can change the data in a variable.
>
> **Now try this!**
>
> Follow the flowchart in Figure 1.8.
>
>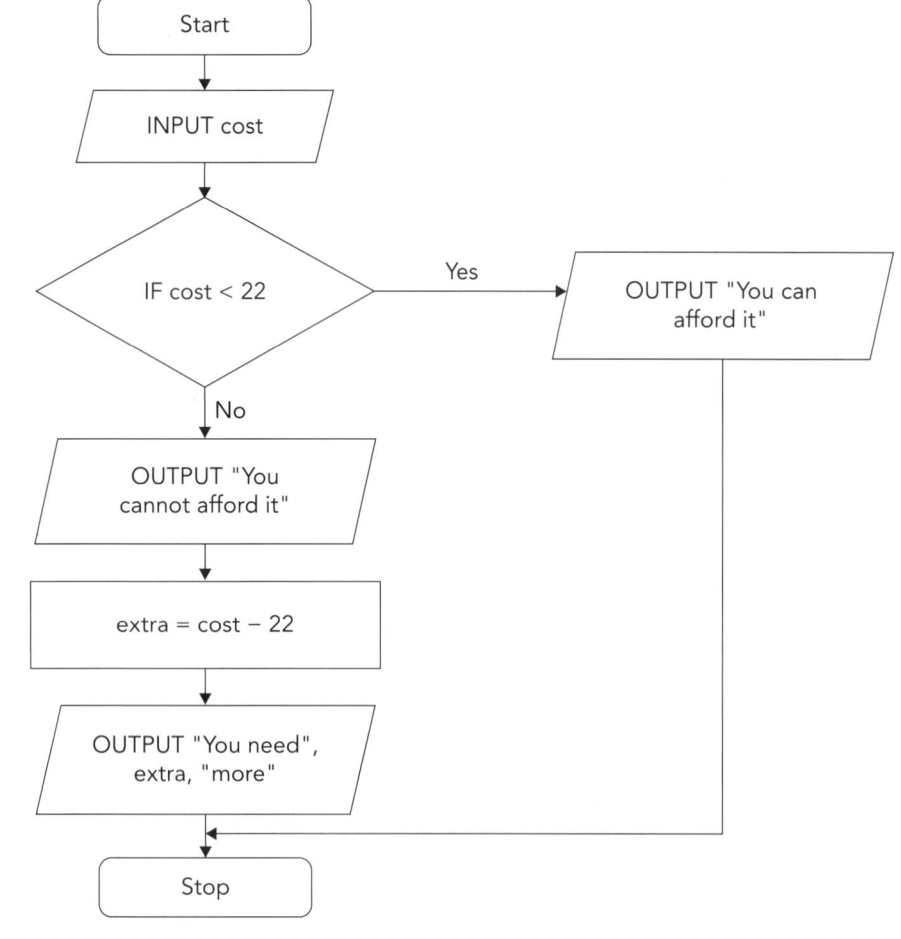
>
> Figure 1.8: Flowchart

1.2 Selection in pseudocode

> **Continued**
>
> 1. Work with a partner to identify the condition in the flowchart.
> 2. Discuss what the output is if the condition is true, and what happens if the condition is false.
> 3. Write down the comparison operator for each of these conditions:
>   a. equal to
>   b. not equal to
>   c. less than
>   d. greater than
>   e. less than or equal to
>   f. greater than or equal to.

Conditional statements

A **condition** is a comparison test that results in true or false. Conditions are used in selection statements. For example, in the flowchart in Figure 1.9, the condition is:

```
IF colour == "purple"
```

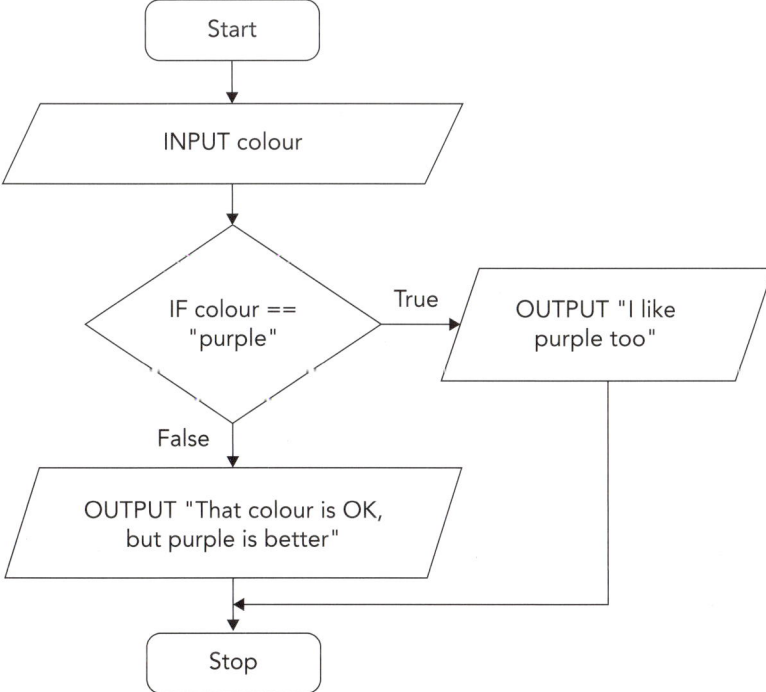

Figure 1.9: A flowchart with a selection statement

1 Computational thinking and programming

A **conditional statement** is a section of code that tells a program to execute different actions depending on whether a condition is true or false.

> If someone has a gluten allergy, they need a gluten-free pizza.

Conditional statements in flowcharts have three elements:

- a condition that can be true or false
- statements that run when the condition is true
- statements that run when the condition is false.

Conditional statements in pseudocode follow the same rules:

- there is a condition that can be true or false
- some statements will run when the condition is true
- some statements will run when the condition is false.

This conditional statement is often called an **IF statement**.

IF THEN

One type of IF statement is an IF THEN statement. In pseudocode, it can use this structure:

```
IF condition THEN
    Statements that run when the condition is True
ENDIF
```

IF THEN statements only have code that runs when the condition is true. If the condition is false, then these statements will not run.

`IF condition THEN` starts the IF statement using the command word IF, followed by the condition and then the command word THEN. The `ENDIF` command shows where the IF statement finishes.

The code inside the IF statement is indented (moved several spaces to the right). This is called **indentation**, and it makes it easier for us to read.

1.2 Selection in pseudocode

We can see which code runs inside the IF statement. The indentation also tells the program when the IF statement finishes. If the condition is false, the program will go to ENDIF. The indentation makes it easy for us to know where to go when following the algorithm.

Example 1

Figure 1.10 shows an example IF THEN statement as a flowchart.

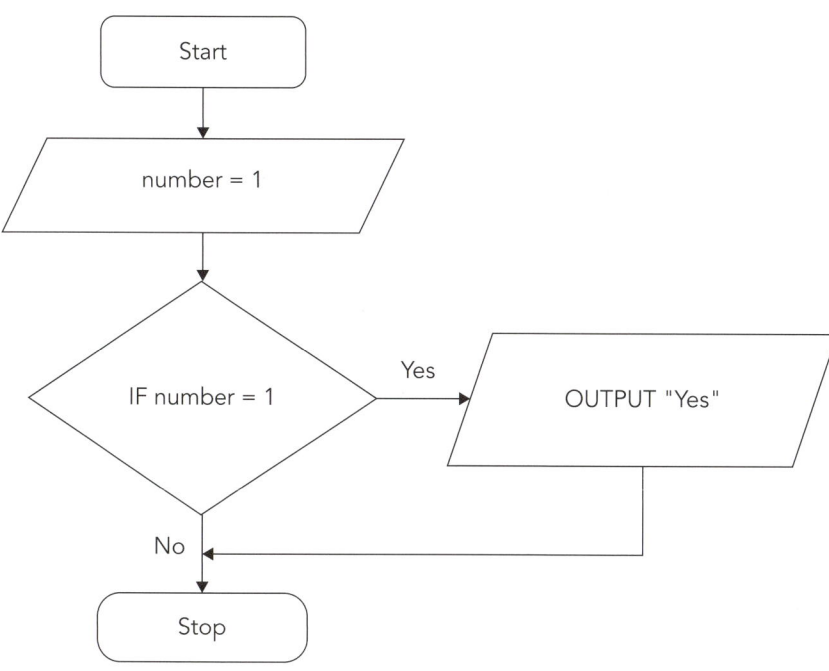

Figure 1.10: Flowchart showing an IF THEN statement

The condition is `number = 1`.

- If this is true, then "Yes" is output.
- If this is false, then this output is not run.

In pseudocode this will be:

```
number = 1
IF number = 1 THEN
    OUTPUT "Yes"
ENDIF
```

Example 2

This program will multiply the number by 2 if the condition is true.

```
OUTPUT "Enter a number"
number = INPUT
IF number > 10 THEN
    OUTPUT number * 2
ENDIF
```

1 Computational thinking and programming

This is pseudocode, and because pseudocode does not have a set syntax, there are lots of other ways the statements can be written. The following three pseudocode algorithms are the same, but they are each written in different pseudocode. These statements are all just as valid.

1
```
answer = 10
IF answer = 10 THEN
    OUTPUT "Correct"
ENDIF
```

2
```
answer = 10
if answer == 10 then
    OUTPUT "Correct"
```

3
```
answer = 10
if answer = 10:
    OUTPUT "Correct"
```

Unplugged activity 1.3

Compare the three different examples of IF THEN statements that have just been shown.

Identify the features that are the same between the programs and the features that are different.

Programming task 1.3: Investigate, Predict and Run

You will need: a pen and paper

Investigate: Read this pseudocode algorithm:
```
INPUT first
INPUT second
IF first > second THEN
    OUTPUT first
ENDIF
```

1. Identify the condition in this algorithm.
2. Identify the code that will run when the condition is true.

Predict: What do you think will be output if the numbers 10 and 2 are entered in this order?

Run: Walk through the code with the inputs 10 and 2 to check if your prediction was correct.

IF THEN ELSE

An IF THEN ELSE statement has some code that runs only when the condition is true. It also has some code that only runs when the condition is false.

In pseudocode, it can use this structure:

```
IF condition THEN
    Statements that run when the condition is True
ELSE
    Statements that run when the condition is False
ENDIF
```

Example 1

Have another look at the flowchart in the Getting started activity (Figure 1.8). This flowchart outputs "You can afford it" only when the condition is true. When the condition is false, it outputs a different message and performs a calculation. Here is that flowchart in pseudocode. Compare the two.

```
INPUT cost
IF cost < 22 THEN
    OUTPUT "You can afford it"
ELSE
    OUTPUT "You cannot afford it"
    extra = cost - 22
    OUTPUT "You need", extra, "more"
ENDIF
```

Example 2

This pseudocode algorithm will output which of the values is the larger.

```
first = 10
second = 20
IF second < first THEN
    OUTPUT first, "is larger"
ELSE
    OUTPUT second, "is larger"
ENDIF
```

Here are two examples of IF THEN ELSE statements.

1 Computational thinking and programming

Programming task 1.4: Investigate, Predict and Run

You will need: a pen and paper

Investigate: Read this pseudocode algorithm:

```
OUTPUT "Enter the number of marks you got in the test out of 50."
INPUT mark
percentage = (mark / 50) * 100
IF percentage > 40 THEN
    OUTPUT "You passed!"
ELSE
    OUTPUT "Sorry, you didn't pass this time."
ENDIF
```

1. Identify the condition in this algorithm.
2. Identify the code that will run when the condition is true.
3. Identify the code that will run when the condition is false.

Predict: What number do you predict can be input to make `"You passed!"` be output?

What number do you predict can be input to make `"Sorry, you didn't pass this time."` be output?

Run: Walk through the code with both of the numbers you identified to see if you were correct.

34

1.2 Selection in pseudocode

We learnt that we can write IF THEN statements in different ways. IF THEN ELSE statements can also appear in different ways. Here are some examples:

1.
```
answer = 10
IF answer == 10 THEN
    OUTPUT "Correct"
ELSE
    OUTPUT "Incorrect"
ENDIF
```

2.
```
answer = 10
if answer = 10 then
    OUTPUT "Correct"
else
    OUTPUT "Incorrect"
```

3.
```
answer = 10
if answer = 10:
    OUTPUT "Correct"
else:
    OUTPUT "Incorrect"
```

Unplugged activity 1.4

You will need: one large piece of paper, or several pieces of paper that you can join together

1. You are going to create a diagram to give someone a recommendation based on their answers to some questions. In groups of two or three, write a quiz that will ask the user simple questions that can only have two answer options (such as 'yes' and 'no').
2. After each question in the diagram, the user will move on to another question. The question they go to next will depend on the answer to the previous question.
3. This will continue until they end up at a box that gives a recommendation.

You can choose the topic for what to recommend. For example, you could recommend a sport they should play, a film they might enjoy or a book they might want to read.

Once you have written your quiz, create the diagram showing the outcome of the answer to each question. Remember to include another question or a recommendation after every answer to every question.

1 Computational thinking and programming

Continued

A short example is shown in Figure 1.11.

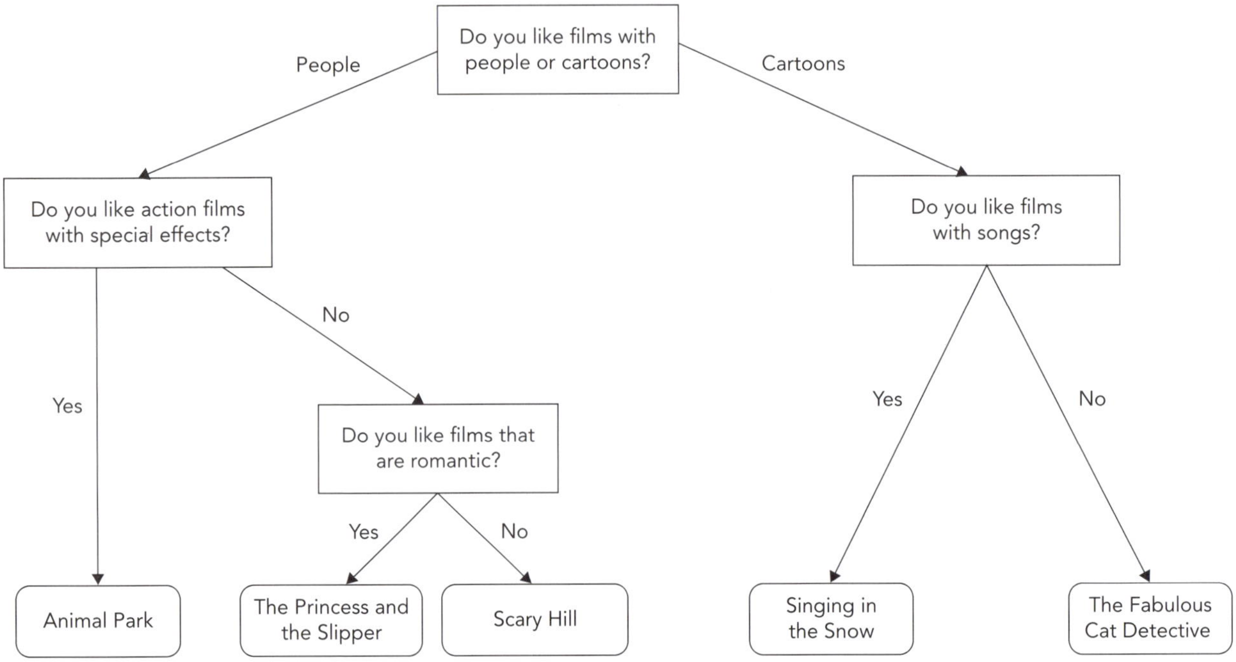

```
                    Do you like films with
          People    people or cartoons?    Cartoons
         ┌──────────                ──────────┐
         ▼                                    ▼
  Do you like action films              Do you like films
  with special effects?                 with songs?
    │              │                      │           │
   Yes             No                    Yes          No
    │              ▼                      │           │
    │        Do you like films that       │           │
    │        are romantic?                │           │
    │          │        │                 │           │
    │         Yes       No                │           │
    ▼          ▼        ▼                 ▼           ▼
  Animal    The Princess  Scary       Singing in   The Fabulous
  Park      and the       Hill        the Snow     Cat Detective
            Slipper
```

Figure 1.11: An example quiz diagram for recommending films

1.2 Selection in pseudocode

> **Continued**
>
> You need to work together to plan your diagram. Choose the outputs first and then the questions that will get to those outputs.
>
> Remember that each question can only have two options. They don't have to be 'yes' and 'no', but there can only be two.
>
> Once you have drawn your diagram, test it to make sure it works.
>
> Swap your diagram with another group and test their diagram.
>
> Discuss in your group how an algorithm can be written to automate this process. It will need to ask questions, take answers and then decide what to do next based on the previous answer.
>
> **Peer assessment**
>
> Individually, give your group a rating for how well you worked together on this activity as a mark out of 10.
>
> Share your rating with your group and explain why you gave it.

ELSEIF

An **ELSEIF statement** is a selection statement where there is more than one condition. If the first condition is false, then the second condition is checked.

If the second condition is false, then the third is checked and so on. There can be as many ELSEIFs as needed.

Here's an example of its structure in pseudocode.

```
IF condition1 THEN
    Statements that run when condition1 is True
ELSEIF condition2 THEN
    Statements that run when condition1 is False
    but condition2 is True
ENDIF
```

Each condition is different. Condition 1 is always tested first. If this condition is true, then the statements directly below it will run. When condition 1 is true, condition 2 will not be tested.

If condition 1 is false, then condition 2 is tested. If condition 2 is true, the statements directly below it will run.

An ELSEIF statement is the same as having multiple IF statements in a flowchart that run when the condition of each previous IF is false. Read the flowchart in Figure 1.12.

1 Computational thinking and programming

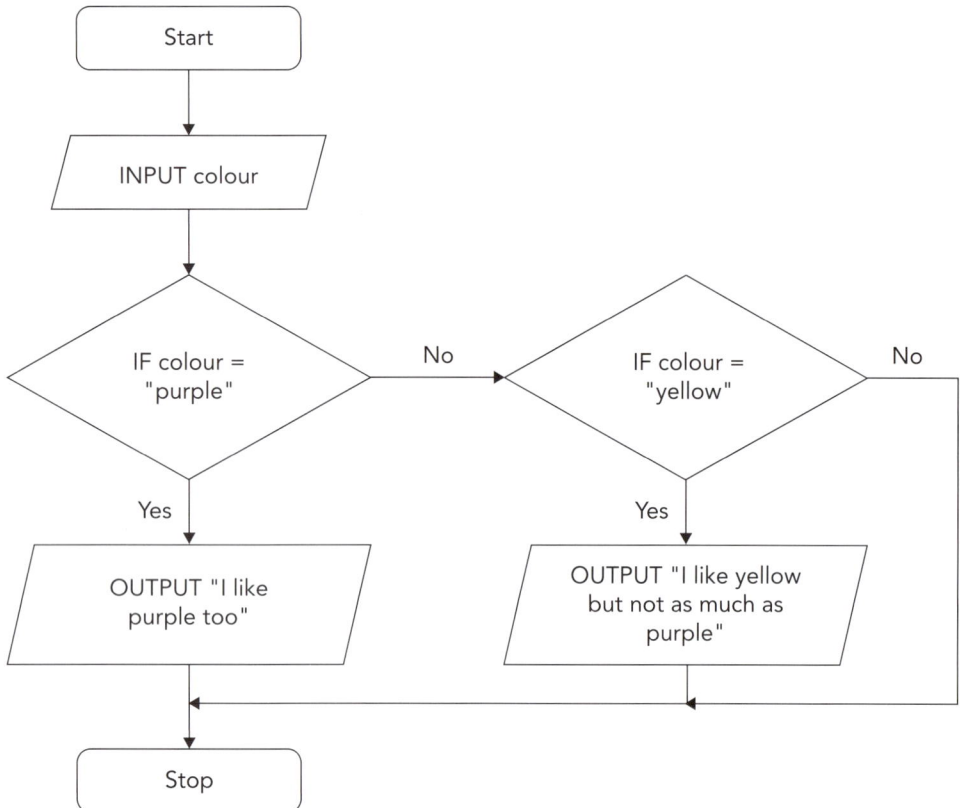

Figure 1.12: ELSEIF flowchart

This has two conditional statements. If the first condition is false (the colour is not purple), then the second condition is tested.

Condition 1: If the user enters "purple" then "I like purple too" is output.

Condition 2: If the user does not enter "purple" then the 'No' arrow is followed. If the user has entered "yellow" then "I like yellow but not as much as purple" is output.

If both conditions are false then nothing is output.

Here is this flowchart in pseudocode:

```
INPUT colour
IF colour = "purple" THEN
    OUTPUT "I like purple too"
ELSEIF colour = "yellow" THEN
    OUTPUT "I like yellow but not as much as purple"
ENDIF
```

1.2 Selection in pseudocode

Multiple ELSEIFs

You can have any number of ELSEIF statements in one IF statement.

The following pseudocode has three conditions (and therefore two ELSEIF statements). This pseudocode algorithm will output a different message each time you enter one of the three weak passwords.

```
OUTPUT "Enter a new password"
INPUT password
IF password = "password" THEN
    OUTPUT "password is not a strong password"
ELSEIF password = "1234" THEN
    OUTPUT "1234 is not a strong password"
ELSEIF password = "password123" THEN
    OUTPUT "password123 is not a strong password"
ENDIF
```

Figure 1.13: A strong password is one that is hard to guess

ELSE and ELSEIF

You can also add an ELSE into the ELSEIF statement. The ELSE statement will always be the last option and you can only have one.

In the multiple ELSEIF code above, if none of the conditions were true, then the code would just stop. The code in the ELSE statement will run when none of the conditions are true.

1 Computational thinking and programming

Example 1

We can put an ELSE in the password-checking algorithm. If the password is acceptable, a message can be output. For example:

```
OUTPUT "Enter a new password"
INPUT password
IF password = "password" THEN
    OUTPUT "password is not a strong password"
ELSEIF password = "1234" THEN
    OUTPUT "1234 is not a strong password"
ELSEIF password = "password123" THEN
    OUTPUT "password123 is not a strong password"
ELSE
    OUTPUT "That password is accepted"
ENDIF
```

Input 1

The user enters `"1234"`.

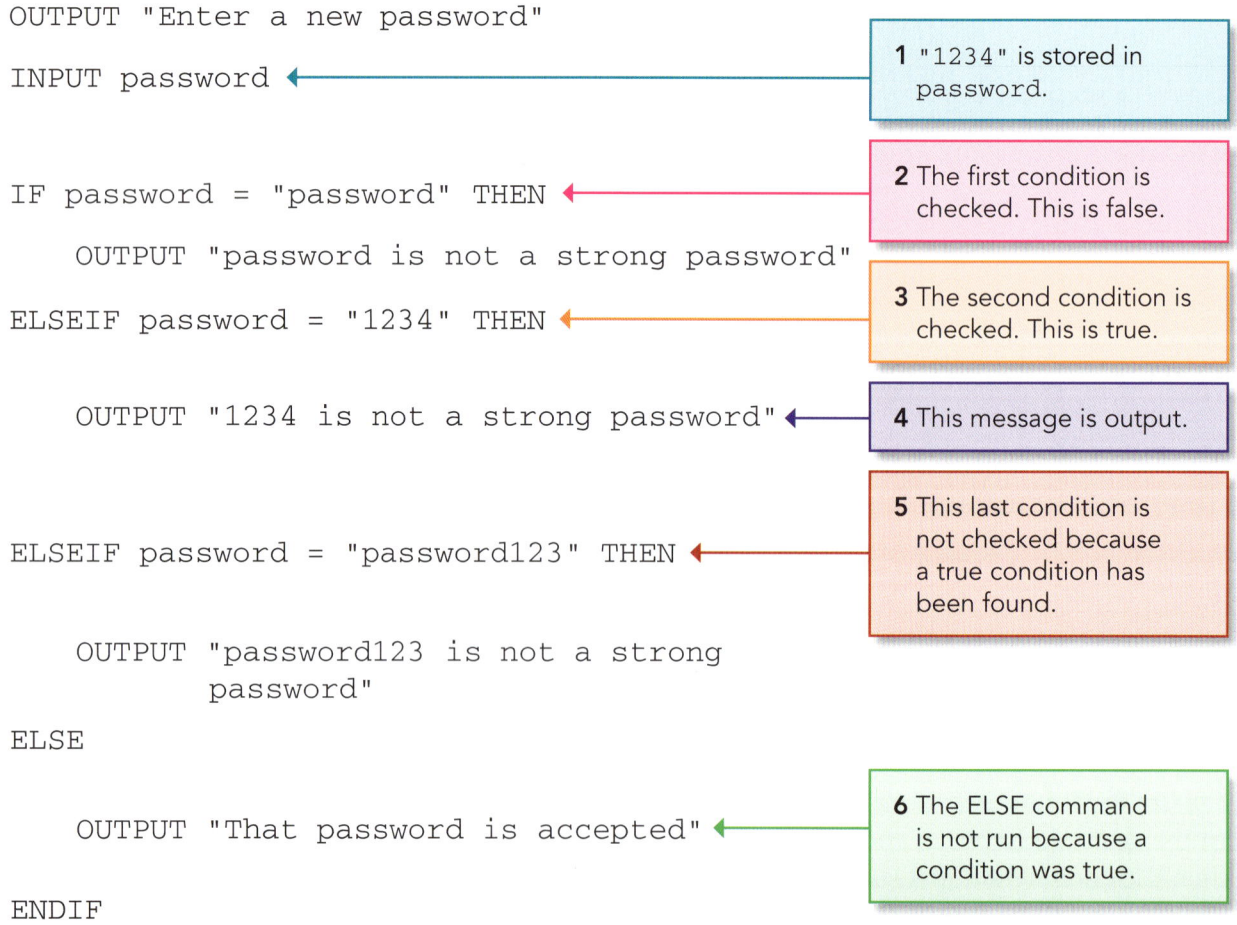

```
OUTPUT "Enter a new password"
INPUT password
```
1 "1234" is stored in password.

```
IF password = "password" THEN
```
2 The first condition is checked. This is false.

```
    OUTPUT "password is not a strong password"
ELSEIF password = "1234" THEN
```
3 The second condition is checked. This is true.

```
    OUTPUT "1234 is not a strong password"
```
4 This message is output.

5 This last condition is not checked because a true condition has been found.

```
ELSEIF password = "password123" THEN
    OUTPUT "password123 is not a strong
            password"
ELSE
    OUTPUT "That password is accepted"
```
6 The ELSE command is not run because a condition was true.

```
ENDIF
```

1.2 Selection in pseudocode

Input 2

The user enters `"password"`.

```
OUTPUT "Enter a new password"
INPUT password

IF password = "password" THEN

    OUTPUT "password is not a strong password"

ELSEIF password = "1234" THEN

    OUTPUT "1234 is not a strong password"


ELSEIF password = "password123" THEN


    OUTPUT "password123 is not a strong
            password"
ELSE

    OUTPUT "That password is accepted"
ENDIF
```

1 `"password"` is stored in password.

2 The first condition is checked. This is true.

3 This message is output.

4 This condition is not checked because a true condition has been found.

5 This last condition is not checked because a true condition has been found.

6 The ELSE command is not run because a condition was true.

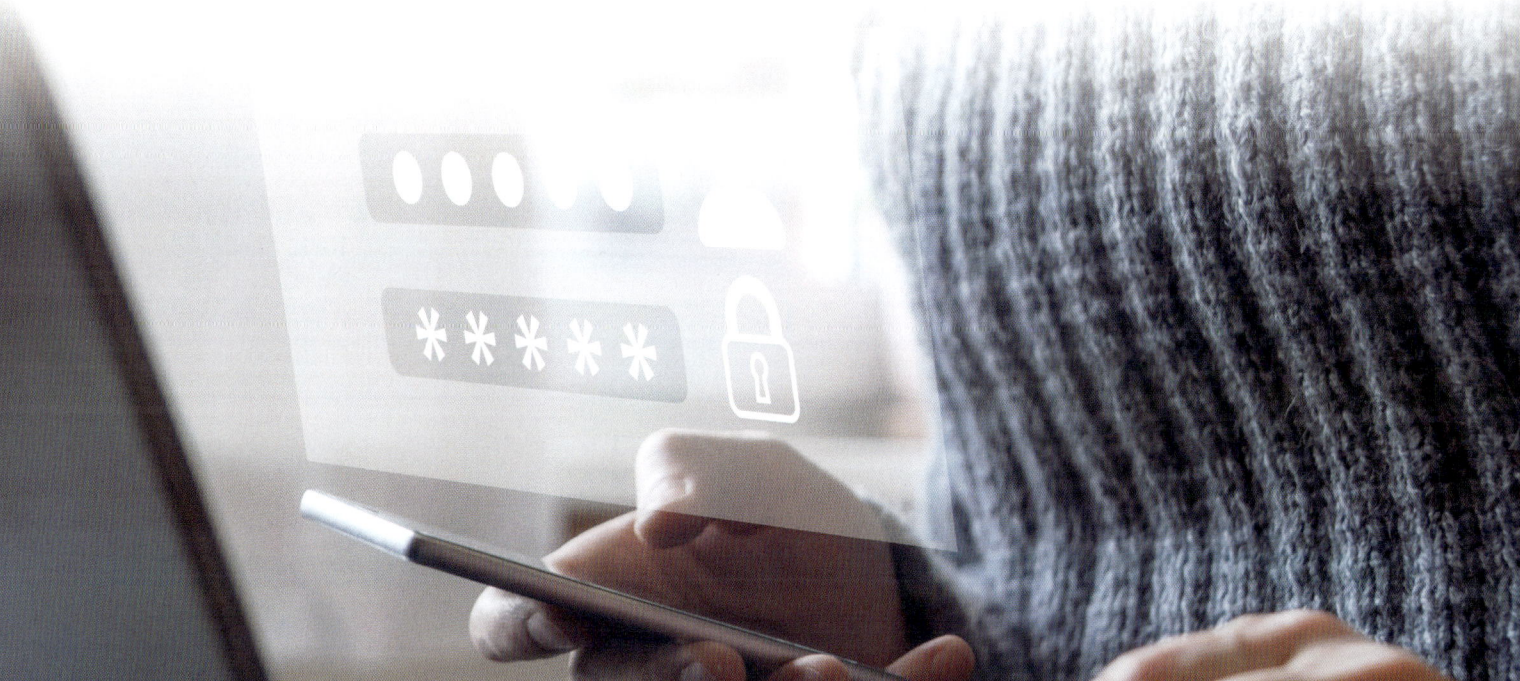

1 Computational thinking and programming

Input 3

The user enters `"12P5ww"`.

```
    OUTPUT "Enter a new password"

    INPUT password



IF password = "password" THEN
    OUTPUT "password is not a strong password"




ELSEIF password = "1234" THEN




    OUTPUT "1234 is not a strong password"
ELSEIF password = "password123" THEN

    OUTPUT "password123 is not a strong password"



    ELSE



    OUTPUT "That password is accepted"

    ENDIF
```

1 `"12P5ww"` is stored in password.

2 The first condition is checked.
This is false, `"12P5ww"` does not equal `"password"`.

3 The second condition is checked. This is false, `"12P5ww"` does not equal `"1234"`.

4 This condition is checked.
This is false, `"12P5ww"` does not equal `"password123"`.

5 The ELSE command runs because none of the conditions were true.

6 This line of code runs. `"That password is accepted"` is output.

1.2 Selection in pseudocode

Unplugged activity 1.5

> **You will need:** a pen and paper

You looked at the flowchart in Figure 1.14 earlier. A message needs to be output if purple was not entered and yellow was not entered.

Work with a partner and write down a suitable message to output. Identify where in the flowchart this output box would be placed.

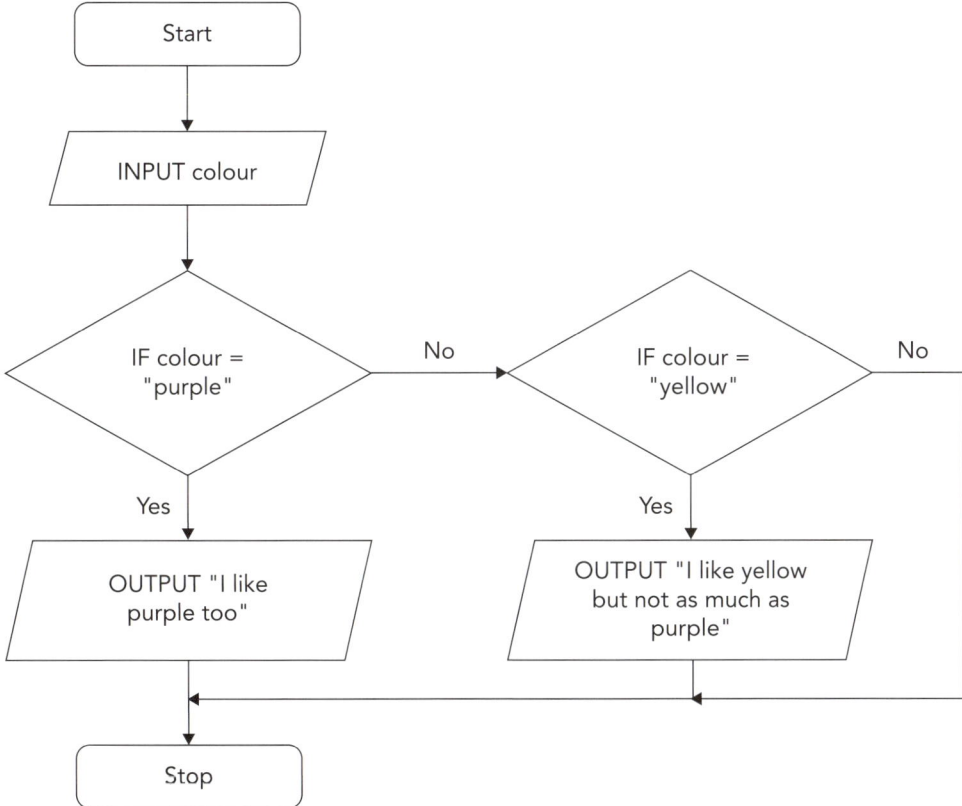

Figure 1.14: Flowchart for programming task

1 Computational thinking and programming

Continued

The pseudocode for this flowchart is shown below. There are two gaps in the code (numbered 1 and 2) that need completing.

```
INPUT colour
IF colour = "purple" THEN
    OUTPUT "I like purple too"
ELSEIF colour = "yellow" THEN
    OUTPUT "I like yellow but not as much as purple"
1_____
    OUTPUT 2_____
ENDIF
```

Work with your partner to identify the key word that needs to go in gap 1, and the code that will be put in gap 2 to output your message.

Unplugged activity 1.6

Individually, revisit the quiz you created in Unplugged activity 1.4. Now that you know how ELSEIF statements work, you can have more than two possibilities for each question. Each answer to your question would be another ELSEIF.

Rejoin your group from Unplugged activity 1.4 and discuss how you would change your diagram. You can edit your diagram to show how this would work, or recreate part of the diagram with multiple options.

Activity 1.2

You will need: a desktop computer, laptop or tablet with audio or video-presentation software and equipment

Create a group of up to four people.

You will be planning and creating an audio or video presentation about selection.

The presentation will need to include:

- a description of conditional statements
- the logical operators
- IF statements
- IF THEN ELSE statements.

1.2 Selection in pseudocode

> **Continued**
>
> In your presentation, you need to give examples in pseudocode as well as real-life examples that are not part of programs. A real-life example for an IF statement could be:
>
> > IF it is raining today THEN I will wear a coat.
>
> Write a script for your presentation and create your presentation using appropriate software. The presentation can be an audio voiceover, or a video with one or more of your group members.
>
> When you have finished, show your presentation to the other groups and watch their videos. Be ready to answer any questions that your classmates might ask.
>
> ### Self-assessment
>
> 1. How well did your group work together?
> 2. How did your group overcome any differences or disagreements?

1 Computational thinking and programming

Programming task 1.5: Investigate, Predict and Run

You will need: a pen and paper

Read this pseudocode algorithm:

```
OUTPUT "Enter one letter"
INPUT letter
IF letter = "a" THEN
    OUTPUT "a is a vowel"
ELSEIF letter = "e" THEN
    OUTPUT "e is a vowel"
ELSEIF letter = "i" THEN
    OUTPUT "i is a vowel"
ELSEIF letter = "o" THEN
    OUTPUT "o is a vowel"
ELSEIF letter = "u" THEN
    OUTPUT "u is a vowel"
ELSE
    OUTPUT letter, "is not a vowel"
ENDIF
```

Investigate: Answer the following questions:

1. How many conditions are in this pseudocode algorithm?
2. When will the output in the ELSE statement run?

Predict: Write down your prediction for the output when each of these inputs is used:

i   A   #   b   u

Run: Walk through the code with the five inputs you predicted the output for.

ELSEIF statements can also appear in different ways. Here are two examples of the same algorithm:

Example 1

```
answer = 10
IF answer = 10 then
    OUTPUT "Correct"
ELSEIF answer > 10 then
    OUTPUT "Too large"
ELSE OUTPUT "Too small"
```

Example 2

```
answer = 10
IF answer = 10:
    OUTPUT "Correct"
ELSEIF answer > 10:
    OUTPUT "Too large"
ELSE:
    OUTPUT "Too small"
```

In the following example, the ELSEIF has been split into a second IF statement. If the first condition is false, then the ELSE runs. Inside the ELSE is a second IF that is separate and will run on its own.

Example 3

```
answer = 10
IF answer = 10:
    OUTPUT "Correct"
ELSE
    IF answer > 10:
        OUTPUT "Too large"
    ELSE:
        OUTPUT "Too small"
```

Did you know?

IF statements are only one type of conditional statement. They are the most common conditional statement, and most programming languages have IF statements.
Another type is a 'case statement' (also called select case or switch case). This allows one variable to be checked against multiple values. Here's an example of a case statement:

```
number = 3
SELECT number
    CASE 1: OUTPUT "First"
    CASE 2: OUTPUT "Second"
    CASE 3: OUTPUT "Third"
    CASE 4: OUTPUT "Fourth"
END SELECT
```

The value in number is used: if this number is 1 then `"First"` is output, if it is 2 then `"Second"` is output and so on.

Not all programming languages have case statements. For example, Python does not have case statements.

1 Computational thinking and programming

Unplugged activity 1.7

You will need: a pen and paper

Work with a partner to create a breakfast menu. Each item needs a number and a name.
For example:

> Number: 1   Name: toast

Write an algorithm using English-style statements to output the menu choice the user has chosen. This can be in pseudocode if you feel confident to try it.

An example of English-style statements:

If the user enters 1, output 'You have chosen toast'. Else if the user enters 2 output . . .

Join with another pair and test your algorithm on each other. Give them a copy of the menu and ask for their choice. Input their choice into your algorithm to output what they want to eat.

Extend your algorithm to give other options. For example, if they enter toast, they could have a choice of toppings:

If the user enters 1, output 'You chose toast'. You could then ask: 'Would you like butter or jam? Enter 1 for butter, 2 for jam.'
If the user enters 1 output 'You chose butter' else output 'You chose jam'.

If the user didn't choose 1 (toast), output 'You chose . . .'

1.2 Selection in pseudocode

Programming task 1.6: Investigate and Modify

You will need: a pen and paper

Investigate: Read this pseudocode algorithm and the flowchart in Figure 1.15, which has been created to do the same actions.

```
OUTPUT "What is 2 * 2?"
INPUT answer
IF answer = 4 THEN
    OUTPUT "That's correct"
ELSEIF answer > 4 THEN
    OUTPUT "Too high"
ELSE
    OUTPUT "Too low"
ENDIF
```

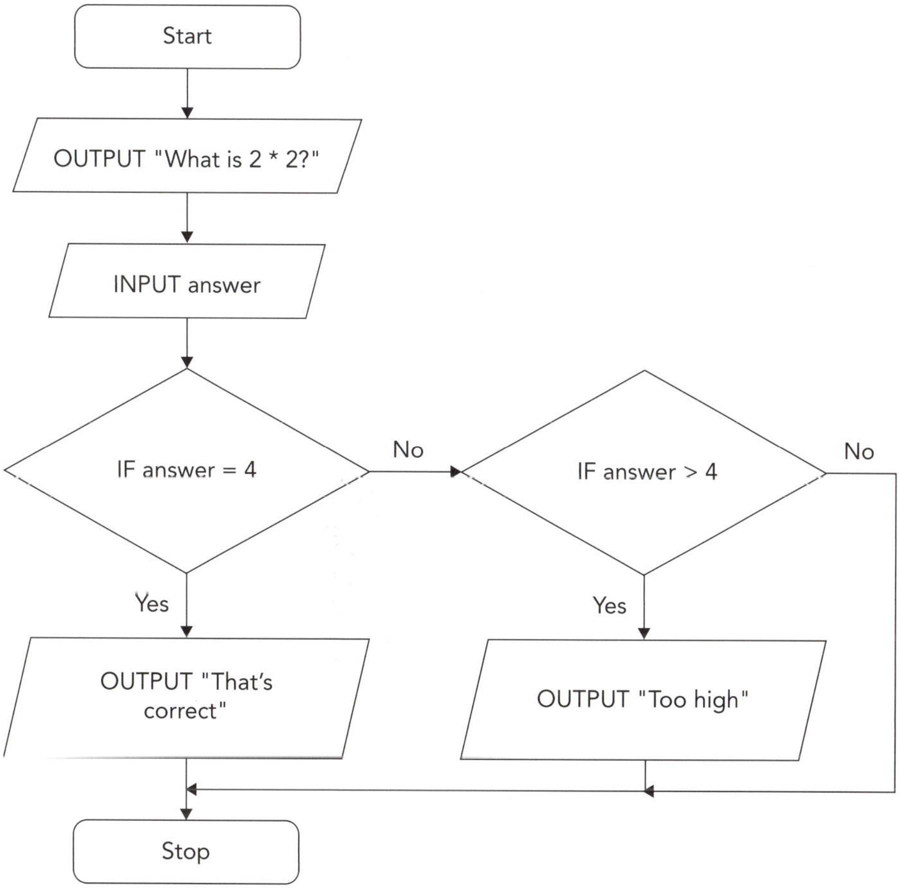

Figure 1.15: Flowchart for programming task

1 Computational thinking and programming

> **Continued**
>
> Work with a partner to match each pseudocode statement to its matching flowchart command. The flowchart is missing one part of the pseudocode.
>
> **Modify:** Change the flowchart so that it includes the missing part of the pseudocode.

Boolean operators

You have already been introduced to the **Boolean** operators AND, OR and NOT. A reminder of their rules is shown in Table 1.4. Boolean means relating to a system of logic that uses only two values: true and false. The result of a logic gate can only ever be true or false.

Boolean operator	Format	Rules
AND	one condition on either side	If both conditions are true, the result is true. Otherwise, the result is false.
OR	one condition on either side	If one, or both, conditions are true, the result is true. It is false only when both conditions are false.
NOT	one condition	If the condition is true, it makes it false. If the condition is false, it makes it true.

Table 1.4: Boolean operators and their rules

Boolean operators in pseudocode

The Boolean operators are used by writing their name in the condition. AND and OR need one condition on either side. NOT needs a condition after it.

The commands can be in uppercase letters (AND, OR, NOT) or in lowercase letters (and, or, not). Sometimes symbols might be used instead. For example:

- AND can be &&
- OR can be ||
- NOT can be !

However, when you are writing pseudocode, all you need to remember is the words AND, OR and NOT.

AND

Here's an example of AND being used in pseudocode:

```
01  total = 97
02  IF(total > 90 AND total < 100) THEN
03      OUTPUT("Just in range")
04  ELSE
05      OUTPUT("Incorrect amount")
06  ENDIF
```

The IF statement on line 02 has two conditions:

- IF total > 90
- IF total < 100

These two conditions are separate and each one is either true or false.

Run 1

Condition 1: total > 90   This is true: the value in total is 97, which is more than 90.

Condition 2: total < 100   This is true: the value in total is 97, which is less than 100.

Replace each condition with its result.

    IF(total > 90 AND total < 100)
    IF(True   AND True)

True AND true is always true.

The condition on line 02 is true and "Just in range" is output.

Run 2

What will happen if we change the value in total? Line 01 is changed to:

```
01  total = 100
```

Condition 1: total > 90   This is true: the value in total is 100 which is more than 90.

Condition 2: total < 100   This is false: the value in total is 100 which is not *less than* 100.

Replace each condition with its result.

    IF(total > 90 AND total < 100)
    IF(True   AND False)

True AND false is always false.

The condition on line 02 is false. The ELSE statement on line 04 is run and the output is "Incorrect amount".

1 Computational thinking and programming

OR

Here is an example of OR being used in pseudocode:

```
01  total = 50
02  IF(total > 100 OR total < 0) THEN
03      OUTPUT("Out of range")
04  ELSE
05      OUTPUT("Accepted")
06  ENDIF
```

The IF statement on line 02 has two conditions. The first is if total > 100. The second is if total < 0. These two conditions are separate and each one is either true or false.

Run 1

Condition 1: `total > 100` This is false: the value in `total` is 50, which is less than 100.

Condition 2: `total < 0` This is false: the value in `total` is 50, which is more than 0.

Replace each condition with its result.

```
    IF(total > 100 OR total < 0) THEN
    IF(False        OR False)
```

False OR False is always false.

The condition on line 02 is false. The ELSE is run and `"Accepted"` is output.

Run 2

What will happen if we change the value in `total`? Line 01 is changed to:

```
01  total = 105
```

Condition 1: `total > 100` This is true: the value in `total` is 105, which is more than 100.

Condition 2: `total < 0` This is false: the value in `total` is 105, which is more than 0.

Replace each condition with its result.

```
    IF(total > 100 OR total < 0) THEN
    IF(True         OR False)
```

True OR False is always true.

The condition on line 02 is true. The output is `"Out of range"`.

1.2 Selection in pseudocode

NOT

Here's an example of NOT being used in pseudocode:

```
01  quantity = 0
02  IF NOT(quantity = 0) THEN
03      OUTPUT("Still some remaining")
04  ELSE
05      OUTPUT("No items remaining")
06  ENDIF
```

The IF statement on line 02 has one condition with a NOT before it.

Run 1

Condition: `quantity = 0`   This is true: the value in `quantity` is 0.
Replace the condition with its result.

```
    IF NOT(quantity = 0) THEN
    IF NOT(True) THEN
```

NOT true gives false.
The condition on line 02 is false. The ELSE is run and
`"No items remaining"` is output.

Run 2

What will happen if we change the value in quantity? Line 01 is changed to:

```
01  quantity = 5
```

Condition: `quantity = 0`   This is false: the value in `quantity` is 5, which is more than 0.
Replace the condition with its result.

```
    IF NOT(quantity = 0) THEN
    IF NOT(False) THEN
```

NOT false gives true.
The condition on line 02 is true. The output is
`"Still some remaining"`.

1 Computational thinking and programming

Programming task 1.7: Predict and Investigate

You will need: a pen and paper

Look at the three algorithms shown here.

Algorithm 1

```
INPUT colour
IF NOT(colour = "red") THEN
    value = 1
ELSE
    value = 2
ENDIF
```

Investigate 1: Read this pseudocode algorithm and identify the three parts of the conditional statement and the Boolean operator.

Predict 1: What will be stored in the variable `value` if `"blue"` is input?

Algorithm 2

The algorithm has been changed.

```
INPUT colour
IF colour = "red" OR colour = "blue" THEN
    value = 1
ELSE
    value = 2
ENDIF
```

Investigate 2: Identify the two conditions and the Boolean operator in this algorithm.

Predict 2: What will be stored in the variable `value` if `"blue"` is input?

1.2 Selection in pseudocode

> **Continued**
>
> ### Algorithm 3
> The algorithm is changed again.
>
> ```
> value = 0
> INPUT colour1
> INPUT colour2
> IF colour1 = "red" AND colour2 = "blue" THEN
>     value = 1
> ELSEIF colour2 = "red" OR colour1 = "purple" THEN
>     value = 2
> ENDIF
> ```
>
> **Investigate 3:** Identify the conditions and the Boolean operators in this algorithm.
>
> **Predict 3:**
>
> 1. What will be stored in the variable `value` if `"blue"` and then `"red"` are input?
> 2. What will be stored in the variable `value` if `"red"` and then `"blue"` are input?
> 3. What will be stored in the variable `value` if `"blue"` and then `"purple"` are input?

Brackets

In the Boolean pseudocode examples, you might have noticed **brackets** are being used more. Brackets are the symbols ( ). The brackets work in the same way as they do in mathematics. The code in the brackets runs first, then the code outside the brackets runs afterwards.

This is more important when you start using multiple Boolean operators in one conditional statement. Here is one example that shows why brackets are important:

```
IF value1 > 10 AND NOT value3 = 20 OR value2 < 20 THEN
```

Some of these statements have more **precedence** than others – they are higher priority, or more important. Precedence means the statement will run first or before other statements.

When you are solving a maths problem, the operators have the following order of precedence:

1. Equations in brackets ( ) are solved first.
2. Equations that use multiplication × or division ÷ are solved next.
3. Equations that use addition + or subtraction − are solved third.

1 Computational thinking and programming

Boolean operators have the following precedence:

1. NOT will always run first.
2. AND will always run second.
3. OR will always run third.

In this example, the NOT will run first, then the AND, then the OR.

Remember that BIDMAS means:
Brackets
Indices
Division
Multiplication
Addition
Subtraction.

```
           2    1                3
IF value1 > 10 AND NOT value3 = 20 OR value2 < 20 THEN
```

Brackets can be used to change this order, for example:

```
IF value1 > 10 AND NOT(value3 = 20 OR value2 < 20) THEN
```

1. Now the OR will run first because it is inside the brackets.
2. The NOT now applies to the result of the OR.
3. Then the AND will run last.

You will not need to read pseudocode that has this many Boolean operators, but you need to know why brackets are important and what to do if you see them.

Unplugged activity 1.8

You will need: a pen and paper

Write a condition that uses multiple logical operators. For example:

```
number = 2 OR NOT number = 3 AND next < 20
```

Rewrite the same statement using brackets in different places, for example:

```
((number = 2 OR NOT (number = 3)) AND next < 20)
```

How many different combinations can you make?

Swap your answers with a partner.

Read your partner's answers and try to find another possible combination.

1.2 Selection in pseudocode

Questions 1.3

1. What are the three components of a conditional statement?
2. What is the pseudocode command word used in all conditional statements?
3. What will this algorithm output?
    ```
    start = 3
    start = start * 2
    IF start > 10 THEN
        OUTPUT "Larger than 10"
    ELSE
        OUTPUT "Smaller"
    ENDIF
    ```
4. Read this pseudocode algorithm:
    ```
    first = INPUT
    second = INPUT
    IF first = second THEN
        OUTPUT "same"
    ELSEIF first > second THEN
        OUTPUT "first"
    ELSE
        OUTPUT "second"
    ENDIF
    ```
    a. What will this algorithm output when the numbers 1 and 3 are input?
    b. What will be output if the numbers 10 and 10 are input?
    c. When will the output be `"same"`?
    d. When will the output be `"first"`?
    e. When will the output be `"second"`?
5. Read this pseudocode algorithm:
    ```
    OUTPUT "Enter 1 for a joke, 2 for a fact."
    choice = INPUT
    IF choice = 1 THEN
        OUTPUT "Why was the computer sneezing?"
        OUTPUT "It had a virus."
    ELSEIF choice = 2 THEN
        OUTPUT "The first ever computer was as big as a room."
    ENDIF
    ```

1 Computational thinking and programming

a   What will be output when 2 is input?
b   What will be output when 1 is input?
c   What will happen when 3 is input?
d   How can the algorithm be changed so when a different value is entered, the message "Not valid" is output?

Summary checklist

☐ I can identify the key words in pseudocode for conditional statements.
☐ I can identify the three parts of a conditional statement in pseudocode.
☐ I can follow a pseudocode algorithm that uses an IF THEN statement.
☐ I can follow a pseudocode algorithm that uses an IF THEN ELSE statement.
☐ I can follow a pseudocode algorithm that uses an ELSEIF statement.
☐ I can follow a pseudocode algorithm that includes AND in a conditional statement.
☐ I can follow a pseudocode algorithm that includes OR in a conditional statement.
☐ I can follow a pseudocode algorithm that includes NOT in a conditional statement.

> 1.3 Searching algorithms

In this topic you will:
- understand why searching algorithms are needed
- learn how to perform a linear search.

Key words
linear

linear search

searching algorithm

Getting started

What do you already know?

- There are many ways to search for something. You could search randomly, or you could search methodically (using a step-by-step approach), looking at one place at a time before moving on to the next space.

- How you search for something might depend on what you are looking for. For example, if you have lost your mobile phone and you know where you last saw it, then you might start looking in that place first. If you have no idea, then you might want to start at the front door and search throughout your entire house as you walk through it!

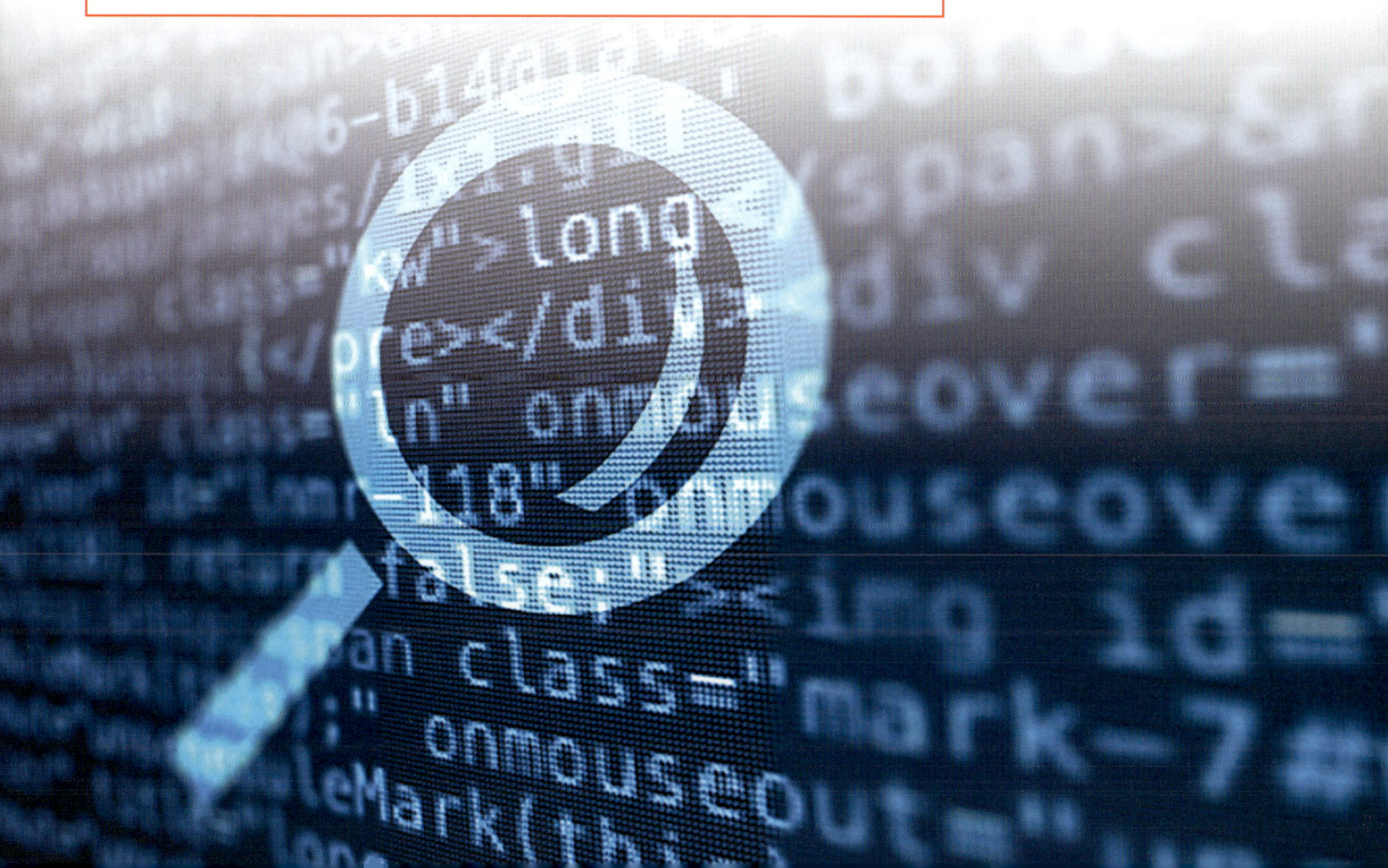

1 Computational thinking and programming

Continued

Now try this!

Work with a partner for this task. You will need a set of cards that each have one of these pairs of numbers and colours written on them: 1 Blue, 2 Blue, 3 Blue, 1 Red, 2 Red, 3 Red, 1 Green, 2 Green, 3 Green.

Place each card face down on the table so you cannot see the number and colour. Make sure you don't know where any particular card is.

Find the 3 Blue card.

Once you have found the card, discuss with your partner what you did to find the card. What steps did you follow? Did you turn the pack face up? Did you turn over one card at a time? Did you drop the cards on the table and spread them out?

Next, mix up the cards. This time you need to find the 2 Green card, but don't search just yet! There are some rules this time.

1. The cards need to stay face down, so you cannot see the value of each card.
2. You can only look at the value of one card at a time. If you turn one card over, you need to turn the card face down before you can look at another card.

Now try to find the 2 Green card.

Discuss the steps with your partner and identify how your search was different from the first time.

1.3 Searching algorithms

Searching algorithms

A computer program might need to search a set of data to find something. Here are some examples of when a program might need to search:

- **Users of a website have accounts with a username and password.** When the user tries to log in, they enter their username and password. There will be a file containing all the usernames and passwords for that system. The program has to search that file for the username the user enters, and then compare the matching password to the one the user enters.

- **A user needs to find a file that they created but cannot remember where they saved it.** The user enters the filename or a keyword in the computer. The software then has to search through every file in the computer to find the ones that match the data the user entered.
- **You need to do some research on the internet for your homework.** You open a web browser and enter the key words into a search engine. The search engine program looks for those key words in the web pages on the internet and then displays your results.

Each of these programs uses a **searching algorithm**. A searching algorithm is a series of steps, or instructions, that are followed to search for the item.

1 Computational thinking and programming

> **Did you know?**
>
> Searching algorithms can be valuable. Search engines use searching algorithms. A search engine with an algorithm that finds the most accurate results in the quickest time might get more users.
>
> What's more, if you know how the search engine's algorithm chooses the first website to display in its list of results, then you can change your website so it is picked up first, and that will get you more users.
>
>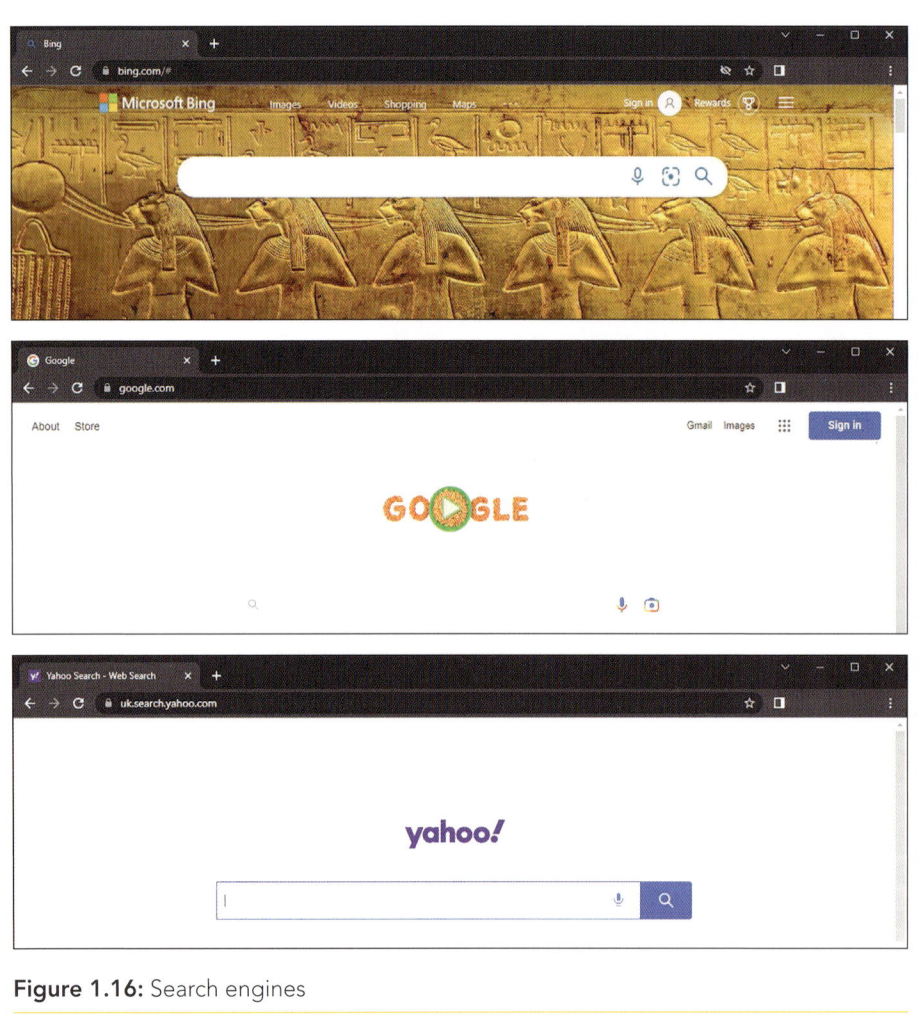
>
> **Figure 1.16:** Search engines

There are many different searching algorithms. Which algorithm will work best depends on the situation. For example, some algorithms are better when there is a very large number of items. Other algorithms only work when the data is in alphabetical or numerical order. It depends on the data.

1.3 Searching algorithms

Did you know?

There is a random search where the algorithm just picks one item in a set of data at random until it finds the one it is looking for. This is like what you did in the Getting started activity where you mixed a pack of cards on a table, then picked up one card at a time in no particular order. You found the card eventually, but this way of searching is not always the fastest.

Activity 1.3

You will need: a desktop computer, laptop or tablet with internet access

Do some research to find the names of as many different searching algorithms as you can. Note these down and then compare your list with a partner. Who found more?

Stay safe!

When you are researching information on the internet, make sure that you only use safe and trusted websites. There are some search engines designed especially for children and young people so that they will not see any unsuitable pages. Ask your teacher or a trusted adult which one you should use if you are unsure.

1 Computational thinking and programming

Linear search

A **linear search** is one type of searching algorithm. The word **linear** means in a straight line, or moving from one point to the next in order. This is what a linear search does. It looks at the first item, then the second, and then the third and so on.

The items, or data, first need to be in a line.

Figure 1.17 shows an example with four cards.

   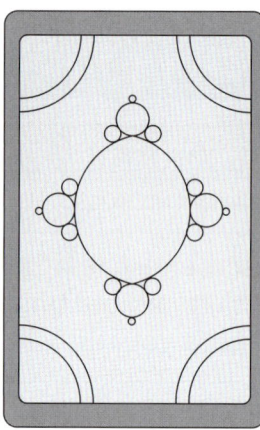

Figure 1.17: Four cards in a row, face down

We are going to look for the 1 Blue card. We can only turn one card over at a time.

1   We start with the card in position 1 and turn it over (Figure 1.18).

 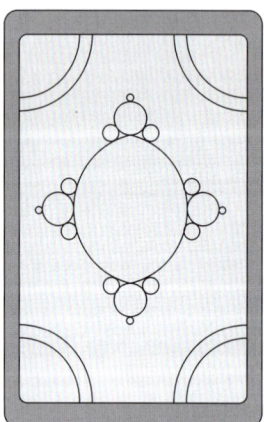 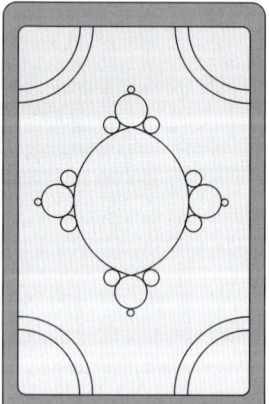 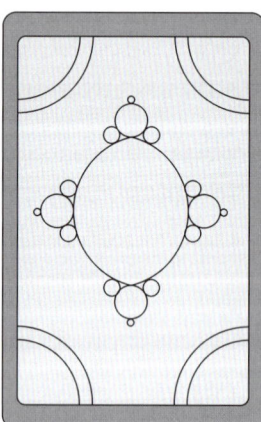

Figure 1.18: 3 Green card in position 1

Is this card 1 Blue?

No, it's 3 Green.

Turn the card back over (like in Figure 1.17).

1.3 Searching algorithms

2   We now move to the card in position 2 and turn it over (Figure 1.19).

 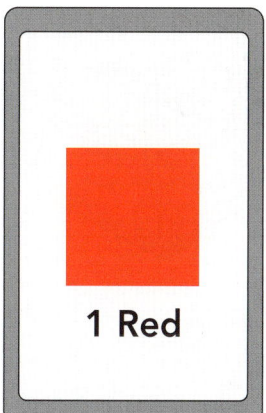  

Figure 1.19: 1 Red card in position 2

Is this card 1 Blue?

No, it's 1 Red.

Turn the card back over.

3   We now move to the card in position 3 and turn it over (Figure 1.20).

   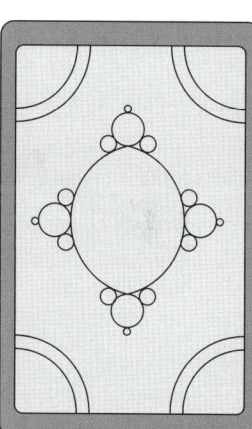

Figure 1.20: 1 Blue card in position 3

Is this card 1 Blue?

Yes, we've found it and can now stop searching.

1 Computational thinking and programming

What happens if the item you are looking for isn't found?
This time we will look for an apple (see Figure 1.21).

Figure 1.21: Four boxes with items inside them

1. Look at the item that is in box 1 in Figure 1.22.

Figure 1.22: Shell in position 1

It's a shell, not an apple.

2. Look at the item that is in box 2 in Figure 1.23.

Figure 1.23: Banana in position 2

It's a banana, not an apple.

3. Look at the item that is in box 3 in Figure 1.24.

Figure 1.24: Mobile phone in position 3

It's a mobile phone, not an apple.

1.3 Searching algorithms

4 Look at the item that is in box 4 in Figure 1.25.

Figure 1.25: Football in position 4

It's a football, not an apple.

5 There are no items left. The apple has not been found.

The linear search can be described using these steps:

Step 1: Look at the first item.
Step 2: Compare it to the value you are looking for.
Step 3: If it is the value you are looking for, stop because you found it.
Step 4: If it is not, look at the next item and go back to step 2.
Step 5: Repeat steps 2 to 4 until you find the value you are looking for, or there are no items left to check.
Step 6: If the item has been found, stop. If you do not find it, go to step 7.
Step 7: If there are no items left, then the value is not there.

Unplugged activity 1.9

You will need: a set of cards (or paper cut into several equal-sized pieces) with a number on one side of each card

You can do this task on your own or with a partner.

1. Mix the cards and place them face down in a row. (The side with the number on is the card's 'face'.)
2. Decide which card you are going to search for.
3. Search for the card using a linear search, following the linear search steps listed previously.
4. Repeat this process with different cards until you are confident using a linear search. If you have been working with a partner, now try it on your own.

1 Computational thinking and programming

Activity 1.4

> **You will need:** a desktop computer, laptop or tablet with animation or presentation software

Create an animation that shows how a linear search finds a value. Your animation could have images of cards or any other item so long as it has a value to look for. Remember: that value cannot be seen until it is turned over.

Unplugged activity 1.10

Work with a partner for this activity.

One of you will give instructions (Person 1), and the other will perform the instructions (Person 2).

Person 1 will tell Person 2 how to look for the number 33 in this set of data:

    20   1   13   66   78   33   12

Person 1 needs to tell Person 2 what to do. For example, Person 1 can ask, 'What is the first value? Is it 33?'

This time is different because you can see all the numbers at the start. The values are not hidden. However, you need to think like a computer. The computer cannot see the numbers, it can only look at one at a time.

If it will help, you can cover up the other numbers to make sure you don't skip any steps.

Then swap roles. Person 2 will give the instructions and Person 1 will follow them. You need to find the number 4 in this data set:

    20   1   13   66   78   33   12

Identify two positive ways you worked on this task.

Identify one thing that you will do differently if you do it again.

How did you remember the steps in a linear search?

1.3 Searching algorithms

Questions 1.4

1. What does a searching algorithm do?
2. Give an example of when a computer uses a searching algorithm.
3. Why are searching algorithms needed?
4. How many searching algorithms are there?
5. Is there one searching algorithm that is always the best?
6. What does linear mean?
7. How does a linear search work?
8. How will a linear search look for the word "horse" in this set of data?
       "cat"   "rabbit"   "mouse"   "sheep"   "horse"
9. How will a linear search look for the number 1 in this set of data?
       3   44   9   50   19   2

> **Summary checklist**
> ☐ I can give an example of when a searching algorithm is used.
> ☐ I can explain why searching algorithms are needed.
> ☐ I can describe how a linear search works.
> ☐ I can use a linear search to search for a value.

1 Computational thinking and programming

> 1.4 Conditional statements in text-based programming

In this topic you will:

- learn how conditional statements are written in Python including IF, ELSEIF and ELSE
- follow programs written in Python that include conditional statements
- change programs written in Python that include conditional statements
- write programs in Python that include conditional statements
- learn how the Boolean operators AND, OR and NOT are used in conditional statements in Python
- follow programs written in Python that include Boolean operators
- write programs in Python that include Boolean operators.

Key words

IF ELSE statement

indent

selection statement

Getting started

What do you already know?

- Conditional statements follow three rules:

  Condition: There is a condition that can be true or false.

  True: Some statements will run when the condition is true.

  False: Some statements will run when the condition is false.

1.4 Conditional statements in text-based programming

> **Continued**
>
> - In pseudocode, conditional statements are IF statements. If the condition is true, the code within the statement runs.
>
> - An IF statement can include an ELSE section. The code in this runs if the condition is false.
>
> - An ELSEIF statement can include multiple conditions. If the first condition is false, the next condition is checked. An ELSEIF statement can also include one ELSE statement that runs if none of the conditions are true.
>
> ### Now try this!
>
> Read this pseudocode program:
>
> ```
> INPUT firstNumber
> INPUT secondNumber
> IF firstNumber > 80 AND secondNumber > 80
>    THEN
>        OUTPUT "Both passed"
> ELSEIF firstNumber > 80 OR secondNumber > 80
>    THEN
>        OUTPUT "One passed"
> ELSE
>        OUTPUT "Neither passed"
> ENDIF
> ```
>
> Work with a partner to identify:
>
> 1. the condition(s)
> 2. the Boolean operators
> 3. the values that need to be entered for `firstNumber` and `secondNumber` so that each different output is displayed.
>
> | Value in `firstNumber` | Value in `secondNumber` | Output |
> |---|---|---|
> | | | "Both passed" |
> | | | "One passed" |
> | | | "Neither passed" |

Note: There might be more than one answer. Can you find all of the values needed? Copy this table and fill in the values.

1 Computational thinking and programming

> **Did you know?**
>
> Conditional statements have lots of different names. They are often called **selection statements** because one set of code is selected to run instead of another. They can also be known as *branching statements*. Each condition has two outcomes and only one is followed. These two outcomes can be seen as two different branches.

Logical operators

You have used logical operators in flowcharts and you have seen them in pseudocode. Table 1.5 shows the logical operators that Python uses.

Operator	Description	Examples
>	Greater than	10 > 2 20 > 19 200 > 0
<	Less than	100 < 200 1 < 2 0 < 10
>=	Greater than or equal to	100 >= 100 120 >= 99 22 >= 1
<=	Less than or equal to	100 <= 100 82 <= 99 1 <= 3
==	Equal to	100 == 100 20 == 20 1 == 1
!=	Not equal to	2 != 1 100 != 99 0 != 10

Table 1.5: Logical operators

1.4 Conditional statements in text-based programming

Conditional statements in Python

The conditional statement in Python is an IF statement. Python also has an ELSE statement and an ELSEIF. These all work in the same way as they do in pseudocode. You need to learn the syntax for each of these in Python so you can follow algorithms that use them. You will also start writing your own conditional statements in Python.

IF

The first statement in the conditional statement is always an IF statement. The format in Python is:

```
if condition:
    code that runs when the condition is True
```

The word `if` is written in lowercase. At the end of the condition is a colon (:).

Indentation

Python has set indentation. In Python, an **indent** is the number of spaces by which a line is moved to the right. Here are some examples of indentation:

This line is not indented.
  This line is indented by 2 spaces.
          This line is indented by 10 spaces.
	This line is indented using the tab key on the keyboard.

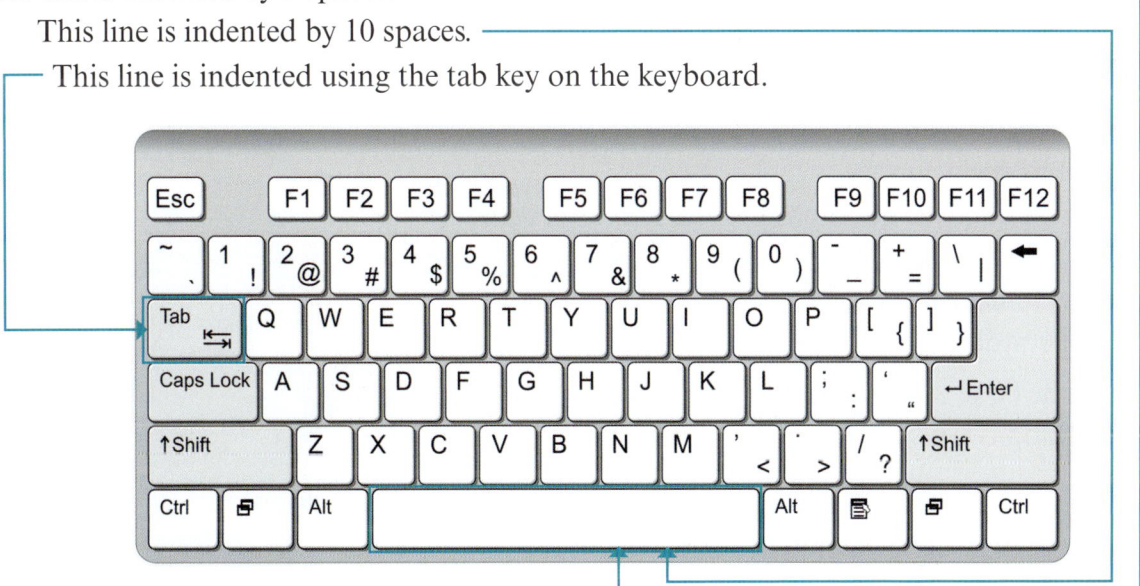

Figure 1.26: Tab key and space key on a keyboard

Indentation is different depending on what IDE you use. The IDE you are using might automatically indent your code for you when you type the colon (:) and press enter. If it does indent for you, you can just go ahead and write the code that runs when the condition is true.

1 Computational thinking and programming

If it does not automatically indent for you when you press enter, use the tab key before you start writing the next bit of code (the code that runs when the condition is true).

Indentation is important in Python. The indent tells Python which code is within the IF statement. For example:

```
if condition:
    this code runs only when the condition is True
    this code also only runs when the condition is True
this code is not indented and will always run
```

The blue text in the example above is the code within the IF statement.

In pseudocode, the statements that run when true are before the ENDIF, for example:

```
IF number > 10 THEN
    OUTPUT number * 2
ENDIF
```

Python does not have an ENDIF. Your indent tells Python which code is inside the IF statement. This pseudocode algorithm in Python will be:

```
if number > 10:
    print(number * 2)
```

In this code, the program will print the value of `number` so long as `number > 10` is true. If `number > 10` is false, the program will not print anything and will stop.

Writing an IF statement

1 You need to decide on the condition. This is the question that can only be true or false and needs to use one of the logical operators.

2 Identify the code that you want to run when the condition is true.

It's helpful to plan your IF statement before you start writing your code.

1.4 Conditional statements in text-based programming

Example 1

A program asks the user to enter the colour that is made when red and blue are mixed, and outputs a message if they get it correct.

1. The condition is if the variable equals purple.
2. If it is true, output `"That is correct"`.

```
colour = input("What colour is made when red and blue are mixed?")
if colour == "purple":
    print("That is correct")
```

Example 2

A program asks the user to enter the percentage they scored on a test, and outputs a message saying whether they passed (got 50% or more) or not.

1. The condition is if the percentage is 50 or more.
2. If it is true, output `"You passed"`.

```
score = int(input("Enter your percentage"))
if score >= 50:
    print("You passed")
```

Programming task 1.8: Predict, Run, Investigate, Modify and Make

You will need: a pen and paper, a desktop computer, laptop or tablet with an IDE for Python, Source file **1.1_programming_task_1.8.py**

Read the program written here.

```
userChoice = input("Do you want to hear a joke?")
if userChoice == "yes":
    print("How do robots eat pizza?")
    print("One byte at a time")
```

Predict: Write down what this program will output when you enter:

1. `"yes"`
2. `"no"`
3. `"YES"`

Remember that when a letter is entered into, or used in, a computer program, that letter is case sensitive. The uppercase letter H does not equal the lowercase letter h.

Run: Enter this program in Python or open Source file **1.1_programming_task_1.8.py** and run it to see if you are correct.

1 Computational thinking and programming

> ### Continued
>
> **Investigate:** Write this program on paper or print a copy of the program. Work with a partner for this task. On your paper, use different colours or shapes to highlight:
>
> - the condition
> - the logical operator
> - the code that will run when the condition is true
> - the code that will always run.
>
> **Modify:** Change this program to output your own joke.
>
> **Modify:** Change this program to tell the user to enter "Y" or "N". If they enter "Y", output the joke.
>
> **Make:** Write a new Python program to:
>
> - output a riddle to the user
> - take the user's answer to the riddle as input
> - output a message if they get the correct answer.
>
> Test your program with a range of data, for example different incorrect answers.
>
>
>
> ### Self-assessment
>
> Did all of your programs work correctly the first time? If not, what have you learnt that will change how you write your next program? Has this changed how you will approach a problem?

1.4 Conditional statements in text-based programming

Programming task 1.9: Predict, Run, Investigate, Modify and Make

You will need: a pen and paper, a calculator, a desktop computer, laptop or tablet with an IDE for Python, Source file **1.2_programming_task_1.9.py**

Figure 1.27: Grocery coupons

Read the program written here.

```
totalCost = float(input("Enter the total cost"))
numberItems = int(input("Enter the number of items bought"))
if numberItems >= 20:
    totalCost = totalCost * 0.9
print("Total cost is", totalCost)
```

Predict: Work with a partner for this task. You can use a calculator if you need to.

Write down what this program will output when you enter:

1	100.00	10
2	100.00	30
3	10.50	20
4	22.85	19
5	96.58	21

Run: Enter this program in Python or open Source file **1.2_programming_task_1.9.py** and run it with the same data to see if you are correct.

1 Computational thinking and programming

> **Continued**
>
> **Investigate:** Answer the following questions about the program.
> - What is the percentage discount given when the value is multiplied by 0.9?
> - What is the logical operator in the conditional statement?
> - Which code only runs when the condition is true?
> - Which code will run when the condition is true and when the condition is false?
>
> **Modify 1:** Change this program to give the discount when the person has bought 10 or more items.
>
> **Modify 2:** Change this program to give the discount when the person has spent $100.00 or more.
>
> **Make:** Write a new Python program to:
> - ask the user to enter the total cost of their items
> - ask the user to enter a code to see if they get a discount
> - give the user a 10% discount if they enter the code 9911
> - output a message if they got the code correct
> - output the total cost (with the discount if it was given, or without the discount if it wasn't given).
>
> Test your program with a range of data, for example different total costs and different codes.

IF ELSE

An **IF ELSE statement** is a conditional statement. The ELSE statement runs when the condition is false. In Python the format is:

```
if condition:
    code that runs when the condition is True
else:
    code that runs when the condition is False
this code is not indented and will always run
```

The word `else` is written in lowercase. The ELSE does not include a condition, and is followed by a colon (`:`).

The code that is in the `else` statement is indented to the same point as the `if`. The code that runs when the condition is false is indented to the same place as the code that runs when the condition is true.

The vertical lines show where the indents line up in this program. The IF and the ELSE are at the same level, and the code inside each part of the IF statement is at the same level.

1.4 Conditional statements in text-based programming

```
if condition:
    code that runs when the condition is True
else:
    code that runs when the condition is False
```

When you have finished writing the code that runs when the condition is true and you have pressed enter, the cursor will be too far indented for the `else:` command. You need to press backspace on your keyboard to remove the indentation.

Figure 1.28: Backspace key on a keyboard

Once you have put the colon after `else`, press enter. The code will indent on the next line. If the code does not indent, it might be because you are missing the colon, or you have spelt `else` incorrectly.

> **Note:** Remember some IDEs don't indent, but if yours normally does, make sure you have keyed the code in correctly.

In pseudocode, the statements that run in the ELSE are before the ENDIF. For example:

```
IF number > 10 THEN
    OUTPUT number * 2
ELSE
    OUTPUT number
ENDIF
```

This pseudocode algorithm in Python will be:

```python
if number > 10:
    print(number * 2)
else:
    print(number)
```

1 Computational thinking and programming

Writing an IF ELSE statement

1. You need to decide on the condition. This is the question that can only be true or false and needs to use one of the logical operators.
2. Identify the code you want to run when the condition is true.
3. Identify the code you want to run when the condition is false.

You can plan your IF ELSE statement before you write the code.

Example 1

A program asks the user to enter the colour that is made when red and blue are mixed.

Figure 1.29: Mixing coloured paint can create different colours

The program outputs a message if they get it correct, and it tells them the answer if they get it incorrect.

1. The condition is if the variable equals purple.
2. If it is true, output `"That is correct."`.

1.4 Conditional statements in text-based programming

3   If it is false, output `"Sorry that's incorrect. Red and blue make purple."`.

```
colour = input("What colour is made when red and blue are mixed?")
if colour == "purple":
    print("That is correct.")
else:
    print("Sorry that's incorrect. Red and blue make purple.")
```

Example 2

A program asks the user to enter the percentage they scored on a test and outputs if they passed (got 50% or more). If they did not pass, the program tells them what score they needed to pass.

1   The condition is if the percentage is 50 or more.
2   If it is true, output `"You passed."`.
3   If it is false, output `"You did not pass this time. You needed 50% to pass."`.

```
score = int(input("Enter your percentage."))
if score >= 50:
    print("You passed.")
else:
    print("You did not pass this time. You needed 50% to pass.")
```

Example 3

A program asks the user a maths question and outputs a message if they answer correctly. The program tells them the answer if they get it wrong. The question is: What is 5 × 5?

1   The condition is if the user enters the number 25.
2   If it is true, output `"That's correct."`.
3   If it is false, output `"No, the answer is 25."`.

```
answer = int(input("What is 5 * 5?"))
if answer == 25:
    print("That's correct.")
else:
    print("No, the answer is 25.")
```

1 Computational thinking and programming

Programming task 1.10: Predict, Run, Investigate, Modify and Make

You will need: a pen and paper, a desktop computer, laptop or tablet with an IDE for Python, Source file **1.3_programming_task_1.10.py**

Figure 1.30: My favourite animal is a horse!

Read the program written here.

```
userAnimal = input("What is my favourite animal?")
if userAnimal == "horse":
    print("Yes that's correct.")
else:
    print("No, my favourite animal is a horse.")
```

Predict: Write down what you think this program will output when you enter:

1. Horse
2. horse
3. bird
4. dolphin

Run: Enter this program in Python or open Source file **1.3_programming_task_1.10.py** and run it with the same data to see if you are correct.

1.4 Conditional statements in text-based programming

Continued

Investigate: Write this program on paper, or print a copy of the program. Work with a partner for this task. On your paper, use different colours or shapes to highlight:

- the condition
- the logical operator
- the code that will run when the condition is true
- the code that will run when the condition is false
- the code that will run both when the condition is true and when the condition is false.

Modify 1: Change the animal in this program to your favourite animal instead of a horse.

Modify 2: Change this program to output a different message when the user gets the correct animal, and one when they don't get the correct animal.

Make: Write a new Python program to ask the user a question about yourself, for example a hobby or something that you enjoy doing. Make the program read the answer from the user. Then, output a message if they get the answer correct, and a different message if they get the answer incorrect.

Test your program with a range of different inputs to make sure the correct message is output.

Programming task 1.11: Predict, Run, Investigate, Modify and Make

You will need: a pen and paper, a desktop computer, laptop or tablet with an IDE for Python, Source file **1.4_programming_task_1.11.py**

Read the program written here.

```
first = int(input("Enter a number"))
second = int(input("Enter another number"))
if first >= second:
    print(first, "is the largest number input")
else:
    print(second, "is the largest number input")
```

1 Computational thinking and programming

> **Continued**
>
> **Predict:** Write down what you think this program will output when you enter:
>
> | | | |
> |---|---|---|
> | 1 | 3 | 4 |
> | 2 | 2 | 2 |
> | 3 | 10 | –5 |
> | 4 | –2 | 0 |
>
> **Run:** Enter this program in Python or open Source file **1.4_programming_task_1.11.py** and run it with the same data to see if you are correct.
>
> **Investigate:** Work with a partner to answer these questions:
> - What is the logical operator that is used?
> - What is the condition?
> - What is output when the condition is true?
> - What is output when the condition is false?
>
> **Modify 1:** Change the program to output the smallest number that is input.
>
> **Modify 2:** Change this program to also output the total of the two numbers that are input.
>
> **Make:** Write a new Python program to ask two users to enter their name and age in years. Output the name of the person who is the oldest.
>
> Test your program with a range of different inputs to make sure the correct message is output.

ELSEIF

IF ELSE only allows for two conditions: condition if true and condition if false. If you want to write code that has multiple conditions, you need the ELSEIF statement. In Python, the command is `elif` (the 'se' is not included). If the first condition is false, then the second condition is checked. Here is how ELSEIF is structured in Python:

```
if condition1:
    code that runs when the condition is True
elif condition2:
    code that runs when condition1 is False and
    condition2 is True
this code is not indented and will always run
```

The command `elif` is written in lowercase letters and is followed by the condition (for example `number > 10`) and then a colon (`:`).

```
elif number > 10:
```

1.4 Conditional statements in text-based programming

The `elif` is indented to the same point as the `if`. The code that runs when condition1 is false but condition2 is true is indented to the same place as the code that runs when condition1 is true.

```
if condition1:
    code that runs when the condition is True
elif condition2:
    code that runs when the condition is False
```

As you saw when learning about `else`, when you finish writing the code that runs when condition1 is true and press enter, the cursor will be indented too far. You need to press backspace on your keyboard to remove the indentation before writing the `elif` and condition 2 (see Figure 1.28).

Once you have put the colon after condition2, press enter. The code will indent on the next line. If the code does not indent when you are expecting it to, it might be because you are missing the colon, or you have spelt `elif` incorrectly.

Here's an example with one ELSEIF in pseudocode:

```
IF number > 10 THEN
    OUTPUT number * 2
ELSEIF number < 0 THEN
    OUTPUT "That is too small"
ENDIF
```

This pseudocode algorithm in Python will be:

```
if number > 10:
    print(number * 2)
elif number < 0:
    print("That is too small")
```

Multiple ELSEIFs

A conditional statement in Python can have any number of `elifs`. Here's an example of a pseudocode algorithm with multiple ELSEIFs.

```
OUTPUT "Enter the name of a primary colour"
INPUT answer
IF answer = "red" THEN
    OUTPUT "Red is a primary colour"
ELSEIF answer = "blue" THEN
    OUTPUT "Blue is a primary colour"
ELSEIF answer = "yellow" THEN
    OUTPUT "Yellow is a primary colour"
ENDIF
OUTPUT "The end"
```

Figure 1.31: The primary colours **a:** red, **b:** blue and **c:** yellow

1 Computational thinking and programming

This algorithm in Python will be:

```
answer = input("Enter the name of a primary
                colour")
if answer == "red":
    print("Red is a primary colour")
elif answer == "blue":
    print("Blue is a primary colour")
elif answer == "yellow":
    print("Yellow is a primary colour")
print("The end")
```

The conditions will run in the order written. In the primary colour example, the first condition is:

```
if answer == "red":
```

If this condition is true (the data stored in `answer` is `"red"`) then `"Red is a primary colour"` will be output and then `"The end"` will be output.

If the first condition is false, the second condition will run. This is:

```
elif answer == "blue":
```

If this condition is true (the data stored in `answer` is `"blue"`) then `"Blue is a primary colour"` will be output and then `"The end"` will be output.

If the second condition is false, the third condition will run. This is:

```
elif answer == "yellow":
```

If this condition is true (the data stored in `answer` is `"yellow"`) then `"Yellow is a primary colour"` will be output and then `"The end"` will be output.

If the third condition is false, then there are no more parts and the program will output `"The end"`.

Primary colours can be blended to make new ones.

1.4 Conditional statements in text-based programming

> **Unplugged activity 1.11**
>
> **You will need:** a pen and paper, scissors
>
> A program takes as input the names of two sports teams that competed in a contest. It also takes the score each team got. The program outputs the name of the team that won, or outputs that it was a draw (a 'draw' means that both teams scored the same).
>
> The program has got mixed up and is in the wrong order. It is also missing the required indentations. You need to work with a partner to put the program back into the correct order. Copy the code sections onto individual pieces of paper and then rearrange them in order. Make sure you indent any code that is inside an IF statement (move the code further to the right).
>
> ```
> print(team2Name, "wins")
> print("It's a draw")
> team1Name = input("Enter the name of team 1")
> elif team1Score > team2Score:
> print(team1Name, "wins")
> team2Name = input("Enter the name of team 2)
> if team1Score == team2Score:
> team1Score = int(input("Enter team 1's score"))
> elif team2Score > team1Score:
> team2Score = int(input("Enter team 2's score"))
> ```

ELSEIF and ELSE

A conditional statement with any number of ELSEIFs can also have one ELSE. It does not have to have an ELSE – this is optional. It cannot have more than one ELSE.

The ELSE will run when none of the other conditions are true.

The ELSE follows the same format as previously, and it is always the last item in the conditional statement. You cannot have an ELSE and then an ELSEIF after it.

Here's an example of a pseudocode algorithm with multiple ELSEIFs and an ELSE.

My favourite colour is red.

1 Computational thinking and programming

```
OUTPUT "Enter the name of a primary colour"
INPUT answer
IF answer = "red" THEN
    OUTPUT "Red is a primary colour"
ELSEIF answer = "blue" THEN
    OUTPUT "Blue is a primary colour"
ELSEIF answer = "yellow" THEN
    OUTPUT "Yellow is a primary colour"
ELSE
    OUTPUT answer, "is not a primary colour"
ENDIF
OUTPUT "The end"
```

This pseudocode algorithm in Python will be:

```python
answer = input("Enter the name of a primary colour")
if answer == "red":
    print("Red is a primary colour")
elif answer == "blue":
    print("Blue is a primary colour")
elif answer == "yellow":
    print("Yellow is a primary colour")
else:
    print(answer, "is not a primary colour")
print("The end")
```

This time, if the data stored in `answer` is not `"red"` (condition 1), not `"blue"` (condition 2) and not `"yellow"` (condition 3), then the `else:` will run and the data stored in `answer` will be output with `"is not a primary colour"`. Then the program will output `"The end"`.

Activity 1.5

You will need: a pen and paper, a desktop computer, laptop or tablet with an IDE for Python and access to Source file **1.5_activity_1.5.py**

Ask your teacher for Source file **1.5_activity_1.5.py** and open it, or type the Python code from the previous section on ELSEIF and ELSE into your IDE. Work with a partner to make sure you include the correct syntax and indents.

Test your program with a range of different answers and make sure the correct answer is displayed each time.

1.4 Conditional statements in text-based programming

Writing an ELSEIF statement

1. You need to decide on the first condition. This is the question that can only be true or false, and it needs to use one of the logical operators. This will always be tested first.
2. Identify the code that will run when the first condition is true.
3. Identify the next condition. This will be checked only when the first condition is false.
4. Identify the code that will run when the previous conditions are false and this condition is true.
5. If you want more than one ELSEIF statement, repeat Steps 3 to 4.
6. Decide if you need an ELSE. This will run when none of the conditions are true.
7. Decide on the code that will run when the ELSE runs.

As with IF and IF ELSE, you can plan your ELSEIF statement before you write the code. But you need to make more decisions.

Example 1

A program asks the user to enter the colour that is made when red and blue are mixed. It outputs one message if they input `"purple"`, a different message if they input `"green"`, another different message if they input `"orange"`, another different message for `"yellow"` and another different message if they input anything else.

1. The first condition is: If the input equals purple.
2. If condition 1 is true, output `"That is correct"`.
3. If condition 1 is false, condition 2 is: If the input equals green.
4. If condition 2 is true, output `"Green is made from yellow and blue"`.
5. If conditions 1 and 2 are false, condition 3 is: If the input equals orange.
6. If condition 3 is true, output `"Orange is made from red and yellow"`.
7. If conditions 1, 2 and 3 are false, condition 4 is: If the input equals yellow.
8. If condition 4 is true, output `"Yellow is a primary colour"`.

9   If conditions 1, 2, 3 and 4 are all false, output "Sorry, the answer is purple".

```
colour = input("What colour is made when red and blue are mixed?")
if colour == "purple":
    print("That is correct")
elif colour == "green":
    print("Green is made from yellow and blue")
elif colour == "orange":
    print("Orange is made from red and yellow")
elif colour == "yellow":
    print("Yellow is a primary colour")
else:
    print("Sorry, the answer is purple")
```

Example 2

A program asks the user to enter the percentage they scored on a test and outputs whether they got a gold star (80% or more), a silver star (60% or more), a bronze star (50% or more) or if they did not pass (less than 50%).

Figure 1.32: Gold, silver and bronze stars

1.4 Conditional statements in text-based programming

1. Condition 1 is: If the percentage is 80 or more.
2. If it is true, output "Gold star".
3. If condition 1 is false, condition 2 is: If the percentage is 60 or more.
4. If it is true, output "Silver star".
5. If conditions 1 and 2 are false, condition 3 is: If the percentage is 50 or more.
6. If it is true, output "Bronze star".
7. If conditions 1, 2 and 3 are false, output "You needed 50% to pass".

```
score = int(input("Enter your percentage"))
if score >= 80:
    print("Gold star")
elif score >= 60:
    print("Silver star")
elif score >= 50:
    print("Bronze star")
else:
    print("You needed 50% to pass")
```

Example 3

A program asks the user to guess the number the program has stored (50) and outputs a message telling them if they got it correct, or if they guessed too high or too low.

1. The first condition is: If the user enters the number 50.
2. If it is true, output "That's correct".
3. If condition 1 is false, condition 2 is: If the number is more than 50.
4. If it is true, output "Too high".
5. If conditions 1 and 2 are false, condition 3 is: If the number is less than 50.
6. If it is true, output "Too low".

1 Computational thinking and programming

```
number = 50
answer = int(input("Guess what number I have stored"))
if answer == number:
    print("That's correct")
elif answer > number:
    print("Too high")
elif answer < number:
    print("Too low")
```

Example 3 can also be written using an `else` instead of the last `elif`. This is because if the number is not higher than 50, and is not the same as 50, then it must be smaller.

```
number = 50
answer = int(input("Guess what number I have stored?"))
if answer == number:
    print("That's correct")
elif answer > number:
    print("Too high")
else:
    print("Too low")
```

Unplugged activity 1.12

You will need: coloured pens or pencils, a large piece of paper

Create a 'Flowchart to Pseudocode to Python' poster for conditional statements. You can use the examples given in this book, or you can create your own. Your poster needs to include the same algorithm written as a flowchart, in pseudocode and in Python. It needs to show how the same features appear in each style.

Your poster needs to include IF THEN, ELSE and ELSEIF statements.

1.4 Conditional statements in text-based programming

Programming task 1.12: Predict, Run, Investigate, Modify and Make

You will need: a pen and paper, a desktop computer, laptop or tablet with an IDE for Python, access to Source file **1.6_programming_task_1.12.py**

A compass shows whether you are facing north, south, east or west. The degrees can be used to identify which way you are facing. If your compass is greater than or equal to 315° or less than 45°, then you are facing north. If your compass is 45° or more and less than 135°, then you are facing east.

Read this program.

```
degrees = int(input("Enter the number of degrees you are facing"))
if degrees >= 315:
    print("North")
elif degrees >= 225:
    print("West")
elif degrees >= 135:
    print("South")
elif degrees >= 45:
    print("East")
else:
    print("North")
```

> **Continued**
>
> **Predict:** Write down what you think this program will output when you enter:
>
> 1. 0
> 2. 30
> 3. 45
> 4. 90
> 5. 218
> 6. 300
> 7. 358
>
> **Run:** Enter this program in Python or open Source file **1.6_programming_task_1.12.py** and run it with the same data to see if you are correct.
>
> **Investigate:** Write this program on paper or print a copy of the program. Work with a partner for this task. On your paper, use different colours or shapes to highlight:
>
> - the first condition
> - the number of ELSEIF statements
> - what the output is if none of the statements are true.
>
> **Modify:** Some compasses also show if you are facing north-west, north-east, south-east or south-west. Change the program so it outputs if the user is facing north, south, east, west, north-west, north-east, south-west or south-east.
>
> **Make:** Write a new Python program that will take the number of minutes past the hour it is, and then output whether this is nearest quarter past, half past, quarter to or on the hour.
>
> For example, if the user enters 5 the program will output "On the hour".
>
> If the user enters 25 the program will output "Half past".
>
> Test your program with a range of different inputs to make sure the correct message is output.

1.4 Conditional statements in text-based programming

Programming task 1.13: Predict, Run, Investigate, Modify and Make

You will need: a pen and paper, a desktop computer, laptop or tablet with an IDE for Python, access to Source file **1.7_programming_task_1.13.py**

A character in a game has a horizontal position and a vertical position. The user decides which way the character will move. They can move up, down, left or right.

- When the player moves up, the vertical position increases by 1.
- When the player moves down, the vertical position decreases by 1.
- When the player moves right, the horizontal position increases by 1.
- When the player moves left, the horizontal position decreases by 1.

Now read this program.

```
horizontal = 10
vertical = 20
direction = input("Enter U to move up, D to move down,
                L to move left or R to move right.")
if direction == "U":
    vertical = vertical + 1
elif direction == "D":
    vertical = vertical - 1
elif direction == "R":
    horizontal = horizontal + 1
elif direction == "L":
    horizontal = horizontal - 1
else:
    print("Invalid movement")
print("Your horizontal position is", horizontal)
print("Your vertical position is", vertical)
```

Predict: Write down what you think this program will output when you enter:

1. U
2. D
3. L
4. R
5. Up
6. None

1 Computational thinking and programming

> **Continued**
>
> **Run:** Enter this program in Python or open Source file **1.7_programming_task_1.13.py** and run it with the same data to see if you are correct.
>
> **Investigate:** Work with a partner to answer the following questions.
>
> - How many different logical operators are used in the program?
> - How many conditions are used in the program?
> - What inputs will cause `"Invalid movement"` to be output?
>
> **Modify:** Change the program.
>
> - Change the vertical position by 10 when the user wants to move up.
> - Change the vertical position by −10 when the user wants to move down.
>
> **Make:** The player's area only exists from horizontal position 0 to 1000 and from vertical position 0 to 500, as shown in Figure 1.33.
>
>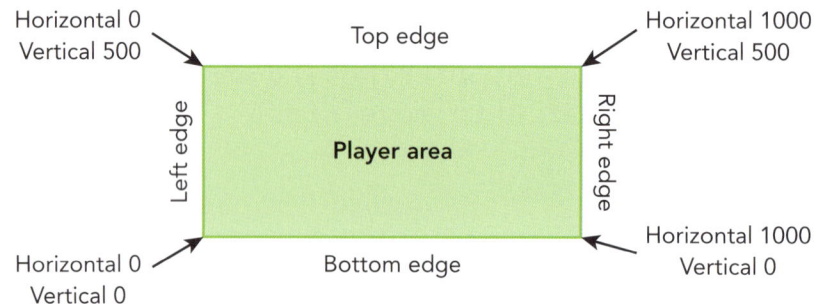
>
> **Figure 1.33:** Player area with horizontal and vertical coordinates
>
> Write a new Python program that:
>
> - takes as input the player's horizontal position as an integer
> - takes as input the player's vertical position as an integer
> - outputs a message if the player is near one of the edges (within 10 positions) and which edge, for example if the horizontal position is 9, they are near the left edge, and if the vertical position is 490, they are near the top edge. If the player is near two edges, these both need to be output (you can use one IF statement for the vertical edges and one IF statement for the horizontal edges).
>
> Test your program with a range of different inputs to make sure the correct messages are output.

1.4 Conditional statements in text-based programming

> **Continued**
>
> **Self-assessment**
>
> Give yourself a rating for how independently you worked on this programming task.
>
> - On my own: I edited and created the program on my own and solved my own problems.
> - With some help: I needed a prompt to help me with some parts of the task, for example to solve a bug.
> - With support: I had help to write some or all of the task, or to fix the errors that I encountered.
>
> Compare how independently you worked on previous programming tasks. Did you find this task more challenging than previous tasks, or are you finding it easier to solve the problems?

Boolean operators in Python

We revisited the three Boolean operators AND, OR and NOT in Topic 1.2. Python has the same three Boolean operators. They are all written in lowercase letters.

- `and` has two conditions: one condition on either side. If both conditions are true, the result is true. Otherwise, the result is false.
- `or` has two conditions: one condition on either side. If one condition is true or both conditions are true, the result is true. It is false only when both conditions are false.
- `not` has one condition: if the condition is true, it becomes false. If the condition is false, it becomes true.

1 Computational thinking and programming

Using and

This example shows the and condition:

```
age = int(input("Enter your age"))
card = input("Do you have a discount card? Enter yes or no")
if(age < 16 and card == "yes"):
    print("You get 10% discount")
else:
    print("You don't get a discount")
```

- If the value stored in `age` is less than 16 and the value stored in `card` is `"yes"`, then `"You get 10% discount"` is output.
- If the age is 16 or more, `"You don't get a discount"` is output. The value in `card` does not change this result.
- If the value in `card` is not `"yes"`, then `"You don't get a discount"` is output. The value in `age` does not change this result.

Using or

This example shows the or condition:

```
answer = input("Do you want to continue? Enter yes or no")
if(answer == "yes" or answer == "YES" or answer == "Yes"):
    print("OK, let's continue")
else:
    print("Bye")
```

- If the value stored in `answer` is `"yes"`, then `"OK, let's continue"` is output.
- If the value stored in `answer` is `"YES"`, then `"OK, let's continue"` is output.
- If the value stored in `answer` is `"Yes"`, then `"OK, let's continue"` is output.
- If the value stored in `answer` is anything else, then `"Bye"` is output.

1.4 Conditional statements in text-based programming

Using not

This example shows the `not` condition:

```
colour = "red"
guess = input("What colour am I thinking of?")
if not(guess == "red"):
    print("No, I'm not thinking of", guess)
else:
    print("Yes!")
```

- If the value stored in `guess` is not equal to `"red"`, then `"No, I'm not thinking of"` is output with the colour that the user entered.
- If the value stored in `guess` is equal to `"red"`, then `"Yes!"` is output.

Programming task 1.14: Predict, Run, Investigate, Modify and Make

You will need: a pen and paper, a desktop computer, laptop or tablet with an IDE for Python, access to Source file **1.8_programming_task_1.14.py**

Read the program here.

```
answer = input("What gets wetter the more it dries?")
if answer == "TOWEL" or answer == "towel" or answer == "Towel":
    print("Correct")
else:
    print("No, it's a towel")
```

Predict: Write down what this program will output when you enter:

1. Water
2. A towel
3. Towel
4. TOWEL
5. towels
6. towel

Run: Enter this program in Python or open Source file **1.8_programming_task_1.14.py** and run it to see if you are correct.

99

1 Computational thinking and programming

Continued

Investigate: Work with a partner to identify the following parts of the program:

- the logical operator(s)
- the Boolean operator(s)
- the code that will run when one of the conditions is true
- the code that will run when none of the conditions is true.

Modify: `"A towel"` and `"towels"` are both correct answers. Change the program to accept both of these as correct answers.

Make: Write a new Python program to ask the user for the answer to a riddle and accept different ways that this answer can be entered.

Programming task 1.15: Predict, Run, Investigate, Modify and Make

You will need: a pen and paper, a desktop computer, laptop or tablet with an IDE for Python, access to Source file **1.9_programming_task_1.15.py**

Figure 1.34: Enjoying a film

1.4 Conditional statements in text-based programming

> **Continued**
>
> This program identifies a film for the user to watch. The user enters their age and a type of film. The film options are listed in this table:
>
> | Film | Minimum age | Type of film |
> |---|---|---|
> | The Brockhurst Diaries | 18 | Drama |
> | The Day You Arrived | 15 | Drama |
> | Potato Pie | 0 | Drama |
> | A Family for Francesca | 12 | Comedy |
> | Any Minute Now | 0 | Comedy |
> | A May Wedding | 15 | Romance |
> | Forever Be | 0 | Romance |
>
> Read the program written below.
>
> ```
> age = int(input("Enter your age in years"))
> type = input("Enter Drama, Comedy or Romance")
> if age >= 18 and type == "Drama":
>     print("The Brockhurst Diaries")
> elif age >= 15 and type == "Drama":
>     print("The Day You Arrived")
> elif type == "Drama":
>     print("Potato Pie")
> elif age >= 12 and type == "Comedy":
>     print("A Family for Francesca")
> elif type == "Comedy":
>     print("Any Minute Now")
> elif age >= 15 and type == "Romance":
>     print("A May Wedding")
> elif type == "Romance":
>     print("Forever Be")
> ```
>
> **Predict:** Identify what you think will be output when a user enters:
>
> 1. 15   "drama"
> 2. 28   "Romance"
> 3. 35   "Drama"
> 4. 12   "Comedy"

1 Computational thinking and programming

> **Continued**
>
> **Run:** Enter this program in Python or open Source file **1.9_programming_task_1.15.py** and run it with the same data to see if you are correct.
>
> **Investigate:** Answer the following questions about the program.
>
> - Which Boolean operator(s) is/are used in the program?
> - What is output if the user does not enter any of the three types of film?
>
> **Modify:** Make the following changes to the program.
>
> - Output a suitable message if the user has not input a valid type of film.
> - Allow the user to enter the type of film in different ways, for example `"Drama"` or `"drama"`.
> - Add another type of film of your choice. First create a table with a minimum of two films with an age and type, then edit your program.
>
> **Make:** Write a new Python program that:
>
> - asks the user to enter a type of music to listen to
> - asks the user to enter the maximum number of minutes they want the song to last
> - outputs a song that matches their inputs.
>
> Create a copy of this table and write the names of your chosen songs, the type of music and the length in minutes (add more rows if you wish).
>
> | Song title | Type of music | Length in minutes |
> |---|---|---|
> | | | |
> | | | |

Questions 1.5

1. What is the command word for a conditional statement in Python?
2. How do you identify the code that you want to run when the condition is true in Python?
3. How many ELSE statements can one IF statement have in Python?
4. Identify the output that this program will give:

```
value = 10
if value < 10:
    print("Tortoise")
else:
    print("Hamster")
```

1.4 Conditional statements in text-based programming

5   Identify the output that this program will give:

```
data1 = "yes"
data2 = "no"
total = 0
if data1 == "no":
    total = 10
elif data2 == "no":
    total = 20
print(total)
```

6   Identify the output that this program will give:

```
data1 = "yes"
data2 = "yes"
total = 0
if data1 == "no":
    total = 10
elif data2 == "no":
    total = 20
print(total)
```

7   In an ELSEIF statement, when does the second condition get tested?

8   Write a Python program to ask the user to enter the year group they are in at school and output a message about that year.

Common errors

You might have already had some errors when writing your programs, or you might not have had any yet. It is OK for programs to have errors. Even the best programmers make errors all the time. How you find and correct the errors is how you learn to program, like making a mistake when you bake a cake – you know what not to do next time!

Figure 1.35: We all make mistakes

1 Computational thinking and programming

Each line of Python code in Table 1.6 has an error in it.

Code	Error	Correction
`IF variable == 10:`	The command word should be in lowercase.	`if variable == 10:`
`if value = 1:`	The logical operator needs two equals signs.	`if value == 1:`
`if data == 30`	The condition is missing the colon at the end.	`if data == 30:`
`if variable1 => 2:`	The parts of the logical operator are the wrong way round – it should be >=.	`if variable1 >= 2:`
`if data == 10:` `print("Yes")`	"Yes" should be output when the condition is true, but this line is not indented.	`if data == 10:` `    print("Yes")`

`if data < 3:`
`    print("yes")`
`else:`
`        print("no")`
	The `else` and `if` should have the same indent, and the code that runs when the condition is false should have the same indent as the code that runs when it is true.	`if data < 3:`
		`    print("yes")`
		`else:`
		`    print("no")`

`if data < 3:`
`    print("yes")`
`else`
`    print("no")`
	A colon is missing after the `else`.	`if data < 3:`
		`    print("yes")`
		`else:`
		`    print("no")`

`if data < 3:`
`print("yes")`
`else:`
`    print("no")`
	The code that runs when the condition is true is not indented.	`if data < 3:`
		`    print("yes")`
		`else:`
		`    print("no")`

`if value == 10:`
`    print("Y")`
`else if value == 11:`
`    print("N")`
	The command for ELSEIF is `elif`.	`if value == 10:`
		`    print("Y")`
		`elif value == 11:`
		`    print("N")`

`if data1 < 3:`
`    total = 3`
`else:`
`    total = 10`
`elif data1 < 10:`
`    total = 4`
	The `else` has to be the last part of the conditional statement, it cannot be followed by an `elif`.	`if data1 < 3:`
		`    total = 3`
		`elif data1 < 10:`
		`    total = 4`
		`else:`
		`    total = 10`

(Continued)

1.4 Conditional statements in text-based programming

Code	Error	Correction

`if var == 0:`
`    dat = 10`
`elif var == 1:`
`    dat = 11`
`else:`
`    dat = 12`
`else:`
`    dat = 13`
	A conditional statement can only have one `else`.	`if var == 0:`
		`    dat = 10`
		`elif var == 1:`
		`    dat = 11`
		`else:`
		`    dat = 12`

`if var == 0:`
`    dat = 10`
`    elif var == 1:`
`        dat = 11`
`else:`
`    dat = 12`
	The `elif` and the `else` need to be aligned with the `if` and the code within the `elif` needs to be aligned with the code that runs when the `if` is true.	`if var == 0:`
		`    dat = 10`
		`elif var == 1:`
		`    dat = 11`
		`else:`
		`    dat = 12`

`if first > 0 and:`	Boolean `and` requires a second condition.	`if first > 0 and first < 10:`
`if new > 1 AND old < 100:`	Boolean `and` needs to be in lowercase letters.	`if new > 1 and old < 100:`
`if new > 1 not:`	Boolean `not` needs to be before the condition. The condition should be in brackets.	`if not(new > 1):`

Table 1.6: Common errors in Python

Summary checklist

- [ ] I can follow a conditional statement in Python that uses IF, ELSEIF and ELSE.
- [ ] I can write a conditional statement in Python that uses IF, ELSEIF and ELSE.
- [ ] I can write a conditional statement in Python that uses multiple ELSEIF conditions.
- [ ] I can follow a conditional statement in Python that uses the Boolean operators AND, OR and NOT.
- [ ] I can write a conditional statement in Python that uses the Boolean operators AND, OR and NOT.

1 Computational thinking and programming

> 1.5 Data in text-based programs

In this topic you will:
- learn the purpose of constants in algorithms
- write an algorithm that includes a constant
- follow algorithms that use the Boolean data type
- write programs in Python that use the Boolean data type.

Key words
Boolean data type

casting

constant

declaration

declare

flag

Getting started

What do you already know?

- You have used variables in different types of algorithms, including in flowcharts, block-based programming languages and text-based programming languages. A variable is a space in memory that is given a name. A program can:
    - store data in that memory space
    - change the data in that memory space
    - read the data in that memory space.

1.5 Data in text-based programs

Continued

- There are different types of data, and sometimes you need to tell a computer program what type of data it should be using.
  - The real data type is for numbers that include decimal points, for example 22.5.
  - The integer data type is for numbers that are only ever whole numbers, for example 12.
  - The string data type is for any combination of letters, numbers and symbols, for example "hello", "123", and "YES!!".

Now try this!

Read this pseudocode algorithm:

```
number1 = 22
number2 = 33
message1 = "The total is"
message2 = "The average is"
total = number1 + number2
average = total / 2
OUTPUT message1, total
OUTPUT message2, average
```

Work with a partner to identify the variables that are used in this algorithm and the most appropriate data type for each one (integer, real or string).

Data types

A computer needs to know the type of data that is being used. For example, the computer needs to know if the data is a number or a word. You have already been introduced to the data types integer, real, character and string.

Use Table 1.7 to remind yourself about these data types.

Data type	Description	Examples
integer	A whole number	0, 22, 34, 998
real	A number with a decimal	0.0, 1.25, 33.598
character	One letter, number or symbol	"h", "0", "!", " "
string	One or more letters, numbers and symbols	"hello", "001", "22.1!!"

Table 1.7: Data types

Boolean data type

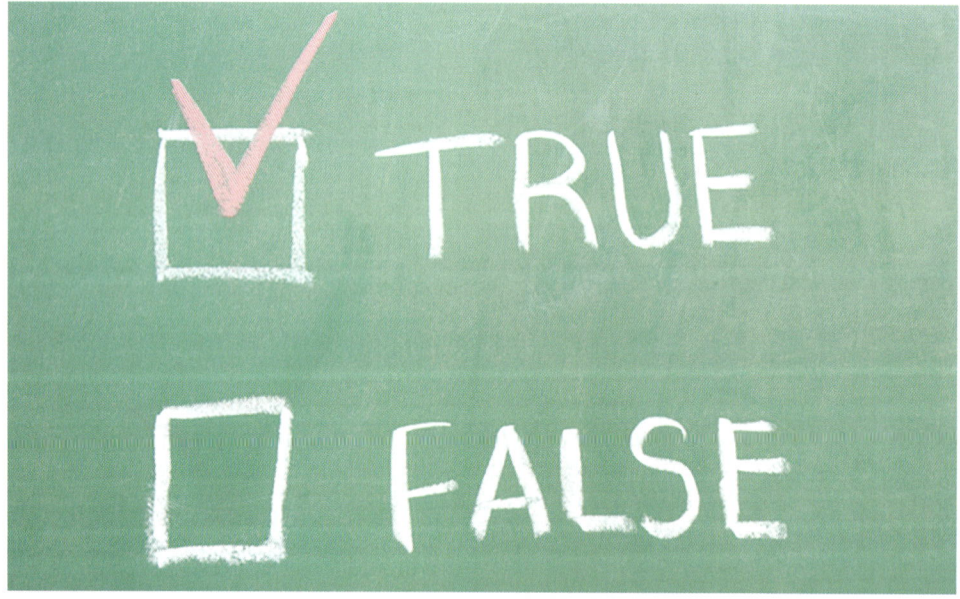

Figure 1.36: Boolean data is either true or false

You should recognise the word 'Boolean' and know that it can be only one of two values: it can be true or it can be false. Data that is the **Boolean data type** is either true or false. There is nothing else.

When you are using a Boolean true or false, the words do not need double quotation marks around them. This tells the computer program that you want it to be the Boolean true and not the word "true".

1.5 Data in text-based programs

In this example, the first variable is a string data type and the second is Boolean.

```
stringVariable = "True"
booleanVariable = True
```

In pseudocode the words true and false can be all lowercase letters (true, false), all uppercase letters (TRUE, FALSE) or just the first letter can be uppercase (True, False). You can decide which to use, but you need to be consistent in each algorithm. If you choose lowercase letters, then you must use lowercase letters each time.

This pseudocode example shows the three different ways true can be written:

```
boolean1 = True
boolean2 = TRUE
boolean3 = true
```

Sometimes a programming language will use 1 and 0 instead of true and false. The 1 and 0 are binary values (you will learn more about binary in Unit 4) and they are the only two options. 1 represents True and 0 represents false.

In Python, the Boolean values start with a capital letter: `True` and `False`

```
pythonBoolean1 = True
pythonBoolean2 = False
```

Unplugged activity 1.13

You will need: a pen and paper

Work on your own for this activity.

Each row in the table has five items of data that need to be stored as the same data type. Decide which data type is most appropriate for each row.

Data set 1	22	13	58	55	888
Data set 2	hello	0000	no!	tomorrow	:)
Data set 3	TRUE	false	maybe	true	FALSE
Data set 4	g	0	!	,	1
Data set 5	false	false	true	true	false
Data set 6	00123	789a	022.05b	12p	£13

Compare your answers with a partner and discuss any differences. If there are some differences, are both data types appropriate, or is one more appropriate than the other?

1 Computational thinking and programming

Programming task 1.16: Predict, Run, Investigate and Modify

You will need: a pen and paper, a desktop computer, laptop or tablet with an IDE for Python, access to Source file **1.10_programming_task_1.16.py**

Read this algorithm with a partner.

```
firstValue = False
secondValue = 20
if secondValue >= 10:
    firstValue = True
print(firstValue)
```

Predict: Identify the value that will be stored in each variable and what the output of the program will be when it runs.

Run: Create this program in Python or open Source file **1.10_programming_task_1.16.py** and run it to see if your prediction was correct.

Investigate: Discuss what will happen if the number in the variable `secondValue` is changed to 0. Identify the variable that has a Boolean data type.

Modify: Change the program so that it outputs `"It is 10 or more"` when the data in `firstValue` is true, and `"It is less than 10"` when the data in `firstValue` is false.

Flags

Boolean data is often used for **flags** in programming. A flag is a variable. The value in the variable identifies whether something has happened or not. If the event has happened, the value in the flag is true. If the event has not happened, the value in the flag is false.

This is similar to a flag in sport. A flag can be raised if an event happens (for example, a foul in football) – we could represent this with true. If the flag is not raised, then the event has not happened – we could represent this with false.

In this Python program, the user is asked to enter their age. If the age is 18 or more, then `age` stores true. If they are under 18, `age` stores false. The variable `age` is a flag. Then, later on in the program, instead of checking the age again, the flag can be used.

Figure 1.37: A linesman flags for offside during a football match

1.5 Data in text-based programs

```
1   input1 = int(input("Enter your age"))
2   if input1 >= 18:
3       age = True
4   else:
5       age = False
```

You can even store the result of a comparison in a variable.

The conditional statement (all the code from line 2 onwards) can be rewritten as this one line:

```
age = (input1 >= 18)
```

Programming task 1.17: Predict, Run, Investigate and Modify

You will need: a pen and paper, a desktop computer, laptop or tablet with an IDE for Python, access to Source file **1.11_programming_task_1.17.py**

You can work individually or with a partner for this task. Read the program written below.

```
answer = int(input("What is 2 * 2?"))
if answer == 4:
    correct1 = True
else:
    correct1 = False


answer = int(input("What is 10 / 2?"))
if answer == 5:
    correct2 = True
else:
    correct2 = False


if correct1 == True and correct2 == True:
    print("You got them both correct")
elif correct1 == True or correct2 == True:
    print("You only got 1 correct")
else:
    print("You got them both incorrect")
```

1 Computational thinking and programming

> ### Continued
>
> **Predict:** Write down the output that you think will be given when the following inputs are entered.
>
> | | | |
> |---|---|---|
> | 1 | 4 | 5 |
> | 2 | 3 | 5 |
> | 3 | 4 | 10 |
> | 4 | 1 | 9 |
>
> **Run:** Create the program in Python or open Source file **1.11_programming_task_1.17.py** and test the program with each of the four sets of test data to check if your predictions were correct.
>
> **Investigate:** Identify each variable that is used in this program and the most appropriate data type for each variable.
>
> **Modify:** Change the program by adding a third question. Store whether the user got the answer correct in a Boolean variable. Output a different message depending on how many questions the user got correct. Test your program.
>
> #### Self-assessment
>
> How confident are you with programming Boolean data types? Give yourself a rating from 1 to 5 about how confident you are:
>
> 1 I am very confident!
> 2 I am confident about most things but still need a little help.
> 3 I am certain about some aspects but not certain about others.
> 4 I am less confident but understand one or two things.
> 5 I am not very confident and still need some help.

> ### Did you know?
>
> If you use a Boolean value in a conditional statement, for example:
>
> ```
> if value1 = True
> ```
>
> you don't need the `= True` part. You can just write it as:
>
> ```
> if value1
> ```
>
> because `value1` is true so the condition is true.

Constants

If something is constant, it means that it does not change. In programming, a **constant** is similar to a variable. A constant has an identifier (name) that points to a space in memory where you can store a value. You can access the value in the constant. However, you cannot change the value in the constant later in the program. This is why it is called a constant. It stays the same.

An example of a constant is pi (π). In maths, you have learnt that the circumference of a circle can be found by using the formula $2\pi r$, which is two times pi times the radius of the circle.

Pi is a constant that stores the number 3.141592 . . . (which we often round down to 3.14). So every time you see pi (π) in a formula, you know that you have to use the number 3.14.

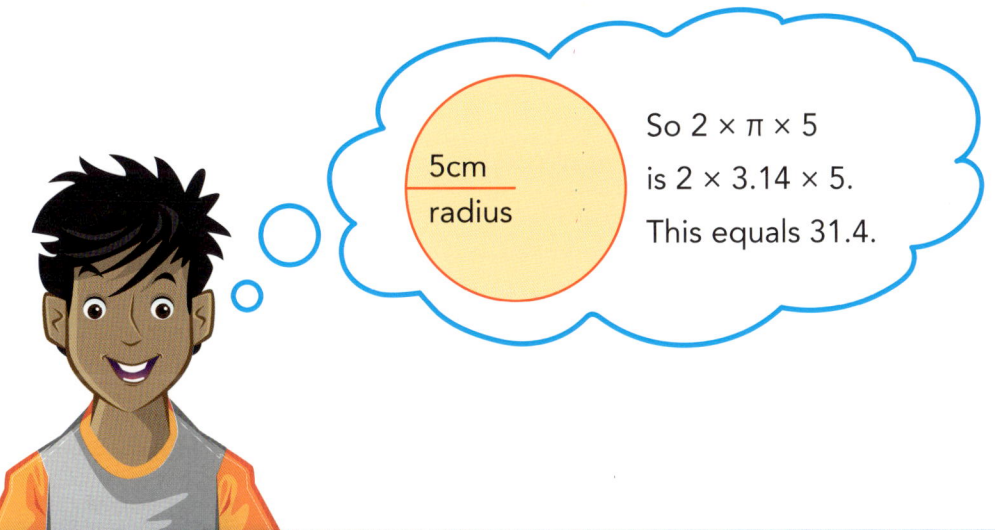

Unplugged activity 1.14

You will need: two boxes or containers, some pens and paper or some items (like a pencil, a ball or a book) that can be placed inside the boxes or containers

Work in pairs or groups for this activity.

Give a box a name, for example "myBox", and write this name on the box or on a sticker to put on the box.

1 Computational thinking and programming

> **Continued**
>
> Take it in turns to give each other instructions to use the variable (the box). For example:
>
> - Store data in myBox. For example, if your data was the string "Red", you would write the word on a piece of paper and place that paper in the box.
> - Remove data from myBox. For example, take out the paper that has been placed in myBox.
> - Output the data. For example, take out the paper from myBox, say what it says, then put it back in myBox.
> - Change the data. For example, take the paper from myBox, change the word (for example to "Yellow") and then put it back in myBox.
>
> Do this twice. The first time you give each other instructions, use the box as a variable. This means you can do all four of the types of instruction listed above. You can store data, retrieve data, delete data and change the data.
>
> The second time you do this, use the box as a constant. This means you can store data (if there is nothing already in there) and you can output the data, but you cannot remove or change the data while you are doing this activity. You can still tell another learner to do these tasks, but they need to say 'no.'
>
> Now you will need a second box or container. Give it an identifier. Decide as a group which box is the variable and which is the constant.
>
> Take it in turns to tell each other to perform one of the four actions with one of the boxes. If an invalid instruction is given to you for the constant, you need to say 'no.'

When do we need constants?

There are several reasons why constants are useful when writing algorithms and programs.

If you store a value in a constant, you know it will not be changed accidentally later in the program. By storing it as a constant, you can use its identifier in your code whenever you need that value, instead of writing the value every time. This also means you won't accidentally write an incorrect value.

It's quite easy to write 1243 as 1234 if you are doing it lots of times.

Another reason to use a constant is that, if you ever need to change the value the constant stores, you only need to do it once – on the line of code where you assigned it. To do this you will need to stop the program, change the code, then run the program again. In Unplugged activity 1.14, if you wanted to change the value of the data you stored in your constant, you would have had to stop the whole activity, change the data, then start the whole activity from the beginning.

1.5 Data in text-based programs

However, you do not always need to use constants. Each time you create a constant, you are taking a space in memory. If you use the value instead, you will use less memory. However, the amount of memory used for constants is very small. It only becomes important to think about this when you are writing longer programs where memory is limited.

Identifying constants

Constants can be used for any piece of data that is written directly into your code. Here are three examples.

Example 1

```
INPUT number
result = number * 10
OUTPUT result
```

The second line has the number 10. We could store this as a constant and then we could refer to it using its identifier.

Example 2

```
INPUT firstItemWeight
OUTPUT "The cost is", firstItemWeight * 2.5
INPUT secondItemWeight
OUTPUT "The cost is", secondItemWeight * 2.5
```

This pseudocode algorithm multiplies each weight input by 2.5. This value can be put into a constant to make sure you don't accidentally write the value incorrectly, for example as 25 instead of 2.5.

The code also has the message "The cost is" twice, so this could be a constant as well.

Example 3

```
INPUT grade
IF grade >= 80 THEN
    OUTPUT "Distinction"
ELSEIF grade >= 50 THEN
    OUTPUT "Merit"
ELSEIF grade >= 30 THEN
    OUTPUT "Pass"
ELSE
    OUTPUT "Try again"
ENDIF
```

1 Computational thinking and programming

This algorithm has three numbers in the IF statement: 80, 50 and 30. Each of these could be stored in a constant and you could use the constant identifier in the IF statements. Then, if the grade boundaries change, for example a distinction drops to 75, the constant can be changed and you will not need to check the IF statement.

Constants in algorithms

A constant is usually **declared** at the start of the program. Declaring means telling the program we want a constant (or variable). We do this by writing a **declaration**: a statement that says what name and value we want the constant to have. Declaring a constant at the start of a program makes the constant easy to find and change if needed.

A constant declaration has four parts:

- a keyword, for example `constant`
- an identifier
- an assignment symbol
- the value to be stored.

In a flowchart, this will be in a process box. For example:

```
constant ten = 10
```

Figure 1.38: Constant declaration in a process box

In pseudocode, this will be written on one line. For example:

```
constant ten = 10
```

In a high-level programming language, there might be a specific word you need to use to declare a constant.

Python has many extra libraries (you will learn about them in Topic 1.6) that give you the ability to use more code. One of these libraries includes constants, but you won't be able to use this library at this stage. For now, you just need to identify that an item will be a constant in Python, so you can use a variable as a constant.

Did you know?
In Python, you cannot make a constant unless you import a special library of additional features you can use.

You can show that you want a variable to be used as a constant by using all uppercase letters for the identifier, for example `MYVARIABLE`. You will still be able to change the value in the program, but using capital letters will remind you not to do this: when you are coding, the value of this variable must stay the same.

1.5 Data in text-based programs

Now, we will rewrite the three examples from the Identifying constants section, this time using constants. We will rewrite each example as a flowchart, in pseudocode and in Python. The first two examples will be given for you, and then you are going to create the flowchart, pseudocode and Python for the third example.

Example 1
Original algorithm:

```
INPUT number
result = number * 10
OUTPUT result
```

The number 10 is going to be stored in the constant `ten`.

Flowchart:
The flowchart has a process box at the start to declare the constant:

- the keyword is constant
- the identifier is ten
- the assignment symbol is =
- the value is 10.

When the number in the constant is used, its identifier is written.

Pseudocode:
In pseudocode, the extra statement is at the start:

- the keyword is constant
- the identifier is ten
- the assignment symbol is =
- the value is 10.

```
constant ten = 10
INPUT number
result = number * ten
OUTPUT result
```

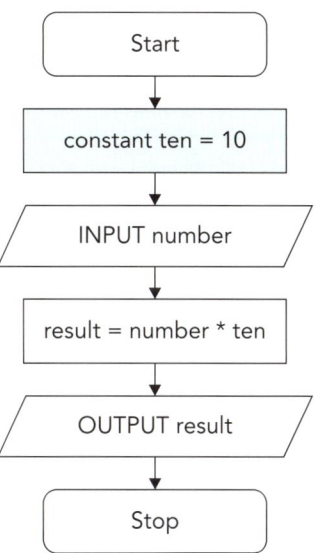

Figure 1.39: Flowchart using a constant

Python:
In Python, the extra statement is at the start:

- the uppercase letters in the identifier show it is a constant
- the identifier is TEN
- the assignment symbol is =
- the value is 10.

```
TEN = 10
number = int(input())
result = number * TEN
print(result)
```

1 Computational thinking and programming

Example 2
Original algorithm:

```
INPUT firstItemWeight
OUTPUT "The cost is", firstItemWeight * 2.5
INPUT secondItemWeight
OUTPUT "The cost is ", secondItemWeight * 2.5
```

The number 2.5 will be put into one constant, and "The cost is" will be put into a second constant.

Flowchart:

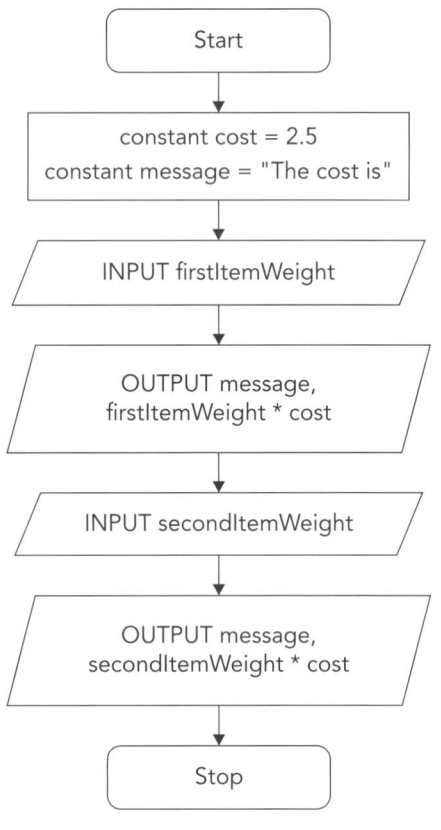

Pseudocode:

```
constant cost = 2.5
constant message = "The cost is"
INPUT firstItemWeight
OUTPUT message, firstItemWeight * cost
INPUT secondItemWeight
OUTPUT message, secondItemWeight * cost
```

Python:

```
COST = 2.5
MESSAGE = "The cost is"
firstItemWeight = int(input())
print(MESSAGE, firstItemWeight * COST)
secondItemWeight = int(input())
print(MESSAGE, secondItemWeight * COST)
```

Figure 1.40: Flowchart, pseudocode and Python code of the same algorithm using a constant

1.5 Data in text-based programs

Programming task 1.21: Predict, Run, Investigate and Modify

You will need: a desktop computer, laptop or tablet with an IDE for Python, access to Source file **1.14_programming_task_1.21.py**

Read this Python program with a partner.

```
data = input("Enter a word")
if bool(data) == False:
    print("No data")
else:
    print("Data")
```

Predict: Discuss what you think will be output if the user enters their name, for example `"Zara"`. Discuss what you think will be output if the user presses enter without typing anything.

Run: Create this program in Python or open Source file **1.14_programming_task_1.21.py** and run it. Enter your name. Run the program again, this time pressing enter without typing anything. Were your predictions correct?

Investigate: Discuss the conditional statement `if bool(data) == False:` and how it works to produce the output.

Modify: Change the program so it asks the user to enter a word again if it is left blank the first time.

How did you approach each programming task?
For example, how did you design your solution?
Would you approach it differently next time? How?

Questions 1.7

1. What are the two values that can be stored in a Boolean data type?
2. What is the difference between the data `"True"` and the data `True`?
3. Identify the data type that should be used for each of these data items.
   a `"Film"`
   b `33.4`
   c `-1999`

d False
e "1"
f "true"

4 Identify the data type of each of the variables in this program.

```
cost = float(input("Enter the cost"))
if cost >= 10.0:
    afford = False
else:
    afford = True
```

Summary checklist

☐ I can describe what a constant is in a program and explain why constants are used.
☐ I can write a program that uses a constant.
☐ I can describe the Boolean data type.
☐ I can identify data that should be stored as a Boolean data type.
☐ I can create a program that uses a Boolean data type.

1.6 Library programs

In this topic you will:
- understand why program libraries exist
- learn what a program library contains
- know how to import a library into a Python program
- be able to call a library function
- understand how to use the return value from a library function.

Key words
call
function
import
parameter
procedure
program library
random number
return

Getting started

What do you already know?

- Programming languages come in different forms, for example block-based languages like Scratch and text-based languages like Python. Users enter the command in text-based languages and use an Integrated Development Environment (IDE) to translate and run the code.

- A library is a place that stores lots of resources for people to access, borrow and use. The most common library you will have used is your school library, where you might have borrowed books.

- A sub-routine is a self-contained algorithm. It has an identifier (name) and you can tell the algorithm to go to the sub-routine by using the sub-routine's identifier. The algorithm will then run the statements in the sub-routine. When it gets to the end of the sub-routine, the algorithm returns to where it was called.

1 Computational thinking and programming

Continued

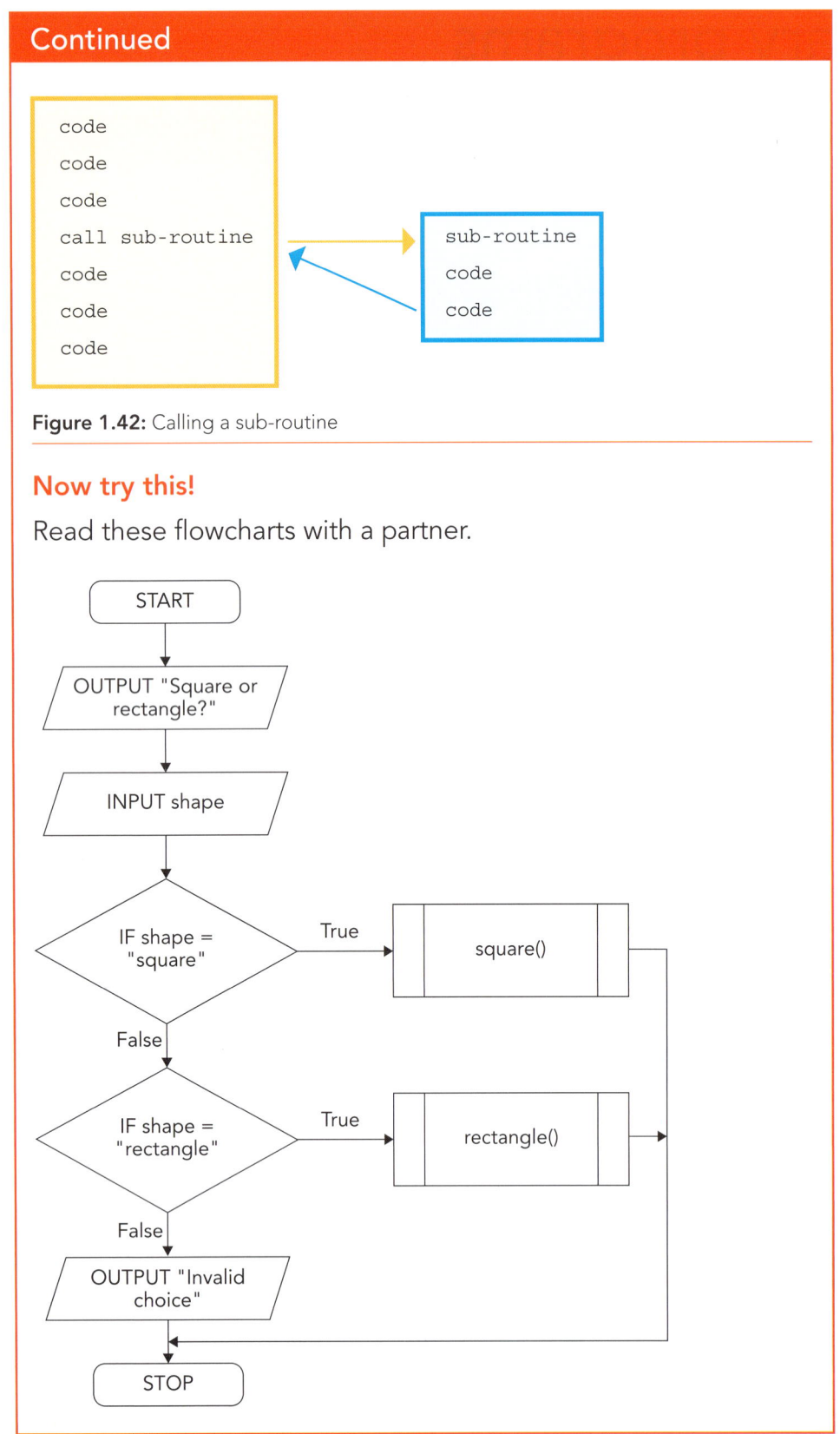

Figure 1.42: Calling a sub-routine

Now try this!

Read these flowcharts with a partner.

1.6 Library programs

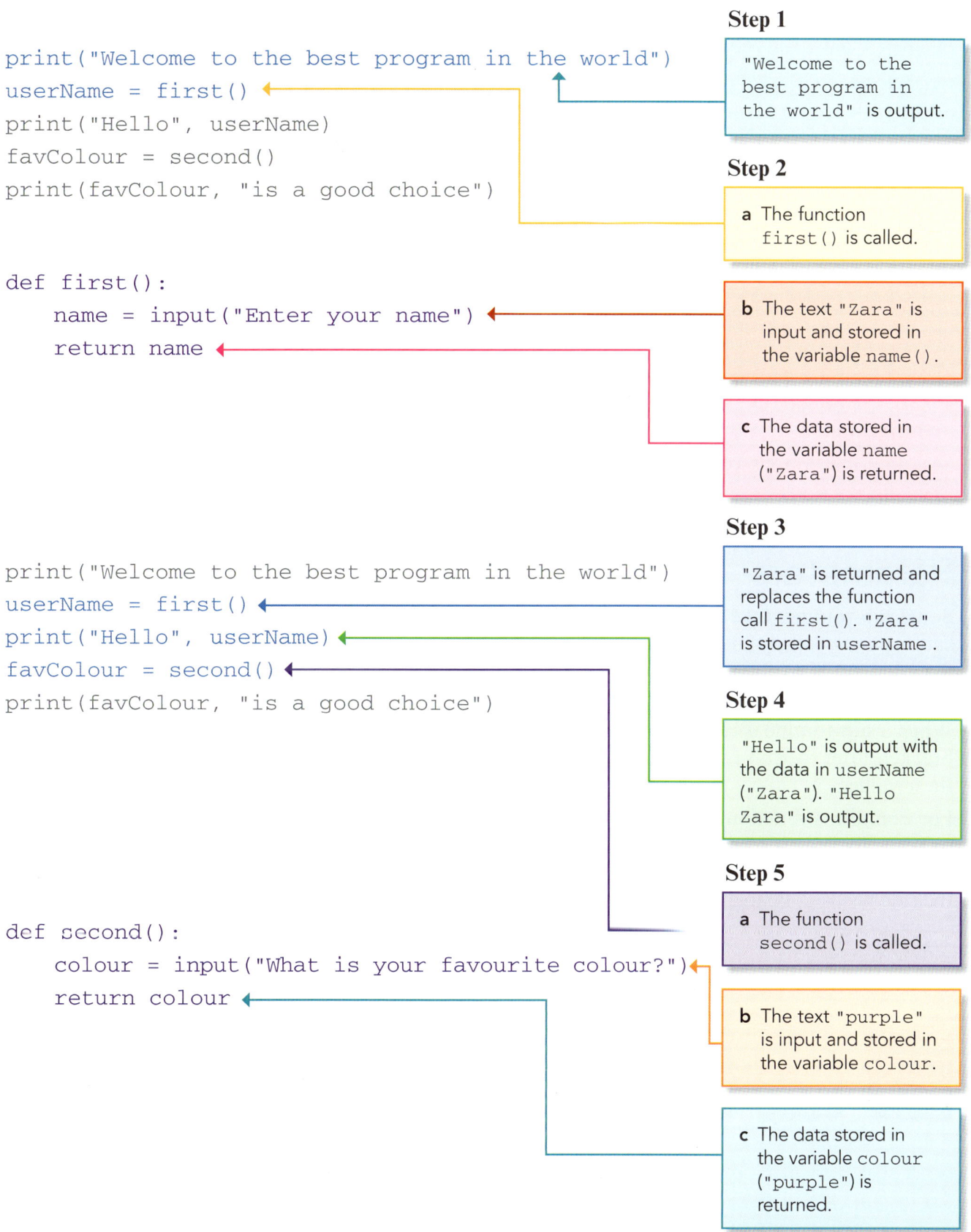

1 Computational thinking and programming

```
print("Welcome to the best program in the world")
userName = first()
print("Hello", userName)
favColour = second()
print(favColour, "is a good choice")
```

Step 6

"purple" is returned and replaces the function call `second()`. "purple" is stored in `favColour`.

Step 7

The data in `favColour` ("purple") is output with "is a good choice". "purple is a good choice" is output.

Not all sub-routines return values. Sub-routines that do not return a value are called **procedures**. Procedures perform a series of instructions but do not need to send anything back to the main program. In some languages, like Python, all sub-routines are called functions. This makes it easier to talk about them, as you do not need to check whether you need a procedure or a function.

You do not need to know the difference at this stage – you can just call them all functions.

Parameters

Some sub-routines take **parameters**. You have just learnt that some sub-routines, called functions, can return a value to the main program. A parameter is a value that is sent to a sub-routine when the sub-routine is called. Some sub-routines will take more than one parameter.

When a sub-routine is called, the parameter value, or values, are in brackets after the sub-routine's name. This allows the sub-routine to use these values.

For example, a function calculates the area of a square, but it needs to know the length of each side of the square. The function takes the length as a parameter. Every time the function is called, the length of the side needs to be included.

1.6 Library programs

This code sends the number 2 to the function `squareArea()`:

```
squareArea(2)
```

The number 2 can now be used in the function `squareArea()` to calculate the area of the square. This area is then returned.

Let's see it in a program.

```
length = int(input("Enter the length of a side"))
area = squareArea(length)
print("The area is", area)
```

In this example, the length of a side of a square is input and stored in the variable `length`.

The data stored in the variable `length` is sent to the function `squareArea()`. You don't know how the function works, but you know if you send it the length of a side it returns the area. This return value is stored in the variable `area`. The data in the variable `area` is then output.

Let's trace it with the input 5.

```
length = int(input("Enter the length of a side"))
area = squareArea(length)
print("The area is", area)
```

Step 1
The number 5 is input and stored in `length`.

Step 2
The function `squareArea()` is called and the data in `length` (5) is sent as a parameter.

Step 3
The function `squareArea()` returns the area (25). This is stored in the variable area.

Step 4
The text "The area is" is output with the data stored in the variable area (25). "The area is 25" is output.

Program libraries

What is a program library?

A **program library** is a collection of sub-routines that have already been written. The programmers who wrote these sub-routines have made them available for you to use in your program.

Figure 1.46: Library full of books

Why do program libraries exist?

There are some algorithms that lots of programmers might want, or need, to use. For example, we know that to find the area of a circle, we need to use the formula πr^2. This is the same for everyone.

Instead of everyone having to rewrite the same code, you can use a library program that performs the task. There is a library called 'math'. In that library, there is a function that will give you the value of pi.

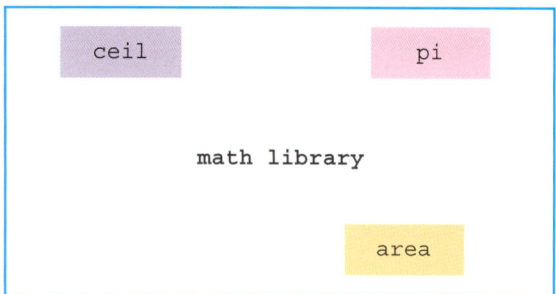

Figure 1.47: Some of the functions in Python's math library

Having these libraries that programmers can download saves time. It also avoids errors. The programmer might get their algorithm wrong and create errors, but the library program has been tested.

Some programmers might need to use an algorithm that they don't know how to write. For example, they might want to output an image to a screen, or make an image move, or use artificial intelligence to predict a result. For these tasks, programmers can use algorithms from a library – created by other people – without needing to know how the algorithms work. This means they can write better programs, be more confident that what they have written will actually work and save valuable time!

Which library do I use?

There are lots of program libraries. Each programming language has its own program libraries. You can think of a program library as a code library, where you can go and get program code to use.

Some libraries have a specific purpose. For example, all the functions in a library might be mathematical functions, graphics functions or even functions for artificial intelligence.

1.6 Library programs

How do I use a library?

When you use a library to help you write a program, you need to tell the program that you want to use a specific library. Each language has a different way of doing this. In some languages, or for some libraries, you have to install the library on your computer before you can use it. Then you can **import** the library into your program so you can use it.

You might think it is cheating to use other people's code in your program, but using libraries isn't cheating. Programmers have spent time developing and testing algorithms so that you don't have to. Professional programmers rely on libraries all the time! Why spend weeks on an algorithm when someone else has already written a perfect algorithm and made it available to you?

Remember though: you still need to correctly access and use the appropriate functions for the program to work, so using a library doesn't mean you can write a program without writing any code at all!

> **Note:** The fact that it's OK to use libraries doesn't mean you can copy anyone's code when you're writing programs for school. You can use library functions where allowed, but you also need to show that you know how to write your own code. There is a big difference between using a library function to help grow your coding knowledge and finding code that is published on the internet, copying it and then claiming it as your own.

1 Computational thinking and programming

Figure 1.48: Learners coding

Benefits and drawbacks

✓ Libraries are helpful because they make writing programs faster, as people don't have to write every function themselves.

✓ Most libraries have been through lots of testing: lots of different people have used a very large range of data to make sure the functions work. This means they are reliable.

? Although they are already tested, they still need checking. Something might have been missed, so you need to make sure they give you the answer you need.

✗ Be careful which libraries you download and use. Anyone can publish a program library. You need to check you can trust them because they could include code that can damage a computer, for example a virus.

Python libraries

To use a library in Python, at the start of your program you use the command `import` then the name of the library. There are some libraries for Python that you have to download and install on your computer. You will not need to do this for the libraries we are going to use.

1.6 Library programs

Some of the most common Python libraries are listed in Table 1.10.

Library	Description
math	Provides mathematical values and algorithms, for example the value of pi and code for rounding numbers
random	Generates random numbers
Pandas	Allows you to use more data structures (ways to store data in a program) and change the data
TensorFlow	Provides artificial intelligence functions, such as machine learning
Numpy	Provides mathematical functions and data structures, like arrays

Table 1.10: Commonly used Python libraries

> ### Activity 1.7
>
> **You will need:** a desktop computer, laptop or tablet with internet access
>
> Work with a partner. Use a search engine to find the names of two other Python libraries and what each library specialises in. As a challenge, find a function in each library and explain what it does.

Did you know?

At the time this book was written, there were over 137 000 Python libraries that people could import into their programs.

In this chapter, you will learn how to import the math and random libraries into a Python program and how to use some of the functions they include.

The math library

The math library has mathematical values and functions for you to use in your programs. Some of these functions include:

- floor
- ceiling
- pi

To import the math library, you need this code at the top of your program:

```
import math
```

The math library has many different functions, but you'll only be learning about three: floor, ceiling and pi.

1 Computational thinking and programming

The floor function

The math function `floor()` rounds a number down to the nearest whole number. The rounded number is then returned to the program that called the function.

Table 1.11 shows some data before and after rounding down:

Before rounding down	After rounding down
22	22
3.1	3
4.55	4
99.8563	99

Table 1.11: Data before and after rounding down

The syntax for calling the function is:

```
math.floor(number)
```

For example:

```
math.floor(22.6)
```

The function returns a value.

This value will not be saved unless you do something with it. You could print it, for example:

```
print(math.floor(22.6))
```

In this line of code, the function call is `math.floor(22.6)`

The function returns the value 22 (22.6 rounded down).

Imagine the function call is replaced with the value:

```
print(22)
```

The output from the program is 22.

You could store the return value in a variable instead.

```
roundedNumber = math.floor(100.2)
```

The function call `math.floor(100.2)` will return 100. When reading the code, you can imagine it being replaced with this number, for example:

```
roundedNumber = 100
```

The variable `roundedNumber` stores 100.

1.6 Library programs

Unplugged activity 1.16

You will need: a pen and paper

Write out each of these statements, replacing the function call with the returned value (the rounded number).

```
print(math.floor(30.8))
variable1 = math.floor(15.5)
variable2 = math.floor(33.6696)
print(math.floor(2.003))
print(math.floor(777.5))
data1 = math.floor(15.5)
print(math.floor(2.0))
total = math.floor(0.03) + math.floor(22.3)
```

Programming task 1.22: Predict, Run, Investigate, Modify and Make

You will need: a pen and paper, a desktop computer, laptop or tablet with an IDE for Python, access to Source file **1.15_programming_task_1.22.py**

Read the program below.

```
import math
firstNumber = 2.6543
print("What is", firstNumber, "rounded down to the nearest
      whole number?")
answer = int(input())
if answer == math.floor(firstNumber):
    print("Correct")
else:
    print("Incorrect")
```

Predict: Write down what this program will output when you enter each of these inputs:
1. 2
2. 3
3. 1
4. 20

Run: Enter this program in Python or open Source file **1.15_programming_task_1.22.py** and run it to see if you are correct.

> **Continued**
>
> **Investigate:** Write this program on paper or print a copy of the program. Work with a partner for this task. On your paper, use different colours or shapes to highlight:
>
> - the command that imports the library
> - the name of the library
> - the library function that is called
> - the place where the return value is stored (or used).
>
> **Modify 1:** Change this program so that it uses a different value for `firstNumber`.
>
> **Modify 2:** Change the program to store the rounded down number in a different variable before it is used in the selection statement.
>
> **Modify 3:** Change the program to:
>
> - output a second number
> - ask the user to input their answer
> - output whether it is correct.
>
> **Make:** Write a new program to:
>
> - take two real (float) numbers as input
> - round each number down to the nearest whole number
> - add together and output the rounded down numbers.

The ceiling function

The math function `ceil()` (short for ceiling) rounds a number up to the next whole number. The rounded number is returned to the program that called it in exactly the same way that `floor()` returned the value.

Table 1.12 shows some data before and after rounding up.

Before rounding up	After rounding up
22	22
3.1	4
4.55	5
99.8563	100

Table 1.12: Data before and after rounding up

The syntax for calling the function is:

    math.ceil(number)

For example:

    math.ceil(22.6)

1.6 Library programs

Unplugged activity 1.17

You will need: a pen and paper

Write out each of these statements, replacing the function call with the returned value (the rounded number).

```
print(math.ceil(33.5))
variable1 = math.ceil(999.51)
print(math.ceil(100.05))
data1 = math.ceil(22)
print(math.ceil(2.55))
total = math.ceil(0.1234) + math.ceil(333.54)
```

Programming task 1.23: Predict, Run, Investigate, Modify and Make

You will need: some coloured pens or highlighters and paper, a desktop computer, laptop or tablet with an IDE for Python, access to Source file **1.16_programming_task_1.23.py**

Read the program below.

```
import math
firstNumber = 33.426
print("What is", firstNumber, "rounded up to the nearest
    whole number?")
answer = int(input())
if answer == math.ceil(firstNumber):
    print("Correct")
else:
    print("Incorrect")
```

Predict: Write down what this program will output when you enter these inputs:

1. 32
2. 33
3. 34
4. 35

Run: Enter this program in Python or open Source file **1.16_programming_task_1.23.py** and run it to see if you are correct.

1 Computational thinking and programming

> **Continued**
>
> **Investigate:** Write this program on paper or print a copy of the program. Work with a partner for this task. On your paper, use different colours or shapes to highlight:
>
> - the command that imports the library
> - the name of the library
> - the library function that is called
> - the place where the return value is stored (or used).
>
> **Modify 1:** Change this program so that it uses a different value for `firstNumber`.
>
> **Modify 2:** Change this program to ask the user what the value is rounded up and what the value is rounded down. Check both answers and output whether the user was correct.
>
> **Make:** Write a new program to:
>
> - ask the user to enter a real (float) number as input
> - ask the user whether they want the number rounded up or rounded down
> - round the number up or down depending on the input, and output the result.

The pi function

You might need to use the value of pi in a program. The math library has a function that will give you the value of pi.

The syntax for calling the function is:

```
math.pi
```

There are no brackets after the function call. It returns a value in the same way as before.

For example:

```
circleCircumference = math.pi * diameter
```

1.6 Library programs

Programming task 1.24: Predict, Run, Investigate, Modify and Make

You will need: some coloured pens or highlighters and paper, a calculator, a desktop computer, laptop or tablet with an IDE for Python, access to Source file **1.17_programming_task_1.24.py**

Study this table that shows how to perform some useful calculations to do with circles.

Calculation	How to work it out	Equation
Area of a circle	Radius squared (radius * radius) multiplied by the value of pi	πr^2
Diameter of a circle	Twice the radius of a circle	$2r$
Circumference of a circle	Radius multiplied by 2 multiplied by the value of pi	$2\pi r$

Look at this program.

```
import math
radius = 2
area = (radius * radius) * math.pi
print("The area is", area)
```

Predict: You will need a calculator for this task. Remember that pi is approximately = 3.14.

Write down what this program will output when you set the radius to:

1. 1
2. 4
3. 10
4. 15

Run: Enter this program in Python or open Source file **1.17_programming_task_1.24.py** and run it to see if you are correct.

Investigate: Write this program on paper or print a copy of the program. On your paper, use different colours or shapes to highlight:

- the command that imports the library
- the name of the library
- the library function that is called
- the place where the return value is stored (or used).

Modify 1: Change this program to take the radius as input from the user, then calculate and output the area for this circle.

Modify 2: Change this program to also calculate and output the circumference of the circle for the radius entered.

1 Computational thinking and programming

> **Continued**
>
> **Make:** Write a new program to:
> - ask the user whether they will enter the radius or the diameter of a circle
> - ask the user whether they want to calculate the area or circumference
> - calculate and output the area or the circumference for the circle they enter the data for.

> **Activity 1.8**
>
> > **You will need:** a desktop computer, laptop or tablet with internet access
>
> Work with a partner to find one other library function that is in the math library. Find out what the function does and write a program that uses it.
>
> Join with another partner who has identified a different library function from yours. Compare your functions and demonstrate your program.

Random numbers

A **random number** is a number that could be any number – one that is chosen by chance. There is no pattern and you cannot guess which number will appear next.

Random numbers are very useful in programming. If there are several options and the program needs to pick one of them, a random number can be used to decide which to choose.

For example, a computer game character needs to decide whether to move forwards, backwards, left or right. We could generate a random number, either 1, 2, 3 or 4, to decide which way they move. The character could move:

- forwards if the number is 1
- backwards if the number is 2
- left if the number is 3
- right if the number is 4.

Unplugged activity 1.18

You will need: a box, paper, scissors

Cut a piece of paper into six smaller pieces and write one number from 1 to 6 on each piece. Fold your numbered pieces of paper so the number cannot be seen and put them all in the box.

Create a table of actions for someone else to perform. Each number (1 to 6) will need a different action. The actions need to be appropriate for use in the classroom, for example stand up, clap your hands and so on.

Your table might look something like this:

Number	Action
1	Stand up
2	Clap your hands
3	…
4	
5	
6	

Work with a partner or group. Take it in turns to pick a number from the box and then perform the action for that number. Once complete, fold the paper again and put it back in the box.

This is acting like a random number generator. Each number has the same chance of being picked. You don't know which one will be picked. The number is used to decide what action to perform.

1 Computational thinking and programming

To import the random library into a Python program, this code needs to be at the top of your program:

```
import random
```

The randint function

The random function `randint()` will return a random whole number between two numbers that you enter as parameters.

- The first parameter is the lowest one. This is the smallest whole number that can be generated.
- The second parameter is the highest one. This is the largest whole number that can be generated.

Both parameters must be whole numbers, not decimals.

The syntax for calling the function is:

```
random.randint(smallest, largest)
```

For example:

```
random.randint(1, 6)
```

This would return any number between 1 and 6.

Table 1.13 shows the numbers that could be generated for different sets of parameters.

Function call	Parameter 1: lower bound	Parameter 2: higher bound	Possible numbers generated
`random.randint(1, 5)`	1	5	1 2 3 4 5
`random.randint(0, 3)`	0	3	0 1 2 3
`random.randint(11, 16)`	11	16	11 12 13 14 15 16
`random.randint(-2, 1)`	-2	1	-2 -1 0 1

Table 1.13: Possible numbers generated for different randint parameters

One function from the random library that you'll learn about is the randint function.

1.6 Library programs

Programming task 1.25: Predict, Run, Investigate, Modify and Make

You will need: a pen and paper, a desktop computer, laptop or tablet with an IDE for Python, access to Source file **1.18_programming_task_1.25.py**

Read the program written below.

```
import random
numberToGuess = random.randint(0, 3)
guess = int(input("What number am I thinking of?"))
if numberToGuess == guess:
    print("Correct")
else:
    print("No, the number is", numberToGuess)
```

Predict: Write down all the possible numbers that the random number command can generate in this program.

Run: Write the program in Python or open Source file **1.18_programming_task_1.25.py**. Run it multiple times until you know whether your prediction was correct (either all the numbers you predicted have appeared, or you have run it lots of times and you have predicted incorrectly).

Investigate: Answer these questions.

- What is the identifier of the program library used in this program?
- What is the identifier of the function used from the program library in this program?
- What is the lower bound and the upper bound sent to the function?
- What does the function do in this program?

Modify 1: Change this program to increase the possible numbers that can be generated.

Modify 2: Change this program so if the guess is incorrect, it tells the user if the guess was too high or too low.

Make: Write a new program to:

- generate a random number, either 1, 2, 3 or 4
- output a different joke depending on which number is generated.

1 Computational thinking and programming

Activity 1.9

> **You will need:** a desktop computer, laptop or tablet with internet access and with an IDE for Python

The random library also contains a function to generate real (decimal) numbers. It is called `uniform()`.

Work with a partner to find out how the random library function `uniform()` is used.

Write a program that generates a random real number and outputs it to the user.

Peer assessment

Discuss how well you and your partner worked together. Ask yourselves these questions:

- Did one of you do more work than the other?
- Were you leading or supporting?
- Were there any disagreements? How did you resolve these?

How did you approach the programs you had to write? Did you use or look at other programs you have written to help you?

If you encountered any errors, how did you resolve them? Did you try to solve them yourself first or did you immediately ask for help?

Will you use the programs you have written to help you write future programs? How do you think you will do this?

Questions 1.8

1. What is a program library?
2. Why are program libraries used?
3. Why do you have to be careful when using program libraries?
4. What is the command in Python to import a library into your program?
5. What is the function call to round down the number 44.56?

1.6 Library programs

6 What does the function `math.ceil()` do?

7 What will this program output?

```
print(math.floor(9999.9999))
print(math.ceil(9999.9999))
```

8 Which library does this code use?

```
print(random.randint(2, 8))
```

9 What are the possible numbers that this function call could return?

```
random.randint(100, 103)
```

Summary checklist

- ☐ I can describe what a program library is.
- ☐ I can explain why program libraries are used.
- ☐ I can identify a program library for Python.
- ☐ I can import a program library into a Python program.
- ☐ I can call a program library function in a Python program.
- ☐ I can use the return value from a library function (for example, store or output the return value).

1 Computational thinking and programming

> 1.7 Software development

In this topic you will:
- understand what decomposition is and why it is used in programming
- learn how to decompose a problem into sub-problems
- learn how to predict the outcome of an algorithm and test if you were correct
- learn how iterative development is used to write programs
- create test plans for specific programs that use a range of data
- understand why a range of data is needed when testing programs.

Key words
boundary test data

decomposing

decomposition

invalid test data

iteration

iterative

iterative development

normal test data

predict

sub-problems

test plan

Getting started

What do you already know?
- When you are writing a program, you need to test it to make sure it works. You don't just test a program once with one piece of data. You test it lots of times with different data to make sure it works every time.

1.7 Software development

> **Continued**
>
> - A test table can be used to record the results of the tests. A test table might look like this:
>
> | Test data type | Description | Example inputs | Expected output | Result |
> |---|---|---|---|---|
> | | | | | |
> | | | | | |
> | | | | | |
>
> This is not the only way you can design a test table, so you might see them with different headings and more or less information. This sometimes depends on the program.
>
> ### Now try this!
>
> Read this Python algorithm with a partner:
>
> ```
> first = 10
> second = int(input("Enter a number"))
> if first > second:
>     print("Your number is smaller")
> elif second > first:
>     print("Your number is larger")
> else:
>     print("Your number is the same as mine")
> ```
>
> 1 Write down what you think the output will be with the following data as input:
>   a 10
>   b 20
>   c 11
>   d 5
>   e 2
> 2 Write the program in Python.
> 3 Run it with each item of test data.
> 4 Check if the outputs were the same as you thought they were going to be.

Decomposing problems

A large problem can be split into smaller problems. A small problem that we combine with other small problems to solve an overall, larger problem is called a **sub-problem**. It is often easier to solve lots of smaller sub-problems and then put the solutions together to solve the large problem.

This process is called **decomposition**. **Decomposing** means breaking something down into smaller parts. You might have come across this word when learning about decomposing organic material, such as leftover vegetables that rot down over time to produce compost.

Figure 1.49: Taking kitchen waste to the compost heap

Usually there are lots of different ways of decomposing a problem in programming. There might be hundreds of ways of splitting a problem down into smaller problems.

Decomposing non-programming problems

Let's look at a non-programming problem first.

When you decompose a problem, you don't want the individual steps. Writing the steps would be writing the algorithm. Here are two examples.

Example 1

Problem: An intruder alarm system needs to be designed. An intruder is someone who enters a building without permission (they are not allowed to enter).

1.7 Software development

Some steps in this problem could be:

1 Set alarm
    a press button to turn on alarm
    b enter security code
    c press enter
    d sound beep until door closed

2 Check for intruder
    a if door is opened, sound beep
    b if correct code is input within 1 minute, turn beep off, else sound alarm

3 Turn alarm off
    a if correct code is input, turn alarm off.

The decomposition for this problem could be:

1 Set alarm
2 Check for intruder
3 Turn alarm off.

The difference between the sub-problems and the individual steps is that the sub-problems can be broken down into steps to follow, but the steps themselves cannot be broken down any further.

Example 2

Problem: Sofia needs help remembering what she needs to do in the morning to get up and get ready to go to school.

Some steps in this problem might be:

1 open eyes
2 turn off alarm
3 remove bed covers
4 swing legs out of bed
5 stand up.

When decomposing the problem, the sub-problems could be:

1 getting up
2 getting washed
3 getting dressed
4 having breakfast
5 packing bag.

153

1 Computational thinking and programming

Can you tell which of these sub-problems the steps above them belong to? The steps all fit into the sub-problem '1 getting up'.

These sub-problems are independent. Each one can be taken out and used at another time, separate to this solution. For example, having breakfast can be used on a non-school day. It might be in a different position, such as having breakfast before getting dressed, but the steps will probably be the same.

Unplugged activity 1.19

You will need: a pen and paper

Working individually, select one of the five sub-problems from Example 2 – how to wake up in the morning and get ready for school. Write an algorithm to identify the steps that will be involved in this stage.

Figure 1.50: Getting ready for school

1.7 Software development

Unplugged activity 1.20

Figure 1.51: Noughts and crosses

You will need: a pen and paper

Work with a partner for this activity. If you do not know how to play noughts and crosses, then find out how to do this first by asking your teacher.

Decompose the problem 'how to play the game of noughts and crosses' into sub-problems. Each sub-problem should not be a specific step, but should contain multiple steps that can be re-used.

Peer assessment

Join with a second pair and compare the sub-problems you each identified. Give the other learners feedback on their answers. For example, you could identify extra sub-problems that they might be able to include, or that you could include in your own answer.

1 Computational thinking and programming

Decomposing programming problems

You decompose a programming problem in the same way as a non-programming problem. Identify sections of the problem that include multiple steps. These sub-problems can often be re-used in the program, or in other programs. Even in programming, there is not necessarily one correct answer. Everyone could decompose a problem in a different way and they could all be valid.

Problem: How to play a computer game of snakes and ladders

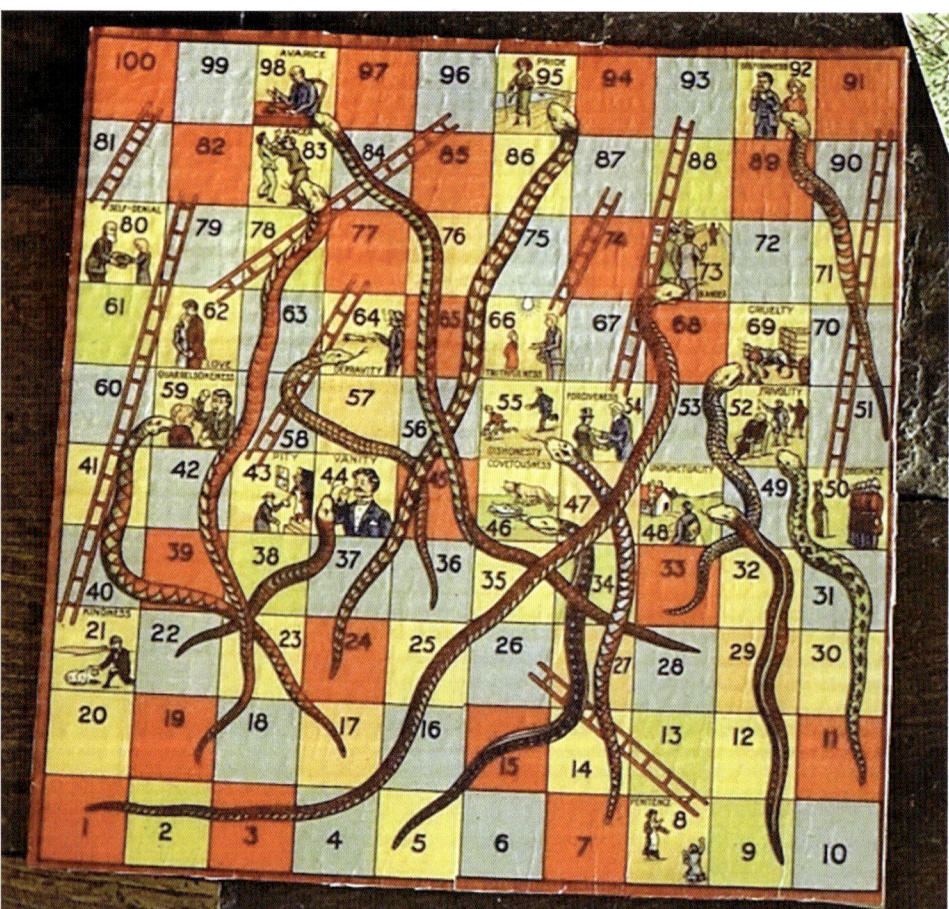

Figure 1.52: Snakes and ladders board

A computer game will allow the user to play the board game snakes and ladders. This problem needs decomposing before we can program it. Here is one way that we can decompose this problem:

Example 1

1. Loading and starting a new game
2. Player making a move
3. Moving the piece

1.7 Software development

4   Checking if on a snake or ladder and moving to the new position
5   Checking if the player has won

Each of these five sub-problems will contain many different steps.

> **Unplugged activity 1.21**
>
> **You will need:** a pen and paper
>
> Working independently, select one of the five sub-problems for the board game snakes and ladders. Write an algorithm to identify the steps that will be involved.

The same snakes and ladders board game problem could be decomposed in a different way. Here's another example:

Example 2

1   Select number of players
2   Set players in first position
3   Display board
4   Roll number block
5   Move player
6   Check if they have won

Did you notice that some of the sub-problems from Examples 1 and 2 are the same? For example, the sub-problem '5 Move player' in Example 2 is the same as the sub-problem '3 Moving the piece' in Example 1.

Others are split down into even smaller problems. For example, in Example 1 the sub-problem '1 Loading a new game' has been split into two in Example 2: '1 Select number of players' and '2 Set players in first position'. Both of these solutions are appropriate.

> **Unplugged activity 1.22**
>
> **You will need:** a pen and paper
>
> Work with a partner for this activity.
> Can you find a third way to decompose the snakes and ladders board game?

1 Computational thinking and programming

Why do we decompose problems?

Earlier we saw that solving a large problem is easier if you break it down and solve the smaller sub-problems. There are also other reasons why we do this.

Decomposing problems into smaller sub-problems is more natural for us as humans. Think about a large task, for example tidying and cleaning the whole home. Would you go in and randomly start tidying and cleaning every room at the same time, or would you split the task up into tidying and then cleaning? And/or you could split it up by room: tidy the kitchen, clean the kitchen, tidy the bedroom, clean the bedroom. Either way gives you smaller problems to tackle one at a time.

Figure 1.53: This bedroom needs tidying!

Lots of people tend to be involved in writing a computer program – sometimes it might be hundreds of people. These people cannot all work together on the same project at the same time. If the problem is decomposed into sub-problems, individual people (or smaller groups of people) can work on solving specific sub-problems. These people can work independently at the same time, and then the programs can be combined once they are finished.

Some programmers specialise in particular areas, for example graphics, artificial intelligence or interfaces. If a problem is divided into sub-problems, these specialists can work on their areas. This means the programs are likely to be better because each person is doing what they do well.

1.7 Software development

Figure 1.54: Group of computer programmers working in an office

Each programmer is working on their own sub-problem at the same time as other programmers. This means the program can be written more quickly.

Dividing a program between many people can also introduce difficulties. The people need to work together to make sure their individual programs will work together. They have to set rules, otherwise they might have lots of problems later when they start combining the programs.

When you decompose problems, you might identify some repeating elements. If you think about the task of cleaning the house, cleaning a window is a repeated task. You might clean a different window in each room, but the steps will be the same. In programming, a sub-routine can be written for each sub-problem, and then some of these sub-routines might be used multiple times. This saves time because the programmers do not have to write the same code lots of times.

Questions 1.9

1. What does decomposition mean?
2. How do you decompose a problem?
3. Why do we decompose problems?
4. Why do we decompose programs?

1 Computational thinking and programming

Iterative development

Programs are written in stages. Unless the program is very small, or you know exactly how to write every part of it, you will only write part of a program. Then you will test that that part works. Depending on what happens in that test, you will change the program or write a new part, then test it again. Then you will change it or write a new part. Then you'll test it again . . .! This continues until you have finished your program.

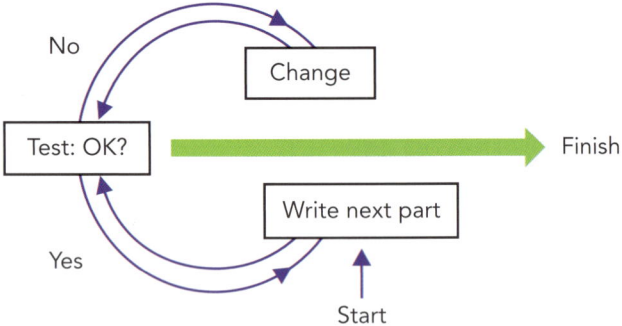

Figure 1.55: Iterative development of a computer program

This process is called **iterative development**. **Iteration** means repeating something. If something is **iterative** it repeats, so iterative development is repeating development.

In programming, this just means that you don't write all of the program code first and then test it all afterwards. Depending on the program, you might write a couple of lines of code and then test them. Then you might add some more code and test that.

For example, imagine you have been asked to write a program that allows two users to play a game called Fire, Water, Earth. In this game, one element wins over another:

- fire beats earth
- earth beats water
- water beats fire.

Figure 1.56: The elements earth, water and fire

1.7 Software development

How will you write the program?

- Will you start writing the code, and keep writing the code until you think you have finished it all and then test it?
- Or will you write a section (a sub-problem), for example inputting the two players' names, and then test that this works?

If the code doesn't work, then it will need changing and retesting. It is easier to change a smaller sub-problem than a larger problem. This is because you will only be testing a small section of code so there are fewer statements to test, and therefore less can go wrong!

> **Did you know?**
>
> There are lots of different software development methodologies (ways of working), for example: rapid application development, waterfall and agile. These all have their own benefits and drawbacks. Developers don't always choose the same method. Many developers will take some features from different methodologies and combine them into a method that works for their programs and how they like to work.

Once the first part of the code is working, you can write the code to allow the first player to choose fire, water or earth. Then test that this works. If it doesn't work, change the code and retest. If it does work, move on . . . and repeat.

This is iterative development. You are doing one part at a time, then testing to make sure it works before moving on.

> **Activity 1.10**
>
> > **You will need:** a micro:bit or a desktop computer, laptop or tablet with access to Scratch, an IDE for Python or presentation software
>
> Work with a partner to write the game of Fire, Water, Earth using iterative development. Choose a suitable technology to create your game. For example, you could use a micro:bit, Scratch, Python or even presentation software.
>
> Keep a brief record of each step that you completed and then tested to show how you used iterative development.

1 Computational thinking and programming

Questions 1.10

1. What does iterative mean?
2. What is iterative development?

Predicting outcomes

Throughout Unit 1, you have been asked to **predict** the outcome of each program – that is, to say what you think will happen when the program runs. You have looked carefully at a program's code and have thought about what the output will be with specific inputs. You then ran the program (or followed the algorithm) to see if your prediction was correct. A prediction identifies what you *think* will be output.

Figure 1.57: A learner thinking

When you predict the outcome of a program, you are guessing what you think will happen when the program runs.

To do this, you need to read the algorithm, but you do not need to run every piece of code in every statement. You might not even read every statement. For example, if a statement outputs a message, you might not need to read that message to predict what the program does. You do not write down the variables or the data that is stored in them at each stage. Instead, you get an overview of the program and identify what the outcomes will be.

The outcome might be an output, or data in the program might be changed. There might be one or more outcomes.

Once you have predicted the outcome, you need to check whether you are correct.

- If you are writing Python code (or code in another programming language), you write your program and then run it.

1.7 Software development

- If you have written an algorithm as a flowchart or in pseudocode, you need to trace the algorithm: follow each step and do the work the program would do at each stage.

Programming task 1.26: Predict and Run

You will need: a pen and paper

Read this program.

```
position = 10
OUTPUT "Enter the number of spaces to move"
INPUT moves
position = position + moves
OUTPUT "Your position is ", position
IF position >= 20 THEN
    OUTPUT "Congratulations, you win!"
ELSEIF position == 19 THEN
    OUTPUT "Nearly there"
ELSEIF position >= 15 THEN
    position = position - 2
    OUTPUT "2 space penalty, move back 2 spaces"
    OUTPUT "Your new position is ", position
ELSEIF position == 13 OR position == 14 THEN
    position = position + 1
    OUTPUT "Extra space awarded! Move forward 1 more place"
    OUTPUT "New position is", position
ELSE
    OUTPUT "You didn't move very far"
ENDIF
```

Predict: What will be the output for each of these inputs?

1. 6
2. 10
3. 15
4. 1
5. 4

Run: Work through this algorithm to check if your predictions are correct.

1 Computational thinking and programming

Programming task 1.27: Predict and Run

You will need: a pen and paper, a desktop computer, laptop or tablet with an IDE for Python, access to Source file **1.19_programming_task_1.27.py**

Read the program written below.

```
item1Cost = 20.5
item2Cost = 15.0
item3Cost = 10.0
answer = input("Did you buy any of item 1?")
total = 0
if answer == "Yes" or answer == "YES" or answer == "yes":
    quantity = int(input("How many did you buy?"))
    total = total + (quantity * item1Cost)
answer = input("Did you buy any of item 2?")
if answer == "Yes" or answer == "YES" or answer == "yes":
    quantity = int(input("How many did you buy?"))
    total = total + (quantity * item2Cost)
answer = input("Did you buy any of item 3?")
if answer == "Yes" or answer == "YES" or answer == "yes":
    quantity = int(input("How many did you buy?"))
    total = total + (quantity * item3Cost)
print("Your total is", total)
```

Predict: Write down what the output will be for each of these sets of inputs:

1	yes	5	NO	YES	10	
2	NO	Yes	6	yes	20	
3	NO	NO	NO			
4	YES	1	YES	2	YES	3

Run: Write this program in Python or open Source file **1.19_programming_task_1.27.py**. Run the program and enter the four sets of inputs. Compare the outputs to your predictions to see if they are correct.

1.7 Software development

Test plans and test data

Test data

When you create a program, do you test it once? Or twice? Or more times? What data do you input? The same data lots of times? Or different data to see what happens?

Just because a program runs with one set of data, that does not mean it will work with every set of data.

Figure 1.58: A programmer testing a program

Make sure to test programs many times and with different sets of data so that you are sure they will run correctly!

Example

A club allows children who are 16 or younger to join. This algorithm outputs whether a person can join or not:

```
age = int(input("Enter your age"))
if age < 16:
    print("You are allowed to join")
else:
    print("Sorry, you are too old to join")
```

To test the program, we will make sure that someone 16 or younger can join.

165

1 Computational thinking and programming

Test data: 10
```
age = int(input("Enter your age"))
if age < 16:
    print("You are allowed to join")
else:
    print("Sorry, you are too old to join")
```

- age = 10
- 10 is less than 16.
- "You are allowed to join" is output.

We could stop testing now, because a person who is 10 is correctly allowed to join. Or we could test it with some other data to make sure it always works.

We could test it with the age of a person who should not join.

Test data: 20
```
age = int(input("Enter your age"))
if age < 16:
    print("You are allowed to join")
else:
    print("Sorry, you are too old to join")
```

- age = 20
- 20 is more than 16.
- "Sorry, you are too old to join" is output.

It works! So shall we stop testing now, because a person who is 20 (more than 16) cannot join? Or should we test it with some more data?

We've tested it with someone who is within the age range and someone who is outside the age range. What about someone who is just young enough? For example, a person who is 16.

Test data: 16
```
age = int(input("Enter your age"))
if age < 16:
    print("You are allowed to join")
else:
    print("Sorry, you are too old to join")
```

- age = 16
- 16 is not less than 16.
- "Sorry, you are too old to join" is output.

This did not work. They should be allowed to join, but the program says they can't. There is an error somewhere.

```
age = int(input("Enter your age"))
if age <= 16:
    print("You are allowed to join")
else:
    print("Sorry, you are too old to join")
```

- The condition was less than, but it should be less than or equal to.

1.7 Software development

We could have tested this program with lots of ages that were under 16, and lots that were over 16, and we would have thought the program worked.

To test a program thoroughly means testing it with a range of data:

- **normal test data** (data that is accepted, or within bounds)
- **invalid test data** (data that is not accepted, or outside bounds)
- **boundary test data** (data that may or may not be accepted, but is on the edge of what is or isn't allowed).

In the age program above, the data for each will be:

- normal data: 1 2 3 4 5 6 7 8 9 10 11 12 13 14 15 16
- invalid data: 17 18 19 …
- boundary data: 16 17

You cannot test every possible piece of data. The ages that are too old to join could go all the way up to 100! That is a lot of tests. Instead, select a reasonable number. For example, if 17 works and 18 works, then maybe jump and try 25, then 50. Because there is one boundary test, if these work, the rest should work.

Unplugged activity 1.23

You will need: a pen and paper

A program asks the user to enter a number from 1 to 100. A message is output if they enter a number from 1 to 100. An error message is output if they enter a number that is less than 1 or greater than 100.

Create a copy of this table:

Normal	Invalid	Boundary

Work with a partner to write the normal test data, invalid test data and boundary test data you will use to test the program. Remember you don't have to use every number. Use a selection of reasonable numbers for each data type.

1 Computational thinking and programming

Test plans

In previous learning, you may have followed test plans that included a range of test data. They might have followed the format of Table 1.14.

Test data type	Description	Example inputs	Expected output

Table 1.14: Test table format

You will now create your own **test plan** for a program, making sure you identify a range of test data.

To create a test plan, follow these steps:

Step 1

Create a table that follows the format of Table 1.14.

Each item of data you identify will be a new row in your table.

You can do this in word-processing software by inserting a table (it might help to change the page layout to landscape to give you more space), or you could use spreadsheet or database software.

Step 2

Insert all of the normal test data you are going to test.

Each example input must be on a new line. You have not written the program yet, so your output must identify what should happen. Table 1.15 shows an example.

Test data type	Description	Example inputs	Expected output
Normal	Input from 1 to 100 allowed	2	Accepted
Normal	Input from 1 to 100 allowed	99	Accepted

Table 1.15: Normal test data

Step 3

Insert all your invalid data. Put each item on a new line, as shown in Table 1.16.

Test data type	Description	Example inputs	Expected output
Normal	Input from 1 to 100 allowed	2	Accepted
Normal	Input from 1 to 100 allowed	99	Accepted
Invalid	Input from 1 to 100 allowed	0	Not accepted
Invalid	Input from 1 to 100 allowed	101	Not accepted

Table 1.16: Invalid test data

1.7 Software development

Step 4

Insert your boundary data. Put each item on a new line, as shown in Table 1.17.

Test data type	Description	Example inputs	Expected output
Normal	Input from 1 to 100 allowed	2	Accepted
Normal	Input from 1 to 100 allowed	99	Accepted
Invalid	Input from 1 to 100 allowed	0	Not accepted
Invalid	Input from 1 to 100 allowed	101	Not accepted
Boundary	Input from 1 to 100 allowed	1	Accepted

Table 1.17: Boundary test data

These tables are just examples. You might have many more items of normal, invalid and boundary test data for your programs.

Activity 1.11

You will need: a desktop computer, laptop or tablet with word-processing, spreadsheet or database software, the test data that you identified in Unplugged Activity 1.23

Create a test plan for the test data that you identified for the program where a user enters a number from 1 to 100.

You will not need to test every number, but each test needs to be on a new row. Make sure you include normal, invalid and boundary test data.

Programming task 1.28: Run

You will need: a desktop computer, laptop or tablet with an IDE for Python and word-processing, spreadsheet or database software, the test plan you created in Activity 1.11, access to Source file **1.20_programming_task_1.28.py**

The following Python program has been written to check if the user has input a number from 1 to 100.

```python
number = int(input("Enter a number from 1 to 100"))
if number >= 1 and number <= 100:
    print("Accepted")
else:
    print("Not accepted")
```

1 Computational thinking and programming

Continued

Run: Create this program in Python or open Source file **1.20_programming_task_1.28.py**. Test the program using your test plan. Include an extra column to identify if the result was correct, for example:

Test data type	Description	Example inputs	Expected output	Result
Normal	Input from 1 to 100 allowed	2	Accepted	
Normal	Input from 1 to 100 allowed	99	Accepted	
Invalid	Input from 1 to 100 allowed	0	Not accepted	
Invalid	Input from 1 to 100 allowed	101	Not accepted	
Boundary	Input from 1 to 100 allowed	1	Accepted	

Activity 1.12

You will need: a desktop computer, laptop or tablet with an IDE for Python and word-processing, spreadsheet or database software, access to Source file **1.21_activity_1.12.py**

A program asks the user what the word for 1024 bytes is. The user enters the answer and the program will output whether they got the answer correct. The user can enter the answer in different ways, for example 'kilobyte' or 'Kilobyte'. Look at the program for the different possible answers.

```
answer = input("What is 1024 bytes?")
if answer == "kilobyte" or answer == "Kilobyte"
   or answer == "KILOBYTE" or answer == "1 kilobyte"
   or answer == "1 Kilobyte" or answer == "1 KILOBYTE":
   print("Correct")
else:
   print("No, it is a kilobyte")
```

Create a test plan for the program. Include normal and invalid data. You will not be able to use boundary data because the answers are either correct or incorrect – there are no answers that are close to being correct or close to being incorrect. In this instance, the answers are not on a scale or in a range, so there are no boundaries.

Create this program in Python or open Source file **1.21_activity_1.12.py**. Test the program using your test plan and complete an actual output column.

1.7 Software development

> How do you approach testing a program?
> How will you use test plans in the future?

Questions 1.11

1. What are the three types of test data?
2. Why do you test a program multiple times?
3. Why do you test a program with different types of data?
4. The following program takes four numbers as input from the user and outputs the largest number and the smallest number. Create and complete a test plan for this program. Include a range of data.

```
number = int(input("Enter the first number"))
smallest = number
largest = number
number = int(input("Enter the second number"))
if number > largest:
    largest = number
if number < smallest:
    smallest = number
number = int(input("Enter the third number"))
if number > largest:
    largest = number
if number < smallest:
    smallest = number
number = int(input("Enter the fourth number"))
if number > largest:
    largest = number
if number < smallest:
    smallest = number
print("The largest number input was", largest)
print("The smallest number input was", smallest)
```

1 Computational thinking and programming

Summary checklist

- [ ] I can explain what decomposition is and why it is used in programming.
- [ ] I can describe how to decompose a problem into sub-problems.
- [ ] I can predict the outcome of a program and test if it was correct.
- [ ] I can describe iterative development.
- [ ] I can write a program using iterative development.
- [ ] I can create a test plan that includes a range of data.
- [ ] I can identify normal, invalid and boundary test data for a program and know why they are needed when testing programs.

> 1.8 Physical computing

In this topic you will:
- learn how to transmit data between two (or more) micro:bits
- write a program to transmit data between two (or more) micro:bits.

Key words
group ID

radio waves

wired transmission

wireless transmission

Getting started

What do you already know?

- A micro:bit is a physical computing device that you can program. The micro:bit has different inputs you can use, and it can produce different outputs.

- To program a micro:bit, you write a program using the MakeCode for micro:bit website, download the program onto your micro:bit and then run the program. You can test your program using the on-screen micro:bit on the MakeCode for micro:bit website to make sure it works before downloading it.

- The micro:bit has blocks that allow for different inputs, for example pressing buttons and moving the micro:bit up or down, or tilting it.

1 Computational thinking and programming

> **Continued**
>
> - The micro:bit has blocks to produce outputs that include using the LEDs and sound output.
> - There are also blocks for calculations, conditional statements and loops (which make blocks repeat).
>
>
>
> **Now try this!**
>
> Using the MakeCode for micro:bit website, write a micro:bit program for each of these tasks:
>
> 1 Output a different image depending on which button is pressed.
>
> 2 Measure the temperature and output a different image depending on what the temperature is (for example, if it is cold, output a snowflake).
>
> 3 Count how many times buttons A and B are pressed and output this number.

Communicating

When you talk to your friends, write an email or even look at someone, you are communicating. There are lots of ways that we can communicate and transmit information to someone else. Like humans who communicate with each other, a device can also transmit data to another device. When you send data from a computer to a printer, for instance, the devices are communicating.

1.8 Physical computing

Figure 1.59: A computer communicating with a printer

Some devices communicate through a physical connection or **wired transmission**. A wire (in a cable) plugs into both devices and the data is sent down the wire. For example, your printer could be connected to your computer by wires.

Some devices communicate wirelessly. This is known as **wireless transmission**. Wireless transmission uses **radio waves**. Both devices have a piece of hardware that can transmit a radio signal and receive a radio signal. For example, your phone could be connected to your headphones by Bluetooth Wireless Technology®.

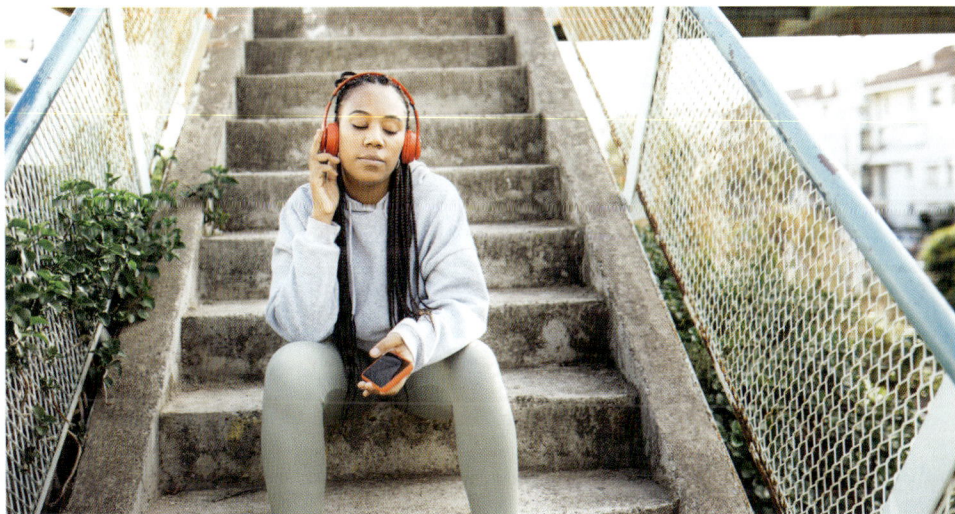

Figure 1.60: Wireless headphones

175

1 Computational thinking and programming

Both devices need to be set up to communicate with each other. This makes sure that they send data in the same language and in the same way, for example using radio waves at the same frequency.

Micro:bit communication

Micro:bits have built-in radio transmitters and receivers. This allows one micro:bit to send data wirelessly to another micro:bit, which can receive the data.

On the MakeCode for micro:bit website, click on the Radio menu to access the radio blocks.

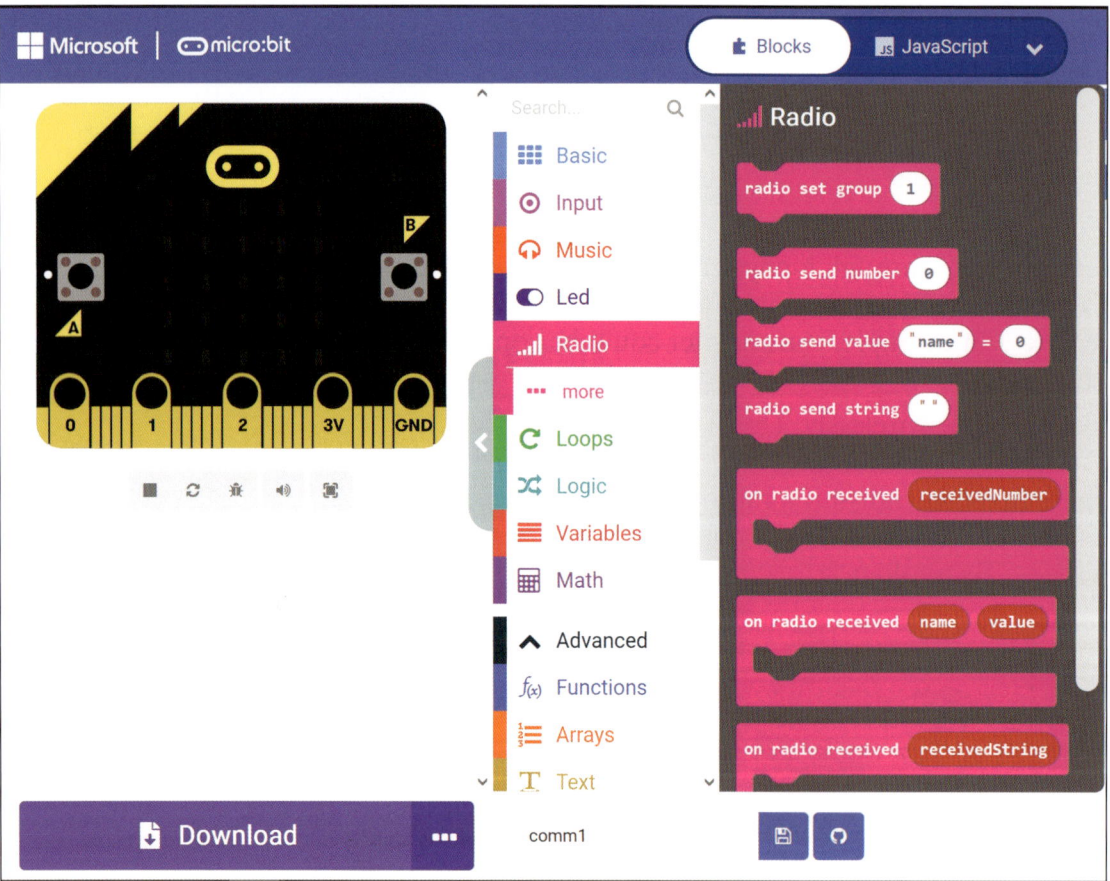

Figure 1.61: Radio menu on the MakeCode for micro:bit website

When you start working with radio blocks, a second micro:bit will appear.

> **Note:** Sometimes you have to write your first code and then run it once before the second micro:bit will appear.

176

1.8 Physical computing

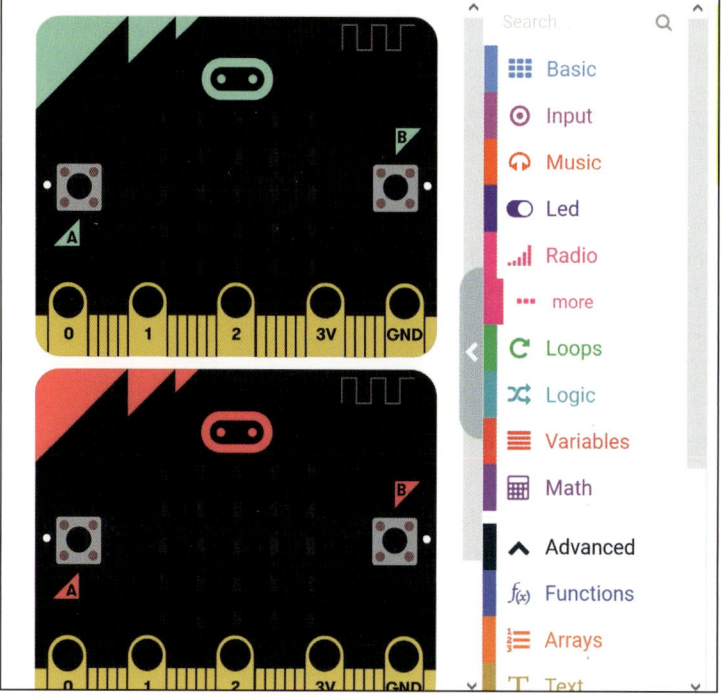

Figure 1.62: Second micro:bit

Activity 1.13

You will need: a desktop computer, laptop or tablet with word-processing, presentation or animation software or video-recording equipment

Work in pairs for this activity. Create a presentation or report about data communication. You could create your presentation using presentation software or animation software, write a report or information booklet using word processing software, or even record a video.

Your presentation or report should include:

- a description of wired and wireless transmission
- examples of devices (including the micro:bit) that can transmit data
- examples of devices (including the micro:bit) that can receive data.

177

We will now look at the different blocks you need to use to get your micro:bits to communicate.

Group ID

Wireless signals can be received by any device that is set up to receive them. If every device transmitted the same way on the same frequency, the devices wouldn't know which device the message was for. Micro:bits use radio groups to identify which device the signals are for. Radio groups are numbered, for example 'radio group 1'. This is known as a **group ID**. If a micro:bit is transmitting in radio group 1, then only micro:bits set to receive radio group 1 transmissions will receive them.

Make sure you are using a different group ID from other people around you, otherwise you will receive their signals and they will receive yours. That could get confusing when your micro:bit starts outputting messages you are not expecting.

Use the 'radio set group' block when the program starts.

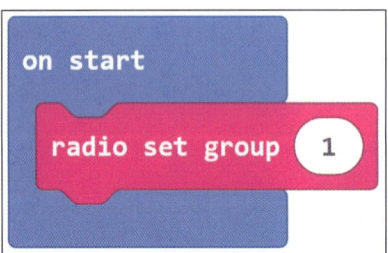

Figure 1.63: 'Radio set group' block

> ### Did you know?
> Any device that can read data is able to pick up wireless signals a computer sends. This is why security is important when transmitting data wirelessly. Data needs to be encrypted so that any other devices in the transmission's path cannot make sense of the data. Encrypting the data will mean that it just looks like jumbled up characters to any device that is not supposed to receive it.

Sending data

Sending a number

The 'radio send number' block shown in Figure 1.64 will send a number that you input to the receiving micro:bit.

The program in Figure 1.65 will transmit the number 10. All devices that are set as radio group 1 will receive the number 10.

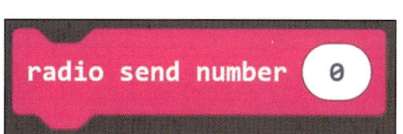

Figure 1.64: 'Radio send number' block

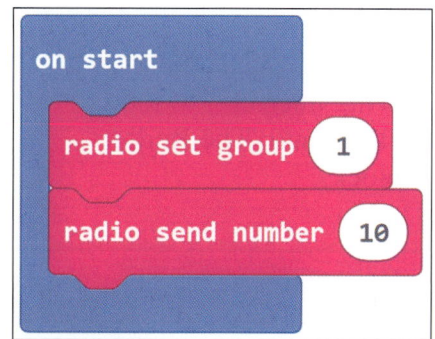

Figure 1.65: Sending number 10 to radio group 1

Sending a string

The 'radio send string' block shown in Figure 1.66 will transmit the text that you enter. The string data type here is the same as the data type you use in text-based programming. A string is a combination of numbers, letters and symbols that always have double quotation marks around them.

The program in Figure 1.67 will transmit the string "Hello" to all devices in radio group 1.

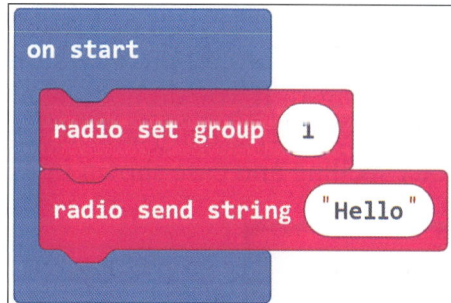

Figure 1.66: 'Radio send string' block

Figure 1.67: Sending string "Hello" to radio group 1

1 Computational thinking and programming

Using a variable

The data that we want to transmit from one micro:bit to the other can be stored in a variable first. We insert the variable's identifier into the block. In the example in Figure 1.68, the string "Hello" is stored in the variable 'Word'. The content of the variable 'Word' is then transmitted to radio group 1.

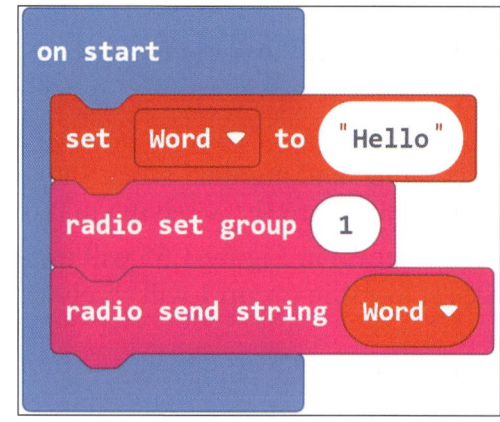

Figure 1.68: Using the variable 'Word'

Receiving data

We also need to program the receiving micro:bit to tell it what to do when it receives a radio signal. The Radio menu has the 'on radio received' block.

Receiving a number

Marcus wants to send a number to Arun's micro:bit. Marcus uses the 'on radio received' block.

This block includes the variable 'receivedNumber'. The number Arun's micro:bit receives from the transmitting micro:bit is stored in this variable. This variable cannot be changed. If you do not already have a variable with the identifier 'receivedNumber', then you will need to make one. Make sure you use the exact spelling and case shown in Figure 1.69.

Figure 1.69: 'On radio received' block

1.8 Physical computing

The program shown in Figure 1.70 sets the radio group ID to 1, then, when the micro:bit receives a number on group ID 1, it stores that number in the variable 'receivedNumber'. It then outputs this data.

Figure 1.70: Program to receive and output a number

Receiving a string

There is also a block for receiving a string – see Figure 1.71.

Figure 1.71: Block for receiving a string

The program shown in Figure 1.72 sets the radio group ID to 1. Then, when the micro:bit receives a string on group ID 1, it stores that string in the variable 'receivedString'. It then outputs this data. You might need to make a new variable with the same identifier (receivedString) before you can use it.

Figure 1.72: Program to receive and output a string

1 Computational thinking and programming

Unplugged activity 1.24

You will need: lots of small pieces of paper

You will need to work in a group for this task. As a group, develop a code or set of codes that will be used to transmit data between computers. The code will stop anyone who doesn't know what the code is from understanding your message.

This code can be a different letter for each letter of the alphabet. Or it could use symbols or other words, for example sending the characters :) means you are happy.

Create a list of the codes that you will use. Make sure everyone in the group has a copy of your codes.

This will work in a similar way to how data is transmitted between devices.

Now work in pairs. Send messages to your partner. Write one word at a time on a single piece of paper and 'transmit' it to your partner (pass that paper to them). Then, write the next word on the next piece of paper and 'transmit' it. Your partner needs to translate your transmitted message using the codes you developed.

Computers can store different codes and then decipher messages sent to them in code.

This is how a computer program can decipher messages (work out what they mean). Data is transmitted, for example through a message in another language like binary. The computer has all the different codes stored. When it receives the message, it can look at the codes and work out what it means.

Programming two micro:bits

Both micro:bits will need a program downloaded onto them. If both micro:bits are going to do the same actions, they can have the same program. However, if one micro:bit is going to send and the second micro:bit is going to receive, then each micro:bit will have a separate program.

Note that, when you are testing your programs on the MakeCode for micro:bit website, either micro:bit can send and either micro:bit can receive. However, when you download your code, make sure that:

- the transmitting code goes to the transmitting micro:bit
- the receiving code goes to the receiving micro:bit.

1.8 Physical computing

Programming task 1.29: Predict, Run, Investigate, Modify and Make

You will need: two micro:bits and a desktop computer, laptop or tablet with access to the **MakeCode for micro:bit website**

One micro:bit is running the code shown in Figure 1.73.

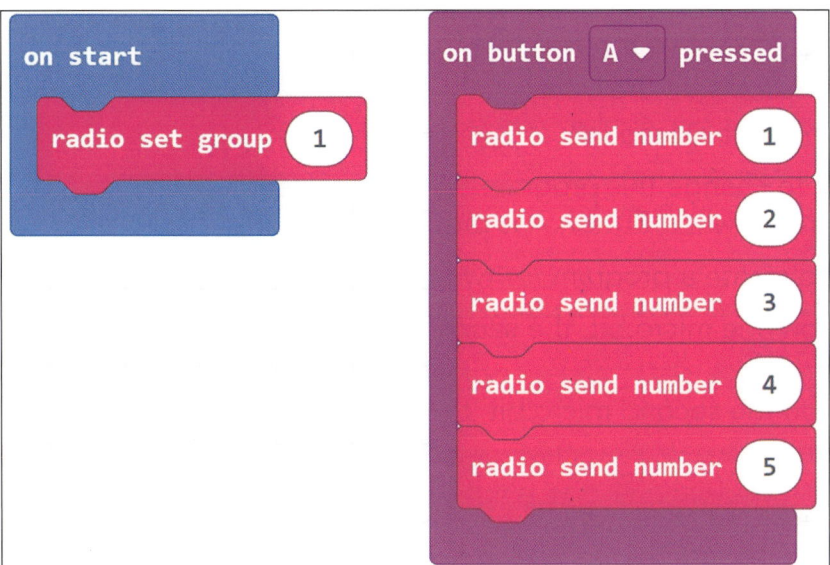

Figure 1.73: Sending micro:bit program 1

A second micro:bit is running the code shown in Figure 1.74.

Figure 1.74: Receiving micro:bit program 1

Predict: What will happen when Button A on the first micro:bit is pressed?
What will appear on the first micro:bit? What will appear on the second micro:bit?

183

1 Computational thinking and programming

Continued

Run: Work with a partner to create and download the program for each micro:bit. You might need to change the group ID for the two micro:bits to make sure you and your partner are not using the same ID as anyone else in your class.

Press Button A on the first micro:bit and test whether your prediction is correct.

Investigate: Work with your partner to answer these questions:

1. Which group ID number did you set your micro:bits to use?
2. When does the first micro:bit transmit the data?
3. What variable is the received data stored in?

Modify: Work with your partner to change this program to display a countdown from 10 to 1 on the second micro:bit when Button A is pressed on the first.

Make: Work with your partner to create a program for two micro:bits.

- When button A is pressed on one micro:bit, the second micro:bit should display 1 2 3 4 5.
- When button A is pressed on the second micro:bit, the first micro:bit should display 5 4 3 2 1.

Self-assessment

Give yourself a rating from 1 to 5 (1 being the least confident and 5 being the most confident) for your confidence in each of these parts of the task:

1. your decision-making
2. the parts that you programmed
3. using radio blocks with the micro:bit.

1.8 Physical computing

Programming task 1.30: Predict, Run, Investigate, Modify and Make

You will need: two micro:bits and a desktop computer, laptop or tablet with access to the **MakeCode for micro:bit website**

One micro:bit is running the code shown in Figure 1.75.

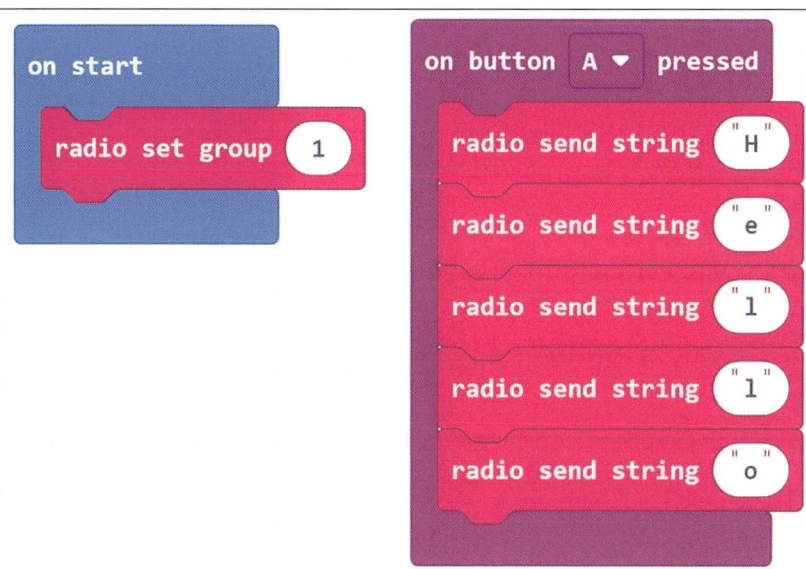

Figure 1.75: Sending micro:bit program 2

A second micro:bit is running the code shown in Figure 1.76.

Figure 1.76: Receiving micro:bit program 2

Predict: What will happen when Button A on the first micro:bit is pressed? What will appear on the first micro:bit? What will appear on the second micro:bit?

Run: Work with a partner to create and download the program for each micro:bit. You might need to change the group ID for the two micro:bits to make sure you are not using the same ID as anyone else in your class.

Press Button A on the first micro:bit and test whether your prediction is correct.

1 Computational thinking and programming

> **Continued**
>
> **Investigate:** Work with your partner to answer these questions:
> 1. How many strings are transmitted?
> 2. How many characters are in each string?
> 3. What is the identifier for the variable where the strings are stored on the receiving micro:bit?
>
> **Modify 1:** Work with your partner to change this program to transmit a different word, one character at a time.
>
> **Modify 2:** Work with your partner to change this program to transmit a different word, one character at a time, when button B is pressed.
>
> **Make:** Work with your partner to create a program for two micro:bits.
> - When one micro:bit is shaken, a message should be output on the second micro:bit.
> - When the second micro:bit is shaken, a different message should be output on the first micro:bit.

Using transmitted data

We learnt previously that the data that is transmitted from one micro:bit to the other is stored in a variable. This variable can be used in calculations or other processes like conditional statements.

The program shown in Figure 1.77 is for the transmitting micro:bit. When button A is pressed, `"heart"` is transmitted. When button B is pressed, `"happy"` is transmitted.

1.8 Physical computing

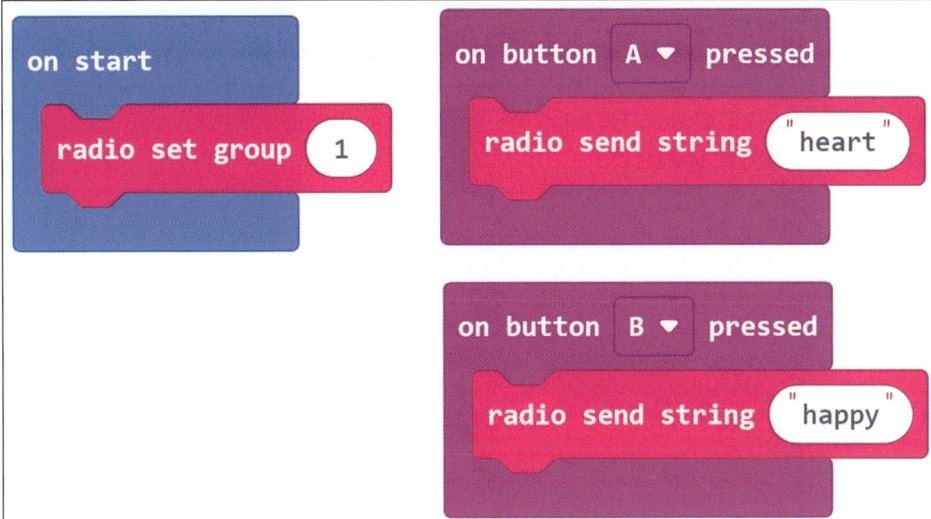

Figure 1.77: Sending micro:bit program 3

The program shown in Figure 1.78 is the receiving micro:bit. The received string is saved in the variable 'receivedString'. The program compares the content of this variable to the string `"heart"`. If the content is equal to `"heart"`, a heart icon is displayed.

If the content is not equal to `"heart"`, it is compared to `"happy"`. If the content is equal to `"happy"`, then a smiley face is output.

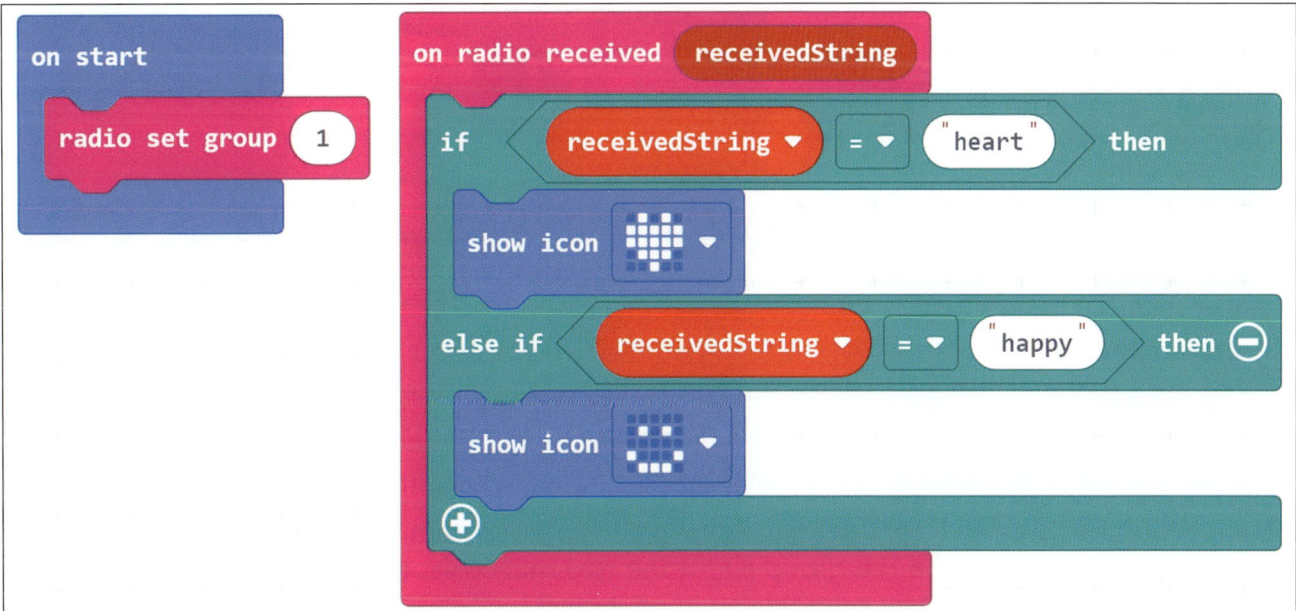

Figure 1.78: Receiving micro:bit program 3

187

1 Computational thinking and programming

Programming task 1.31: Predict, Run, Investigate, Modify and Make

You will need: two micro:bits and a desktop computer, laptop or tablet with access to the **MakeCode for micro:bit website**

One micro:bit is running the code shown in Figure 1.79.

A second micro:bit is running the code shown in Figure 1.80.

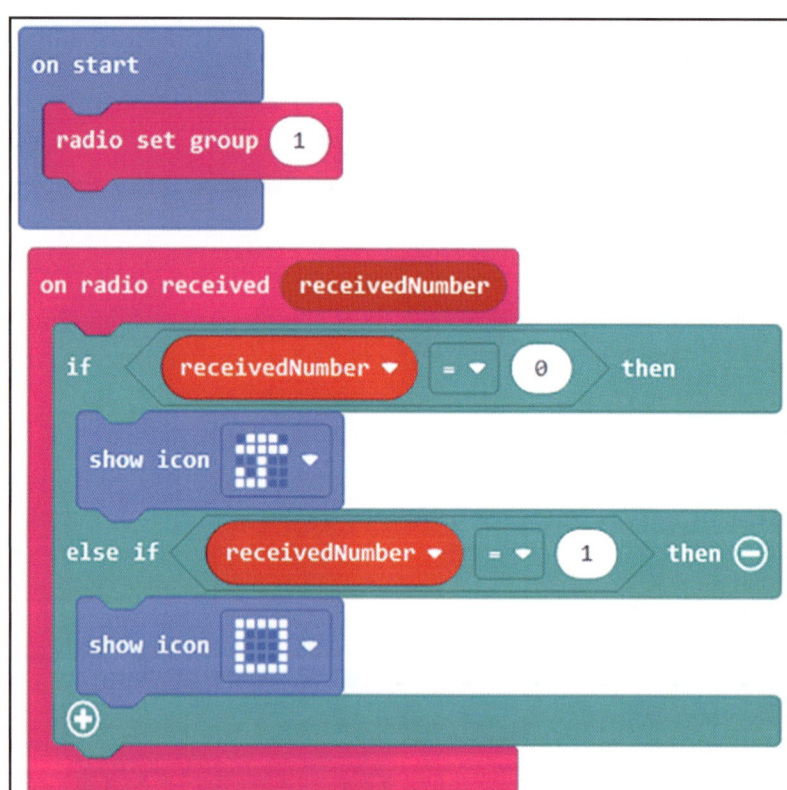

Figure 1.79: Sending micro:bit program 4   Figure 1.80: Receiving micro:bit program 4

Predict: What will happen when Button A on the first micro:bit is pressed? What will appear on the first micro:bit? What will appear on the second micro:bit?

What will happen when Button B on the first micro:bit is pressed? What will appear on the first micro:bit? What will appear on the second micro:bit?

Run: Work with a partner to create and download the program for each micro:bit. You might need to change the group ID for the two micro:bits to make sure you are not using the same ID as anyone else in your class.

- Press Button A on the first micro:bit and test whether your prediction is correct.
- Press Button B on the first micro:bit and test whether your prediction is correct.

188

1.8 Physical computing

> ### Continued
>
> **Investigate:** Work with your partner to answer these questions:
>
> 1. What data is transmitted when button A is pressed on the first micro:bit?
> 2. What data is transmitted when button B is pressed on the first micro:bit?
> 3. What happens when one of the buttons on the second micro:bit is pressed?
> 4. What is the identifier of the variable that stores the data transmitted to the second micro:bit?
> 5. What are the conditions used in the IF statement?
>
> **Modify 1:** Work with your partner to change this program to output a word when 0 is received and a different word when 1 is received.
>
> **Modify 2:** Work with your partner to change this program so the first micro:bit transmits a different number when the micro:bit is shaken, and the second micro:bit outputs a different word when this is received.
>
> **Make:** Work with your partner to create a program for two micro:bits.
>
> - When one micro:bit is tilted in different directions, different data is transmitted.
> - When the second micro:bit receives data, it outputs a different image, sound and/or message depending on the data.

Programming task 1.32: Make

> **You will need:** two micro:bits and a desktop computer, laptop or tablet with access to the **MakeCode for micro:bit website**

Work with a partner to create a way to communicate messages to each other using your micro:bits.

You will first need to decide what words, statements or images can be sent. Each one will need a way of being selected. You can design this using a table. For example:

Motion	Data transmitted	Output

1 Computational thinking and programming

How did you approach the teamwork required in this topic? How did you divide the micro:bit tasks? How did you work with a partner to allow two micro:bits to communicate?

Questions 1.12

1. How is data transmitted from one micro:bit to another?
2. What type of data can be transmitted from one micro:bit to another?
3. Why do you need to make sure you are using a unique group ID when programming two micro:bits to transmit data between each other?
4. When a micro:bit receives data (for example, a number) where is this stored?
5. How can you use the data a micro:bit receives?

Summary checklist

- [ ] I can describe how data is transmitted between two micro:bits.
- [ ] I can program a micro:bit to transmit data to another micro:bit.
- [ ] I can program a micro:bit to receive data from another micro:bit and output this data.
- [ ] I can program a micro:bit to receive data from another micro:bit and use this data to perform another action.

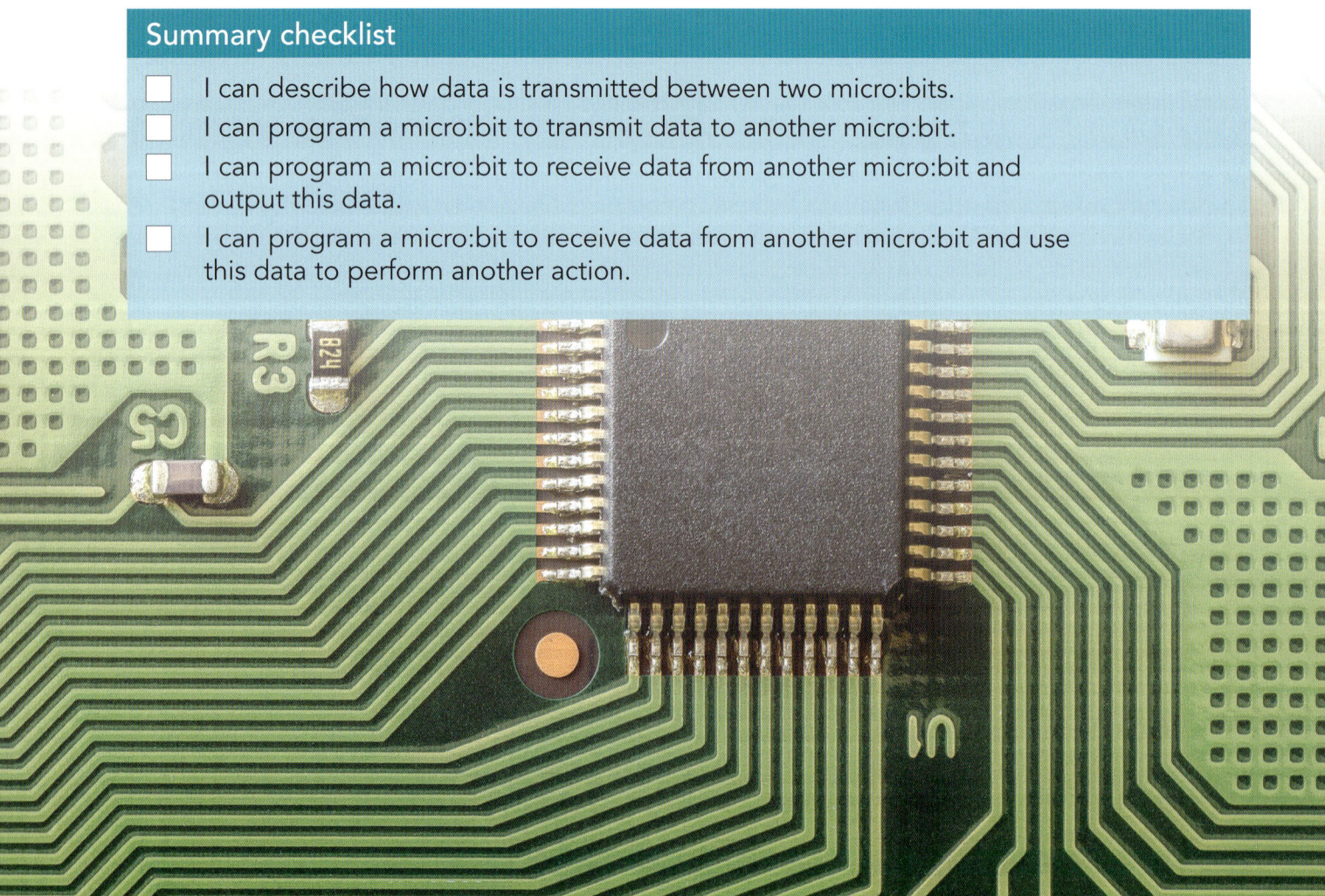

1.8 Physical computing

Project 1: Adventure story

Zara and Sofia like reading adventure stories where the reader gets to decide what will happen next. The reader has to make decisions, and each decision affects what happens to the story's characters. Because of this, there might be several different endings.

Zara and Sofia would like you to design and create an electronic adventure story for the computer. They want to be able to read it and make decisions for the characters.

You need to create the story as a computer program. The program will output the first line, or section, of the story and give the user two or more options to choose from. Each option will lead to a different action.

For example, the first section could be:

Sofia is walking to school and has to pass the dark forest. As she approaches, she hears a laugh coming from the depths of the forest and she stops. Sofia's school is on the far side of the forest, but she usually walks around the forest. What should she do today?

Enter 1 to go through the forest. Enter 2 to go around the forest.

1 Computational thinking and programming

> **Continued**
>
> You will need to work in pairs to:
> - create a plan for the story – this should include what the story is about, the choices at each stage and where each choice leads
> - decompose the plan into sub-problems that can be programmed individually (for example, each new statement and choice can be an individual sub-problem)
> - decide what the user will enter as their choice at each stage
> - decide how long the story will be and when it ends
> - produce a test plan for each choice in the story
> - produce evidence that you have tested each choice in the story.
>
>
>
> Figure 1.81: Adventure story

1.8 Physical computing

Continued

Outcomes

You need to produce:

- a design for the story and each path through the story (the decisions and where each decision takes the reader)
- the input that the user will enter at each stage
- a final program that meets the requirements
- a test plan that includes the data to be entered for each test
- a completed test plan to show how the story was tested.

Challenge

Allow the user to enter their choices in multiple ways. For example, instead of asking them to enter 1 for option 1, or 2 for option 2, ask them what they would like to do (for example, they could enter 'door' to open a door, or 'window' to open a window). Each possible answer they could give will need to be built into the program, so make sure you keep it simple, for example by using only one-word answers.

Project 2: Fire, Water, Earth

You need to work in a group to develop your own version of the Fire, Water, Earth game (see pages 160–161), using two micro:bits.

In your group you need to decide:

- how your version of Fire, Water, Earth will work, including which item beats which other item
- design how the user will input their choice of item
- decide how the choice will be transmitted and compared to the other item
- decide how the result will be output on each micro:bit.

Outcomes

You need to produce:

- an explanation of the rules of your game
- a design (for example, flowcharts or written algorithms) for each micro:bit
- a test plan for how you will make sure each micro:bit allows the game to be played
- a completed test plan with the results of your tests.

Challenge

Extend the game to keep track of how many times each player wins and output this on each micro:bit.

1 Computational thinking and programming

Check your progress 1

1. Which of the following pseudocode commands can be used to read input from a user?
   A   INPUT   B   Enter   C   ReadIn   D   ReadLINE   [1]

2. Write the value stored in `newValue` once this pseudocode algorithm has run.
   ```
   variable1 = 20
   xValue = 200
   newValue = (variable1 + xValue) / variable 1
   ```
   [1]

3. Which of the following outputs will this pseudocode algorithm give when the numbers 10 and then 5 are input?
   ```
   second = 0
   third = 0
   INPUT first
   IF first > 10 THEN
       INPUT second
   ELSE
       INPUT third
   ENDIF
   OUTPUT first, second, third
   ```
   A   1000   B   0010   C   1005   D   00510   [1]

4. What does a searching algorithm do? [1]

5. How does a linear search work? [2]

6. Show how a linear search will search for the number 33 in this set of data:
   12   3   33   19   5   [2]

7. Which of the following is the Python operator for equal to?
   A   =   B   !=   C   <>   D   ==   [1]

8. Which of the following is the Python operator for not equal to?
   A   =   B   !=   C   <>   D   ==   [1]

9. a   Write a Python program that asks two users to enter their name and age. [4]
   b   Change the program so that it outputs the name of the older user or tells the users they are the same age. [5]

10 Which set of blocks is used to program a micro:bit to transmit data? [1]

11 Micro:bit 1 has this program:

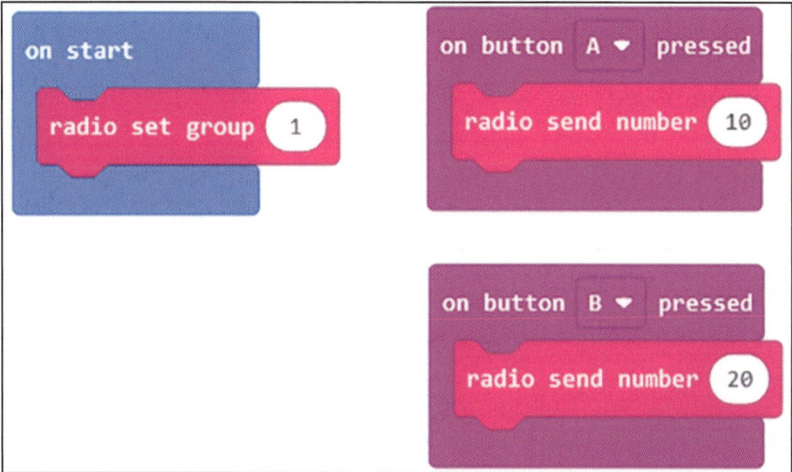

Figure 1.82: Micro:bit 1 program

Micro:bit 2 has this program:

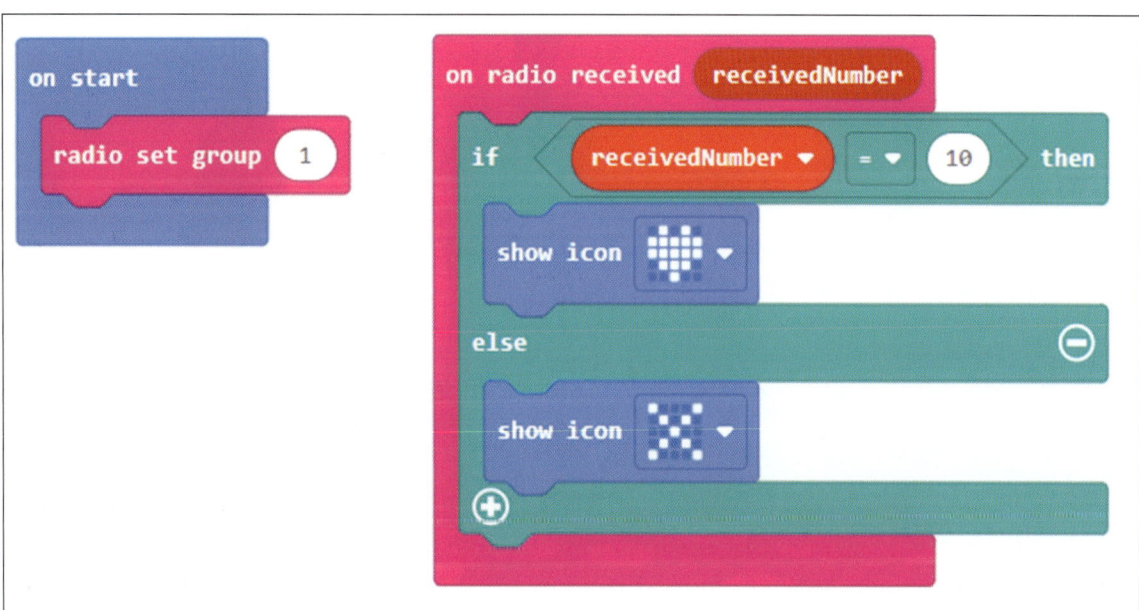

Figure 1.83: Micro:bit 2 program

a What data is transmitted when the user presses Button A on micro:bit 1? [1]
b What data is transmitted when the user presses Button B on micro:bit 1? [1]
c What data is transmitted when the user presses Button A on micro:bit 2? [1]

1 Computational thinking and programming

  d   What is output when micro:bit 2 receives the number 10?   [1]

  e   What is output when micro:bit 2 receives the number 20?   [1]

12 What are the steps that you follow when you develop a program iteratively?   [4]

13 **a**   What is problem decomposition?   [1]

  b   Why are problems decomposed?   [2]

2 Managing data

> 2.1 Modelling

In this topic you will:
- understand the purpose of a simulator
- learn to identify the key features of a simulator
- learn what data a simulator might need
- know how to use a spreadsheet model to do a what-if analysis
- learn how to use the goal seek tool.

Key words

feature

goal seek

key feature

model

simulator

what-if analysis

2 Managing data

Getting started

What do you already know?

- A computer model is a representation of a real-life system or situation.
- Simulators use models to allow users to see how a system would respond to different inputs.
- Simulators can be used in many different areas such as flying, space exploration, health, manufacturing and retail.
- You can change values in a spreadsheet.

Now try this!

Think about the questions:

- *What if* it rains tomorrow?
- *What if* I get a good grade in my exam?

Knowing the answer to questions like these can help you plan for the future. If you know it is going to rain tomorrow, you can plan to take an umbrella out with you. If you know you are going to get a good grade on your exam, you can plan how to celebrate.

We can use a spreadsheet to help us see the answers to these what-if questions. If you were planning a music event at your school, you would want to know if you were going to make a profit. You might ask the what-if question: 'What if I make the cost of a music ticket $10?' Then you can learn information such as how much money will be made from the music event.

You will learn more about this in this unit.

2.1 Modelling

What is a simulator?

Figure 2.1: A person using a driving simulation computer system

A **model** can provide a realistic copy of a real-life system, for example a model aeroplane. A model can also provide an example of a particular setting, for example a model village. Models can be used to help us understand how something will look, feel or work.

A **simulator** is a type of model. Simulators are copies of systems or scenarios that can help people to develop and practise certain skills. For example, a surgeon can use a surgery simulator to practise before they perform surgery on real people. The surgery simulator can help the surgeon to look at all the different things that could happen during the surgery without risking any lives. Can you think of any examples of a simulator that you already know?

Unplugged activity 2.1

You will need: a pen and paper

Write down all the examples of simulators that you know. Try to think of at least five examples.

Compare your list of simulators with a partner.
- How many of the same ones did you think of?
- How many different ones did you think of?

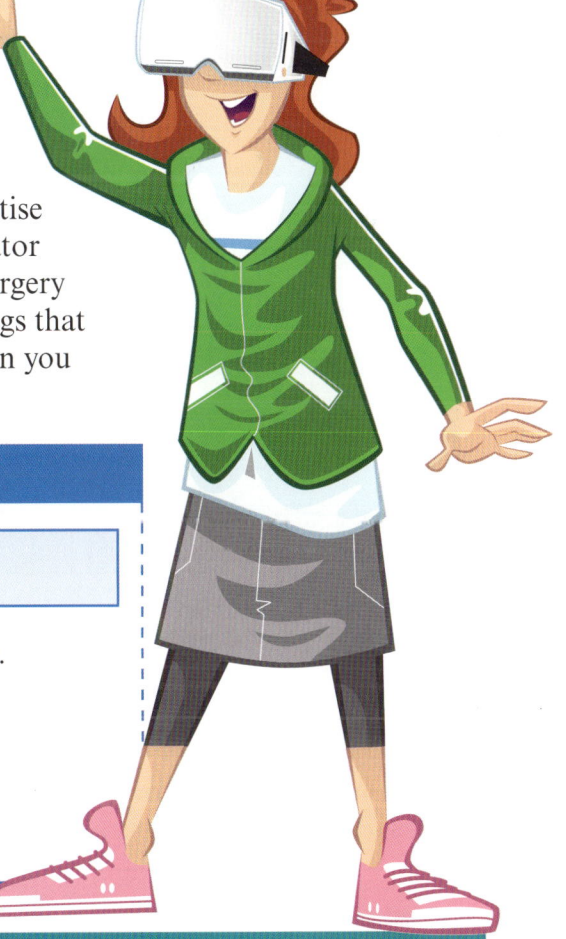

2 Managing data

Another example of a simulator is a flight simulator. A flight simulator allows you to experience what it is like to fly an aeroplane. It allows you to do this safely on the ground. You do not need to get into an actual aeroplane and fly it.

> ### Stay safe!
>
> The flight simulator that you are going to use in the next task is an online simulator. Make sure that you do not click on pop-up adverts when using the online simulator as these could take you to a website that should not be trusted. There should not be any pop-up adverts on this online simulator, so if you do see any, tell your teacher.

Practical task 2.1

Figure 2.2: Using a flight simulator can be a lot of fun

You will need: a desktop computer, laptop or tablet with internet access

Open your internet browser and type in the website address your teacher gives you. This website is an example of a flight simulator.

2.1 Modelling

> **Continued**
>
> To start the flight simulation, click the blue 'Fly' button. There is also an instructions button that you can click on to get some information about how to work the simulator. If you cannot find the 'Fly' button or the instructions button, ask your teacher to help you find them.
>
> Experiment with the flight simulator. Try to get the aeroplane to fly.
>
> - What information can you see on the screen?
> - Can you make the aeroplane move forward?
> - Can you change the speed of the aeroplane?
> - Can you turn the aeroplane left and right?
> - Can you work out what all the different black dials are for?
> - Can you find out how to change to a different aeroplane?
> - Can you find out how to change the camera angle?

All of the different pieces of information that are output on the screen and the options that you can choose are called the **features**. Some of these features can be **key features**. Key features are features that are important or interesting.

A key feature of the simulator is the information that shows you the speed of the aeroplane. This is very important information to know.

> **Unplugged activity 2.2**
>
> **You will need:** a pen and paper
>
> Make a list of all the features that you can find in the flight simulator. Pick the three features that you like the best. Then, pick three features that you think are key features.
>
> Discuss with a partner why you think these three features are the best, and why you think the key features that you have chosen are key features.

Simulators and data

To make most simulators work, we need to give them some data that they can process to give an output. Think about the flight simulator. What data were you able to input into the simulator? You may have:

- used the + and – keys to change the speed
- used the number keys 0 to 9 to set the speed

2 Managing data

- used the arrow keys to turn the aeroplane left and right
- used the mouse to turn the aeroplane left and right
- used the mouse to get the aeroplane to take off into the air.

This is all data that you can give to the simulator that allows you to try and fly the aeroplane. This is also the type of data that a real pilot would need to give to an aeroplane. A real pilot would not do this by using number keys and a mouse, but they would need to set the speed of the aeroplane and turn it in different directions.

A lot of this data is vital to make the aeroplane fly. What would happen if you didn't set the speed for the plane? It would probably just stay still and not move. What would happen if you were not able to turn it left or right? It would only be able to fly in a straight line.

Unplugged activity 2.3

You will need: some pens and a large piece of paper

Work with a partner. Discuss with your partner what other data you can give to the flight simulator. Create a mind map of all the data you can think of. You can use the mind map to put the data into different categories, like this:

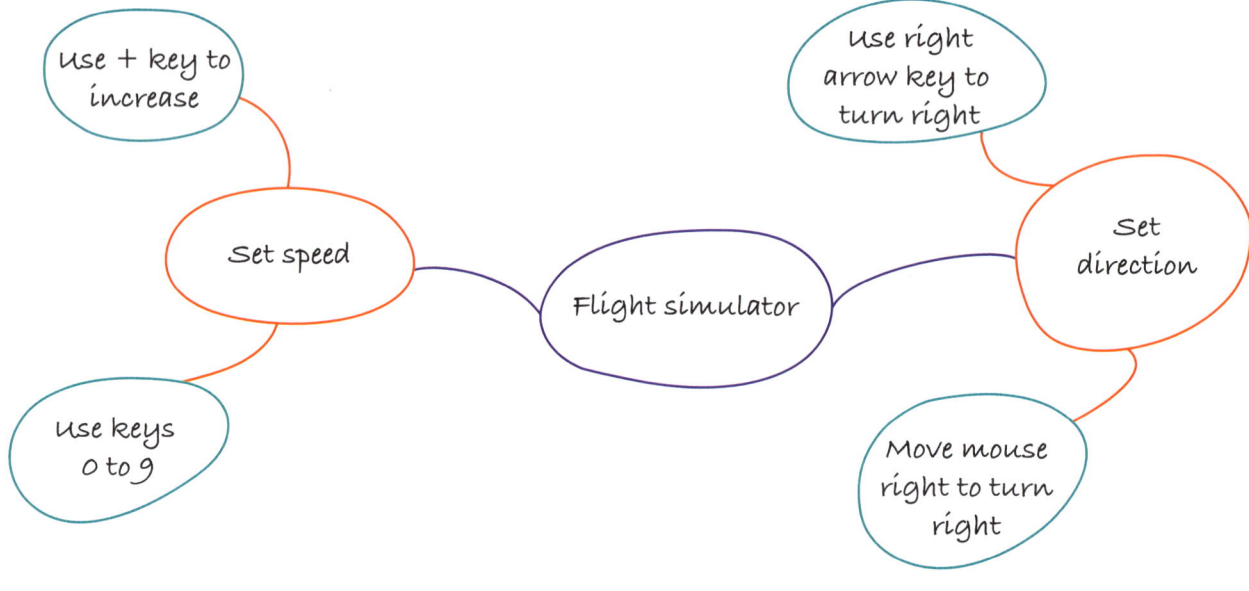

Figure 2.3: An example of a mind map

2.1 Modelling

> **Continued**
>
> **Peer assessment**
>
> Find another pair of learners who have completed the activity and compare your mind maps.
>
> - Do you all have the same data on your mind map?
> - Have they thought of any data that you haven't?
> - Have you structured your diagram in the same way with the same categories, or is your diagram different?
>
> Discuss any differences and explain to each other what data you listed and why you put it into those categories.

> **Did you know?**
>
> One of the earliest known flight simulators was called the Link Trainer. It was created by Edwin Link, who was an American inventor. He began creating it in 1927 and it was available to buy in 1929. He created it because there was a need for a safe way to teach new pilots how to use the controls of an aeroplane.
>
>
>
> **Figure 2.4:** An early flight simulator

2 Managing data

You have thought about some examples of different simulators. You have looked at a flight simulator and thought about the data that is put into it. Now you are going to complete an activity about using a different type of simulator.

Activity 2.1

You will need: a desktop computer, laptop or tablet with internet access

Choose two other people to work with so that you are a group of three. Imagine that you are a team of people who use simulators for planning.

A local zoo called Zoodledoo wants to create a new animal area. It will be home to the lions that will be coming to live at Zoodledoo.

Zoodledoo wants to plan where to put the area for the lions and how to structure it. They want to make sure that the lions have a good home. They also want to make sure that people visiting the zoo get the best experience when seeing the lions.

You and your team have a simulation that can be used to plan where to put the area for the lions. It will simulate:

- what kind of building the lions will live in and what kind of environment they will have, such as the temperature in different kinds of weather

2.1 Modelling

> **Continued**
>
> - what kinds of playful objects the zookeepers can put in for the lions and where these can be placed to create the best entertainment for the lions
> - the safety of visitors to the zoo and how well they are able to see the lions in their environment.
>
> Zoodledoo can provide you with lots of data about what the lions need and the type of customers they get at the zoo. They want to know what data you need.
>
> 1. Research the kind of environment lions need at a zoo. You could research more than one zoo.
> 2. Discuss with your team what data you will need to use for the simulation.
> 3. Create an email for Zoodledoo that will tell them what data you need.
>
> To get you started in your discussion, here are three examples of data that you might need:
>
> - the age range of the visitors who come to the zoo
> - how the zoo will feed the lions
> - how close the visitors can be to the lions.

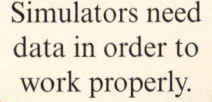

Simulators need data in order to work properly.

> Were you a helpful member of your team? What did you contribute to make sure that you were helpful? How do you think you could be more helpful in group work in future?

You have thought about the data that we need to input into a simulator. We also need data to be able to create the simulator. A programmer will create the computer program for the simulator and will need to use data to do this. For example, if a programmer creates a flight simulator, they will need to use data such as:

- how high the aeroplane will be able to fly
- how fast the aeroplane will be able to fly
- what kinds of controls the user will have.

Spreadsheet models

You may have previously learnt that a spreadsheet can be used to analyse data and model solutions to a problem. For example, you can use a spreadsheet to look at students' test scores and calculate the highest, lowest and average score. You can also use a spreadsheet to see

205

2 Managing data

how much money a business earns from sales and how much money it spends. If the business is not making a profit, for example, you can model a solution that reduces the money it spends to increase the profit.

One way that you can use a spreadsheet to analyse data is by using **what-if analysis**. A what-if analysis is where you ask the question 'What if . . .?' and change values in a spreadsheet to find out the answer. You can do this to see what effect the changes have on other values in the spreadsheet.

For example:

- *What if* you increased the price of the product by $0.50?
- *What if* you saved $10 per week?
- *What if* you wanted to make a profit of $200?

You can change a value in a spreadsheet. For example, an ice cream shop could increase the price of an ice cream from $0.30 to $0.50 in a spreadsheet. You can then see what effect this will have on the profit value.

Practical task 2.2

Figure 2.5: Spreadsheets can be a very useful tool for analysing data

You will need: a desktop computer, laptop or tablet with access to Source file 2.1_keep_it_kool.xlsx

206

2.1 Modelling

> **Continued**
>
> Keep It Kool is a company that sells iced food and drinks. Its main products are:
> - ice cream
> - milkshakes
> - frozen yoghurt
> - iced coffee.
>
> The staff have a spreadsheet model that helps them plan the selling price for each of their products. They have some what-if questions for you to test to see what would happen.
>
> Open Source file **2.1_keep_it_kool.xlsx**. You should see a spreadsheet that looks like this:
>
> **Keep It Kool**
>
> | | Cost to make | Selling price | Number sold | Profit |
> |---|---|---|---|---|
> | **Ice cream** | $0.50 | $2.00 | 20 | $30.00 |
> | **Milkshake** | $0.75 | $2.50 | 20 | $35.00 |
> | **Frozen yoghurt** | $0.65 | $2.75 | 20 | $42.00 |
> | **Iced coffee** | $0.40 | $1.75 | 20 | $27.00 |
> | **Total revenue** | $180.00 | | | |
> | **Total profit** | $134.00 | | | |
>
> Figure 2.6: The Keep It Kool spreadsheet
>
> The first what-if question that Keep It Kool has is:
> - What if we increased the selling price of ice cream to $2.25? How much more profit would we make on ice cream?

2 Managing data

> **Continued**
>
> To test the outcome of this, you need to change the price of ice cream from $2.00 to $2.25. Then look at the profit value for ice cream. It is $30.00 now, but what does it change to?
>
> You should find that the profit for ice cream increases from $30.00 to $35.00. They would make $5 more profit on ice cream.
>
> Keep It Kool have some more what-if questions for you:
>
> 1. What if we increased the selling price of a milkshake from $2.50 to $2.65? How much more profit would we make on a milkshake?
> 2. What if the cost to make frozen yoghurt increased by $0.15? How would this affect the profit for frozen yoghurt?
> 3. What if we sold 30 iced coffees? How much more profit would we make on iced coffee?
>
> Change the values in the spreadsheet to see what the outcome would be for these what-if questions.

The goal seek tool

There is a useful tool in a spreadsheet that you can use to test some what-if questions. It is called **goal seek**. The goal seek tool allows you to set a specific goal and then it works out what the values in the spreadsheet need to be in order to achieve that goal.

For example, if you wanted a profit of $50, how many products would you need to sell? The goal is the profit of $50 and you can use the goal seek tool to set this.

2.1 Modelling

The goal seek tool is on the 'Data' tab in your spreadsheet. Click the 'Data' tab and then click the option 'What-if Analysis'. This opens a menu with the option 'Goal Seek'.

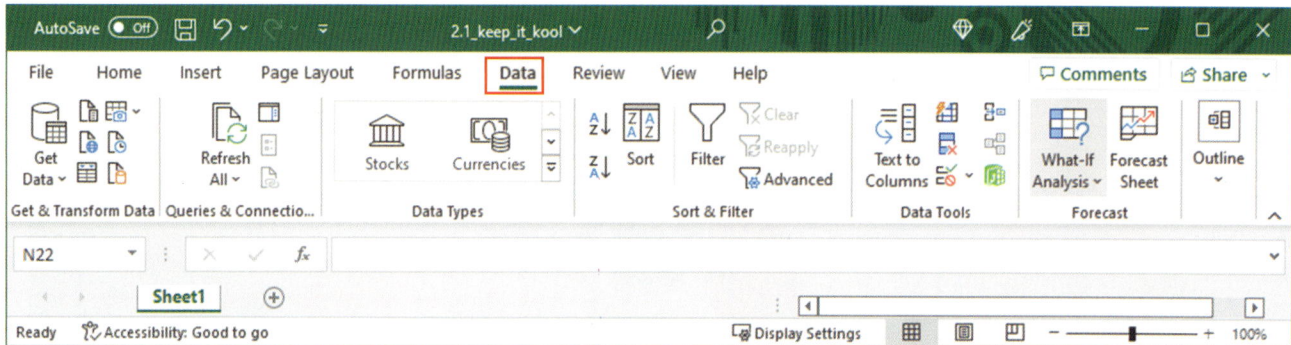

Figure 2.7: 'What-if Analysis' button in Microsoft Excel

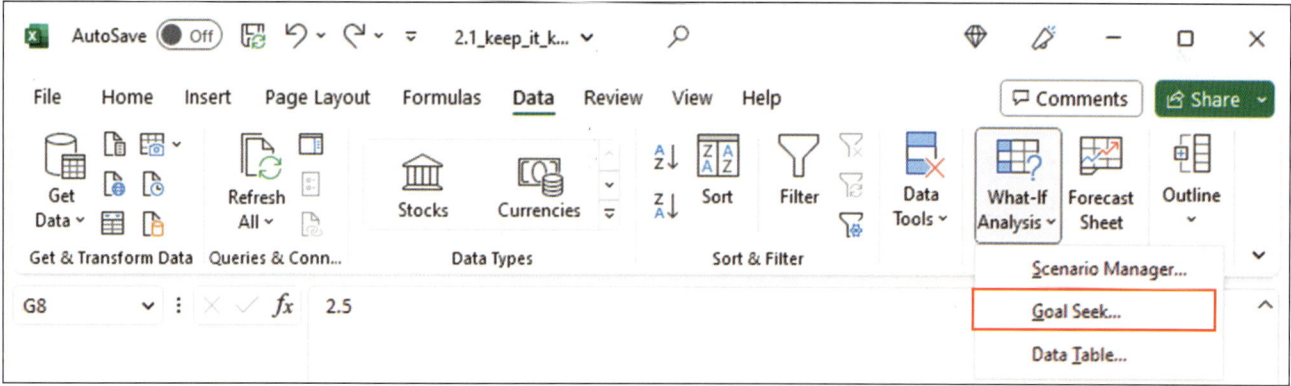

Figure 2.8: 'Goal Seek' menu option in Microsoft Excel

You should then see a 'Goal Seek' box like this:

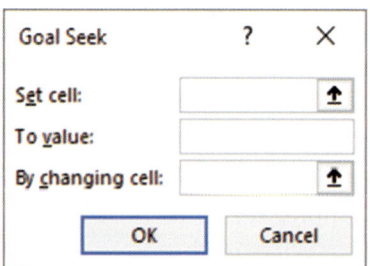

Figure 2.9: The 'Goal Seek' box in Microsoft Excel

The goal seek tool lets you set a goal, such as a profit of $50. We do this by entering the cell reference (for example, A1) of the value in the 'Set cell' field. Then we enter the goal value (for example, 50) in the 'To value' field. Finally, we enter the cell reference of the value that will need to change to reach that goal. This could be the number of a particular product that is sold.

2 Managing data

Practical task 2.3

You will need: a desktop computer, laptop or tablet with access to Source file **2.1_keep_it_kool.xlsx**

Open Source file **2.1_keep_it_kool.xlsx**.

- Make sure the 'Cost to make' value for ice cream is $0.50.
- Make sure the 'Selling price' for ice cream is $2.00.
- Make sure the 'Number sold' for ice cream is 20.

Use the goal seek tool to find out what the selling price for ice cream needs to be in order to have a profit of $50.00.

1. Select cell K6 for the 'Set cell' field.
2. Enter 50 into the 'To value' field.
3. Select cell G6 for the 'By changing cell' field.

Click OK and you should see the selling price for ice cream changes from $2.00 to $3.00. This is because each ice cream would need to be sold for $3.00 to make a profit of $50. Before you answer the following questions, reset the values in the spreadsheet of Source file **2.1_keep_it_kool.xlsx** to the values shown in Figure 2.6.

2.1 Modelling

Continued

Keep It Kool would like you to use the goal seek tool to find the outcome for these what-if questions:

1. What if we wanted to make a profit of $43 for milkshakes? What should the selling price for milkshakes be? (Make sure the number sold is 20.)
2. What if we wanted to make a profit of $105 for frozen yoghurt? How many frozen yoghurts would we need to sell? (Make sure the selling price is $2.75.)

Peer assessment

Compare your answers with the person next to you. Did you get the same answers? If they are different, explain to each other how you got your answers and discuss which are likely to be the correct ones.

Summary checklist

- [ ] I can explain the purpose of a simulator.
- [ ] I can identify the key features of a simulator.
- [ ] I know some examples of the data that may be needed by a simulator.
- [ ] I can change the values in a spreadsheet to test a what-if question.
- [ ] I can use the goal seek tool to test a what-if question that has a goal.

2 Managing data

2.2 Data and databases

In this topic you will:
- learn how to identify what items of data are needed for a purpose
- learn how to identify whether the data is limited and has items missing
- learn how to add a validation check to a field in a database
- learn how to create a data collection form that uses validation
- know how to evaluate whether a database is suitable for a purpose.

Key words

field
format
null
primary key
purpose
record
validation
wizard

Getting started

What do you already know?
- It is really important that a data collection form is effective, otherwise you might not collect the correct data. This means that the questions need to be clearly asked and the form needs to be easy to fill in.

2.2 Data and databases

> **Continued**
>
> - A data collection form can be evaluated to see how effective it is. You can analyse the form to check the following.
>   - Are the instructions clear?
>   - Are the questions asked in a logical order?
>   - Is a format needed so that all users fill in the answer in the same way?
>   - Is there enough space for the user to answer the question?
>   - Are all answer options provided for a multiple-choice question?
> - The basic structure of a database includes a table, a field, a record and a primary key.
> - You can search a database using a single criterion, such as less than or greater than.
> - You can evaluate the effectiveness of a data collection form by analysing things such as whether the instructions are clear and whether they make each user fill in the data in the same format.
>
> **Now try this!**
>
> Your teacher wants a help sheet that they can give to younger students, which identifies all of the different parts of a database. It also needs to have a short description of the purpose of each part.
>
> Use a desktop computer, laptop or tablet and word-processing software to create the help sheet for your teacher.

Data collection

Data is very important. We need to make sure that the data we collect is suitable for its **purpose**. Purpose means the reason why something exists – what is it for? The purpose of data is the reason why we need the data.

2 Managing data

Marcus is a helper in the school library. Some new volunteers are about to start helping at the library too. He will need to decide what different tasks to give to each volunteer. What data will he need to do this?

First, Marcus will need some basic data about each person, such as:

- their name
- their age.

He may also want to know:

- whether they have ever volunteered in a library before
- which tasks they like to complete
- whether they have any disabilities.

He wouldn't need to know:

- their favourite drink
- their favourite colour.

Some of the data may not be as important as other data. Some of the data could also be incomplete and this could affect the tasks that Marcus gives the volunteers.

What would happen if Marcus did not know which tasks the volunteers liked to complete? He might give them a task they don't like doing. The volunteer might not like this task, but they would still be able to do the task.

2.2 Data and databases

What would happen if Marcus did not know a volunteer had a disability? He might give them a task that they are not able to complete, such as lifting heavy books. This could cause the volunteer to get an injury.

What would happen if Marcus gathered data about the volunteers' favourite drinks? It might be a nice thing to know about the volunteers, but it would not affect which tasks Marcus gives them. This data is not necessary or important.

Unplugged activity 2.4

You will need: a pen and paper

A local drinks company that sells healthy drinks needs your help. Imagine that you are doing work experience at this company. The marketing manager needs to send marketing messages to customers about a new drink the company has. The manager only wants to send the marketing messages to the customers that they think will be interested.

You are going to identify the data needed.

- Make a list of the data that is needed about the customers.
- Identify which three items of data are the most important, and then give a reason why for each one.

Figure 2.10: Healthy drinks

2 Managing data

> **Continued**
>
> **Self-assessment**
>
> Look at the list of data that you have written.
>
> - Did you think about all the data that would be needed to send the message to the customers?
> - Did you think about asking what drink the customers like?
> - Did you think about asking for data about how often the customers buy that kind of drink?
> - Was all the data important and necessary? Could the company send the marketing message without that data?

Questions 2.1

1. Why is it important that data collected is suitable for its purpose?
2. What could happen if data is incomplete or missing?

Data validation

You have just learnt how to identify the data that is needed for a purpose. You learnt to think about what data is important and suitable. You are now going to learn how to make sure the data that is collected is accurate.

Why is the accuracy of the data important? You have previously learnt how to create simple queries to search a database. When we search a database, we want to make sure we get the correct results. We want to make sure that all of the **records** are found that should be found. A record is the set of data about a single object in the database, made up of one data item from each **field** (column).

Look at this database:

First name	Last name	Date of birth
John	Jones	11/01/2001
Sue	Begum	16.06.83
Natasha	Johansson	12th October 2002	← Record
Sebastian	Wong	11th January 01
Paulo	Valdez	14/12/1999

↑ Field

Table 2.1: Table showing differently formatted dates

2.2 Data and databases

If we try to find all the people who were born on 11th January in 2001, what will happen?

We could search for records that contain the data 11/01/2001. The result of this would be John Jones. Is he the only person who was born on that day?

We could search for records that contain the data 11th January 01. The result of this would be Sebastian Wong. We already know that John Jones was also born on that day. Why is he not a result in the search?

We could search for records that contain the data 11.01.2001. The result of this would show no records. Why?

It is important for the **format** of all the data in a field to be the same so that we get accurate search results. A field is a collection of the data about one aspect of every record, such as date of birth. The columns in a database table are the fields. The format of the data is the structure of the data in that field. For example, the structure of a date could be DD/MM/YYYY (meaning the day / the month / the year).

To make sure all the data matches, we can create **validation** checks. Validation checks are rules for the data that is entered into a field. These are some validation rules:

Validation check	Description
Presence check	This is the simplest validation rule. This checks that data has been entered into the field. This is used to stop people leaving a field blank.
Format check	This validation rule makes sure the format of the data in a field matches. A format check for the database could be that all dates entered must have the format DD/MM/YYYY.
Length check	This validation rule checks the length of data entered in a field. You may want to set a rule about how long the data item needs to be in a field. For example: you need to enter 12 digits in a telephone number field.
Range check	This validation rule checks that values are within a set limit. You may want to limit entered values to be between 1 and 10.

Table 2.2: Validation checks

These validation rules can be used when creating a data collection form. They will make sure that the data collected is accurate. They will do this by rejecting any data that a user tries to enter until the validation rules are met.

2 Managing data

Practical task 2.4

Figure 2.11: A class reviewing a book

You will need: a desktop computer, laptop or tablet with access to Source file **2.2_book_reviews.accdb**

You are going to complete a database system for book reviews for your class. The database will be used to collect:

- the name of the person reviewing the book
- the age of the person reviewing the book
- the title of the book
- a review score between 1 and 5 for the book.

The fields for the database have already been created. A review ID is automatically given to each record and is set as the **primary key**. The primary key in a database is a field where each record has a unique entry. This means every record is different.

Open Source file **2.2_book_reviews.accdb**. You will see a database.

Your first task is to add some validation rules to make sure the data collected is accurate. The 'Review ID' field will have a number automatically entered. You need to make sure that all the other fields have a presence check on them. This will make sure that there is no data missing from a record.

2.2 Data and databases

Continued

To set a validation rule, you need to have the database in 'Design View'. Look for this symbol:

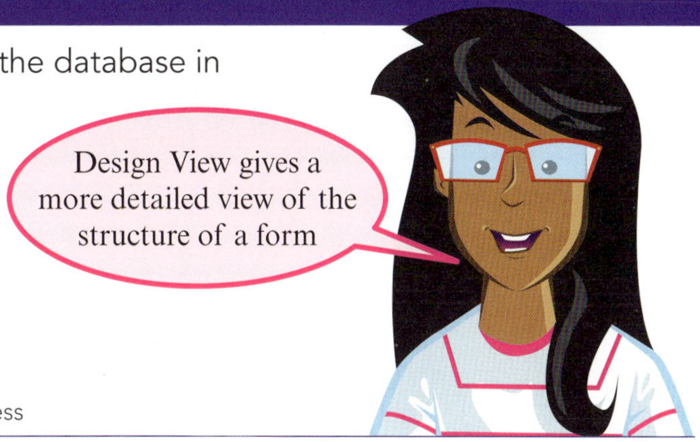

Design View gives a more detailed view of the structure of a form

Figure 2.12: The 'Design View' button in Microsoft Access

Click the symbol and the view will change to 'Design View'.

- Select the 'Reviewer first name' field by clicking on the field name.
- Look for the row in the lower table that is labelled 'Validation Rule'.
- Type the text 'Is Not Null' for the validation rule.

In databases, **null** means unknown or missing. The text 'Is Not Null' is used for validation rules. The system will check that a field has some data in it, or that the field does not have a null entry (no entry). You have set a presence check as the validation rule for this field. To check if it has worked:

- change the view to 'Table View' (click the same 'View' icon as before – be aware that the symbol on this box may have changed to look like a table)
- click 'Yes' to save the table
- type the data for a record but leave the 'Reviewer first name' field blank
- press the enter key to submit the record to the database.

What happens when you do this? You should see an error message that says data needs to be entered.

Set a presence check validation rule for all the other fields in the database.

How did you remember how to set a presence check validation rule? Did you need to refer to the instructions more than once? How do you think you'll remember it in the future?

2 Managing data

> **Practical task 2.5**
>
> **You will need:** a desktop computer, laptop or tablet with access to Source file **2.2_book_reviews.accdb**

You are going to set two more validation rules for the database. These are a length check and a range check. You need to be in 'Design View' again to do this.

Descriptions of length check and range check validation rules are in Table 2.2.

Length check

A person is not likely to have a name that is more than 25 characters long. This means that a sensible length check to put for the name fields would be 25.

Actually, database software automatically gives each field a length check. This is 255 characters. You can find this by looking for the field in the lower table labelled 'Field Size'. You will see that each one is set to 255.

- Change the 'Field Size' for the 'Reviewer first name' to 25. If you get a message saying that some data may be lost from making this change, click 'Yes' when it asks you if you want to continue anyway.
- Change the view to 'Table View'.
- Check that your validation rule works by trying to type more than 25 characters into the 'Reviewer first name' field.

What happens when you try to do this? You should find that it will not let you type any more than 25 characters into the field.

Range check

The review score that can be given to a book is a number between 1 and 5. This means that you do not want people to be able to enter a number lower than 1 or higher than 5. A range check validation rule can be used to do this.

- Click the 'Data Type' field next to 'Review score' to select it.
- Change the 'Data Type' for 'Review score' from 'Short Text' to 'Number' using the drop-down box.
- Look for the row in the lower table that is labelled 'Validation Rule'.
- Type the text '>=1 And <=5' for the validation rule.

This has set a range check as the validation rule for this field. To check if it has worked:

- change the view to 'Table View'
- type an invalid number, such as 6 or 0, into the 'Review score' field
- press the enter key to submit the record to the database.

2.2 Data and databases

> **Continued**
>
> What happens when you do this? You should see an error message that says the data needs to be >=1 and <=5.
>
> Make sure that you save the database with the validation rules that you have created.
>
> 1. Now you will set another length check and another range check. Add a length check for the reviewer's last name. Think about how long the longest surname you know is when considering how many characters it should be.
> 2. Set a range check for the reviewer's age.
> 3. Set either a length check or a range check to any other data you can think of! You could add another field with some new data if you feel confident.
>
> **Self-assessment**
>
> Rate yourself as ☺ (yes), 😐 (almost, but needs work) or ☹ (I can't do this yet) for each of the following statements:
>
> 1. I was able to follow the instructions to set a range check and a length check.
> 2. When I enter a value that should not be possible, an error message pops up.
> 3. I can confidently explain the purpose of a length check and a range check.
> 4. I was able to set a range or length check on an additional piece of data.
> 5. I will remember how to perform both checks in the future.
>
> If you gave yourself a ☹ rating for any of the five statements, what could you do to improve?

Data collection forms

A data collection form can be paper-based or electronic. It is used to collect data that is stored in a database. You will have previously learnt how to evaluate the design of a data collection form. You are now going to learn how to produce an electronic data collection form that uses the validation rules you created.

You are going to use a **wizard** to design and create your data collection form. A wizard is a help tool on the computer that guides you through creating something.

Figure 2.13: A wizard is like an instruction manual on a computer!

2 Managing data

Practical task 2.6

You will need: a desktop computer, laptop or tablet with access to Source file **2.2_book_reviews.accdb**

Open Source file **2.2_book_reviews.accdb.** This is the file that you saved your validation rules in.

- Select the 'Create' tab.
- Click the option 'Form Wizard'.

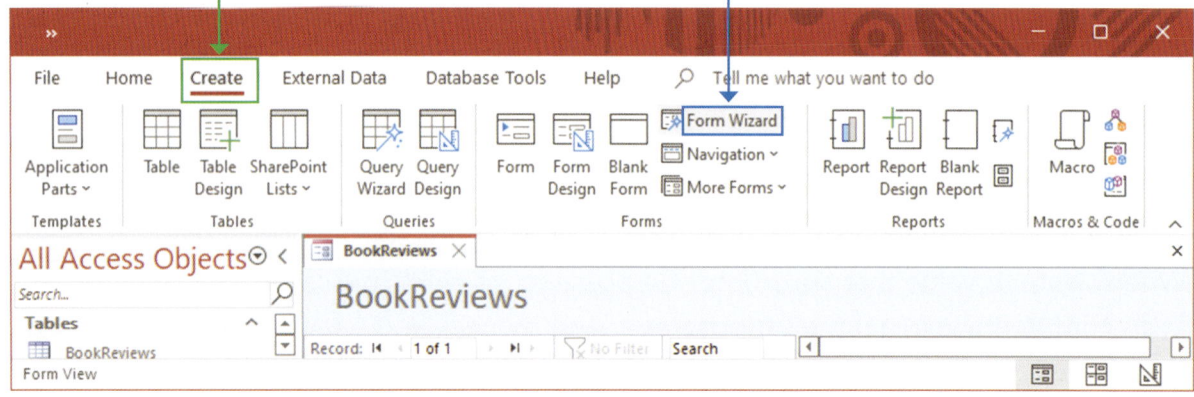

Figure 2.14: 'Form Wizard' button on the 'Create' tab in Microsoft Access

This should open a window that has a list of the fields in your database.

- Click the button that has this symbol >>

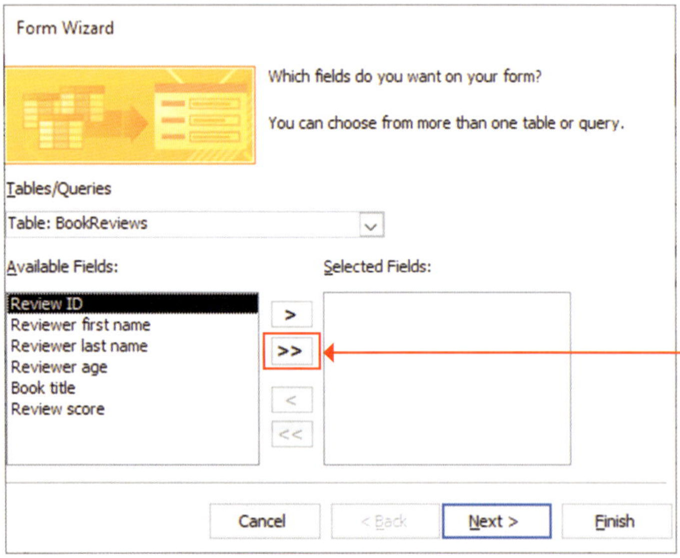

Figure 2.15: Adding fields

2.2 Data and databases

> **Continued**
>
> This should move all the fields from the box on the left into the box on the right. This means that you have chosen all of the fields to be displayed on the data collection form.
>
> **Note:** The single arrow > moves each field across one at a time.
>
> - Click the button labelled 'Finish'.
>
> This should open the data collection form that you have created. You should see all the fields from your database on the form.
>
> You can now use the form to enter data into your database. See if you can use it to enter a record.
>
> If you want to enter more than one record, you will need to move to the next record after you add each one. You can do this by using the arrow pointing to the right at the bottom of the screen.
>
>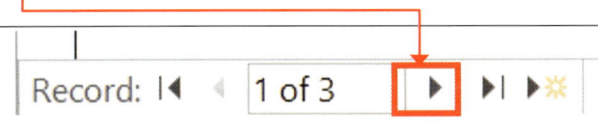
>
> Figure 2.16: Move to the next record
>
> Now that you are an expert, make a help sheet to tell other learners how to create a data entry form using the form wizard. On your help sheet, make sure that you explain each stage in the process. You could use screenshots to help the other learners know which buttons to press.
>
> **Self-assessment**
>
> Ask three learners from your class to use your data collection form to enter a book review into your database. Ask them to check whether all your validation rules are working correctly.

Questions 2.2

1. What is a data collection form?
2. Can you name three different validation rules?
3. Why is validation used?

2 Managing data

Evaluating a database

Companies collect a lot of data that they normally store in a database. They do this so that they can use the data for different tasks in their business. The database needs to be suitable to make sure the data that it stores is accurate and complete. How can you evaluate whether a database is suitable for its purpose? There are things that we can check about the database, for example:

- Checking whether all the data that is stored is necessary. Is all the data needed or is some of it not needed?
- Checking whether the data is accurate. Is all the data stored in a similar way, for example do all the dates have the same format?
- Checking whether validation has been set for the data that will be entered, to make sure all the data is complete and correct.
- Checking whether the data collection form is easy to use and has clear instructions for entering the data.

Let's look at an example of a database. This database stores data about animals and their various features. The table shows the fields in the database and any validation that is set for them.

Field name	Validation
Animal name	
Animal type	Presence check
Animal age	Range check
Animal weight	
Fur description (for example, spots or stripes)	
Other features	

Table 2.3: Database about animals

You are going to think about how suitable this database is for a given purpose.

2.2 Data and databases

Unplugged activity 2.5

> **You will need:** a pen and paper

Zoodledoo are looking for a new exhibit. They want a unique animal – an animal that they haven't already got, with exciting and interesting features.

Figure 2.17: Maybe a red panda could go in your database!

Work with a partner to discuss and evaluate the suitability of this database for searching for this unique animal.

These are some things you should consider in your discussion:
- Is all the data stored about the animals necessary?
- Is there any data missing?
- Will it be possible to find animals that are tall?
- Will it be possible to find animals that can fly?
- Will it be possible to find animals that have certain features?
- Do all the fields have the necessary validation to be able to find the correct data?
- Will all the data be accurate and correct?

If you and your partner answer 'No' to any of the questions, write down an improvement that you would make to the database.

2 Managing data

You have learnt a lot in this chapter about data that is stored in a database, including how to check whether it is necessary, accurate and complete. You also need to be able to identify the data that will need to be stored in a database for a given purpose.

Activity 2.2

Figure 2.18: A games shop needs your database knowledge!

You will need: a desktop computer, laptop or tablet with access to database software

A local games shop needs a database of all the games that it sells. It needs to be able to search the database for information about the games, such as:

- games that are suitable for certain age groups
- games that need a certain number of players
- games that have certain themes
- games that are made by certain companies
- the average length of time that it will take to play each game.

Make a list of all of the fields that would be needed in the database and any validation that would be necessary for each field. Create the database and add the validation that you have identified.

2.2 Data and databases

Continued

Peer assessment

Look at the fields in a partner's database. Which fields did you add that were similar? Which fields did you add that were different? Do you think their database is suitable for the shop? Will all the information about the games be easy to find in the database? Discuss your thoughts about your partner's database with them.

Summary checklist

- [ ] I can identify items of data that will be needed for a certain purpose.
- [ ] I can identify whether a database is suitable for a certain purpose by knowing if the data is limited or has missing items.
- [ ] I know why validation is used.
- [ ] I know how to add three validation rules to a database: a presence check, a length check and a range check.
- [ ] I know how to create a data collection form that uses validation.
- [ ] I know how to evaluate whether a database is suitable for a purpose.

Project: Presentation time!

Figure 2.19: A learner giving a presentation to her peers

2 Managing data

Continued

Sofia has just won an award for creating presentations at an inter-school competition. Members of the computer club have asked her to help create a podcast and presentation. She's asked you to help!

Task 1 Create a podcast

Create a podcast that can be used to teach people how to use a spreadsheet model for what-if analysis.

Make sure your podcast includes:

- an explanation of the purpose of what-if analysis
- some examples of what-if analysis
- how to use the goal seek tool.

You could try to make your podcast more engaging by:

- adding a musical introduction
- adding some sound effects.

If you are not able to create a podcast, you could write a script for the podcast host to read. The script should include the information above about what-if analysis and the goal seek tool. You could also add some notes to your script about sound effects that could be played at certain points.

Task 2 Create a presentation

Create a presentation that can be used to teach people how to add validation to a database and create a data collection form.

Make sure your presentation includes:

- an explanation of the purpose of validation
- some examples of validation rules and why they are used
- how to use a wizard to create a data collection form.

You could try to make your presentation more exciting by:

- adding images
- adding a voiceover
- adding animations.

Ask your teacher if you need support with adding things to your presentation.

2.2 Data and databases

Check your progress 2

1. State the purpose of a simulator. [1]
2. Give two examples of a simulator. [2]
3. State what is meant by a feature of a simulator. [1]
4. Explain what what-if analysis means. [2]
5. Copy the boxes and the terms and definitions onto a piece of paper.
   Draw a line to match each term with the correct definition. [4]

Term	Definition
Field	Helps us gather data from people
Record	A collection of all the fields about a single object in the database – a single row in the table
Validation	A collection of the data about one aspect of every record – a single column in the table
Data collection form	Rules for the data that is entered into a field

6. Copy the table with the descriptions onto a piece of paper.
   Complete the table with the name of the validation rule for each description. [3]

Validation rule	Description
	This rule checks how many characters have been entered.
	This rule checks whether the data entered is within a range of values.
	This rule checks whether data has been entered into a field.

7. What are two things we can check when evaluating the suitability of a database for a given purpose? [2]

3 Networks and digital communication

> 3.1 Types of network

In this topic you will:

- learn to describe the structure and characteristics of a personal area network (PAN)
- learn to describe the structure and characteristics of a local area network (LAN)
- learn to describe the structure and characteristics of a wide area network (WAN)
- learn to describe the characteristics of copper cables and fibre optic cables
- understand how copper cables and fibre optic cables are used in a network
- understand the advantages and disadvantages of wired and wireless networks in terms of their performance and security.

Key words

copper cable

fibre optic cable

HDMI (high-definition multimedia interface)

internet service provider

local area network (LAN)

network

network hardware

personal area network (PAN)

wide area network (WAN)

Getting started

What do you already know?

- You know that devices can be connected together to create a network. You also understand the role of a client and a server in a network.

3.1 Types of network

> **Continued**
>
> - You can explain the role of a range of hardware in a network, including a switch, a router and a wireless access point.
> - You know that networks can have a wired connection or a wireless connection. You know how a range of wireless connections work, including wi-fi, Bluetooth Wireless Technology and cellular.
>
> **Now try this!**
>
> Write down each of the following terms on a separate small piece of paper:
>
> - network
> - client
> - server
> - switch
> - router
> - wireless access point
> - wired connection
> - wireless connection
> - wi-fi
> - Bluetooth Wireless Technology
> - cellular
>
> Work with a partner. You and your partner should fold all your pieces of paper in half and put them into a cup or a hat. Take turns to pick out a piece of paper and give one piece of information about the term on the paper.

Different types of network

A **network** is created when we connect devices together, usually by wires or by wi-fi. A network can vary a lot in size. It could be two devices connected together, like when we connect a computer to a printer. It could also be billions of devices connected together, like the internet. There are three main types of network, each with a different structure. A network can be a **personal area network (PAN)**, a **local area network (LAN)** or a **wide area network (WAN)**.

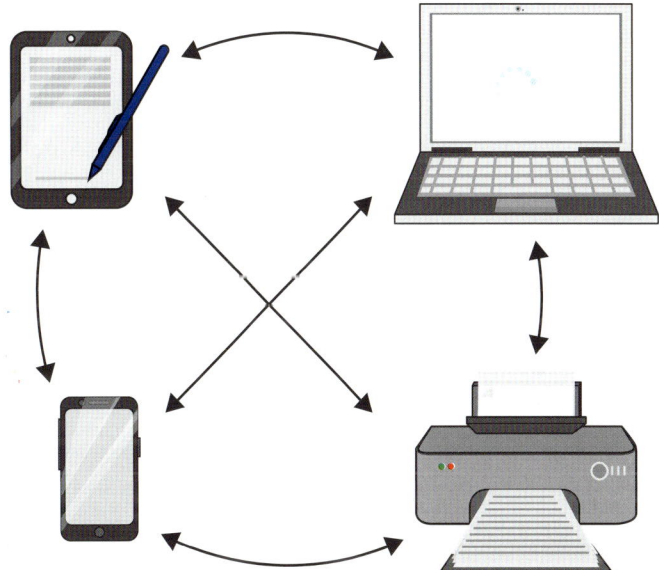

Figure 3.1: Different devices connected together make a network

3 Networks and digital communication

Personal area network (PAN)

A PAN is a network that has a small number of devices – see Figure 3.2 for an example. It often has just two devices connected together. The devices in a PAN are very close together, normally in the same room. In a PAN, devices can be connected using a wireless or wired connection and the purpose of their connection is normally linked to the personal needs of a user. In a PAN, all the **network hardware** belongs to the user. The network hardware is all the physical parts that are needed to create the network, such as the cables or the router.

Figure 3.2: A PAN connecting a smartwatch and earbuds to a mobile phone

Zara has a smartwatch that she uses to track some of her daily habits, such as the number of steps she takes in a day. Zara connects the smartwatch to her mobile phone so that she can see the data the smartwatch collects. This is an example of a PAN. Zara's smartwatch is connected to her mobile phone using a wireless connection. The devices are normally close together and are connected to meet Zara's needs. Zara also owns the wireless access point (WAP) that provides the wireless connection.

Marcus has a laptop that he uses to write a story. He connects the laptop to the printer in his room to print a copy of his story. This is also an example of a PAN. Marcus's laptop is connected to his printer using a wired connection. The devices are close together in the same room and are connected to meet Marcus's needs. Marcus owns the cable that provides the connection.

3.1 Types of network

Questions 3.1
1. How many devices can a PAN have?
2. Where are the devices normally located in a PAN?
3. Who owns the network hardware in a PAN?

Local area network (LAN)

A LAN is a network that can have a small or large number of devices. The devices in a LAN are also close together: they are normally in the same building or site (a small collection of buildings). In a LAN, devices can be connected using a wireless or wired connection and all the network hardware belongs to the user or company.

Arun's family have several devices in their house, including their mobile phones, a tablet and a laptop. Arun's family like to share their photographs and store them on a central storage device. All the devices are connected to each other and to the central storage device. This is an example of a LAN. The devices are connected using a wireless connection, as shown in Figure 3.3. The devices are all within the same building: Arun's family's house. The wireless access point (WAP) that provides the wireless connection belongs to his family.

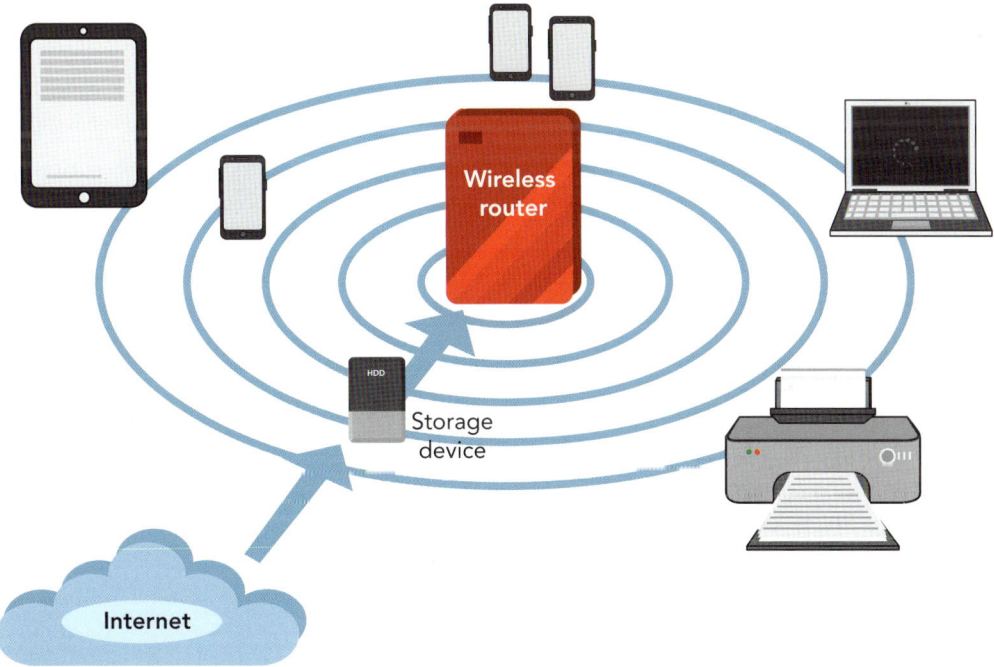

Figure 3.3: A wireless home LAN

A school has several computers in their computer lab, as shown in Figure 3.4. The students need to share data about their school projects.

3 Networks and digital communication

All of the computers are connected to each other. This is an example of a LAN. The devices are connected using a wired connection. The devices are all within the same building, which is the school. The cables that are used to provide the connection belong to the school.

Figure 3.4: A LAN connects computers in a school computing lab

Questions 3.2

1   How many devices can a LAN have?
2   Where are the devices normally located in a LAN?
3   Who owns the network hardware in a LAN?

Wide area network (WAN)

A WAN is a network that can have a small or large number of devices. The devices in a WAN are located over a large area – this could be across a town or city, in several cities or even in several countries. The devices can be very far apart. In a WAN, devices can be connected using a wireless or a wired connection; sometimes both of these are used. Some of the hardware in a WAN belongs to the user, but some may belong to another person or company, such as an **internet service provider (ISP)**. An ISP is a company that provides an internet connection to a house or a business.

Figure 3.5 shows an example of a WAN. Sofia is friends with Marcus. They live on opposite sides of a city. They each have a tablet device that they use to video chat with each other over the internet.

3.1 Types of network

Sofia and Marcus's tablet devices are connected to the WAP in each of their houses using a wireless connection. The WAPs are connected using many different cables that run underground from one side of the city to the other. The WAPs that are used belong to Sofia and Marcus's families. The cables belong to an internet service provider. The devices are connected across the city using the internet.

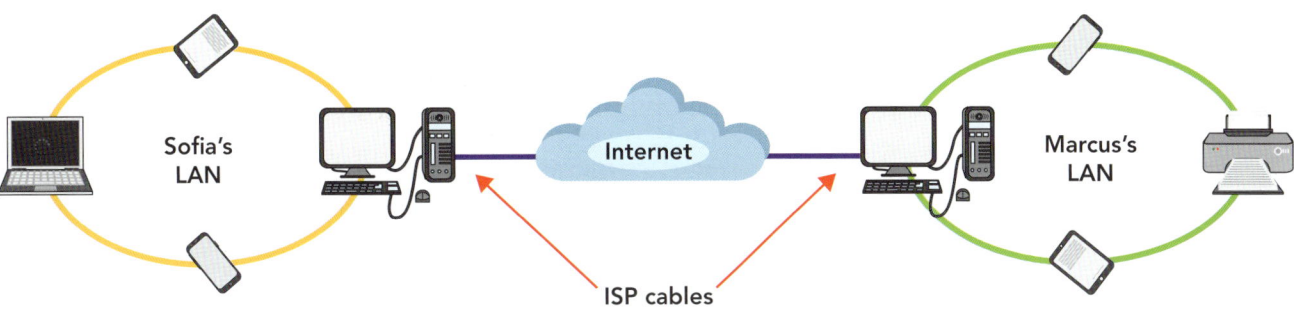

Figure 3.5: Two LANs connected across the internet to form a WAN

A video streaming service provides television programs and movies for people to watch on their televisions or mobile devices. People all over the country are able to watch the videos. The connected devices and computers around the country are an example of a WAN.

Figure 3.6: Watching a film on a tablet

The devices involved could be connected using a wired or wireless connection. If the devices displaying the video are in a person's home, the connection will probably belong to the family. If a device is in a location such as a café, the connection will belong to another person, such as the café owner. Cables connect the router in the house or café to servers in another location, where the videos are stored. These cables will belong to another company such as an ISP or the video streaming service. Some of the connection will use the internet.

> **Did you know?**
>
> The internet is the largest example of a WAN. The internet was first called ARPANET. It was created in the 1970s and was then just a few computers connected together in the cities of Boston, San Francisco and Los Angeles. This gradually expanded and grew into the modern-day internet that connects billions of devices around the world.
>
>
>
> Figure 3.7: Internet connections around the world

Questions 3.3

1. How many devices can a WAN have?
2. Where are the devices normally located in a WAN?
3. Who owns the network hardware in a WAN?

3.1 Types of network

> **Unplugged activity 3.1**
>
> **You will need:** a pen and paper
>
> Write the words 'Type of network' in the centre of your page. Draw a circle around these words to create a bubble for them. Create a mind map around this bubble. The next three bubbles in your mind map are the words PAN, LAN and WAN. Complete your mind map with all the facts you can remember about each of the networks. Aim for three facts per network type. If you can't remember three facts, you could discuss this with the person next to you.
>
> **Self-assessment**
>
> Give yourself a rating from 1 to 3 for the mind map you created.
>
> - I was able to remember one fact about each network without help.
> - I was able to remember two facts about each network without help.
> - I was able to remember three facts about each network without help.

Wired connections

A network can be connected using wireless or wired connections. You have previously learnt about different types of wireless connection, including wi-fi, Bluetooth Wireless Technology and cellular connections. You are now going to learn about two different types of wired connection: copper cables and fibre optic cables.

Copper cables

Copper cables are made of many thin strips of copper wire. Copper cables are the traditional cables that are used in a network.

3 Networks and digital communication

Sofia has some facts for you about copper cables.

FACTS:

- Transmit data using electrical signals that travel down the copper wires.
- Speed of data transmission can be up to approximately 300 mbps.
- Cheap to make.
- Easy to install – many countries already have lots of copper cabling installed.
- Can suffer from electromagnetic interference (when electrical signals disturb another electrical signal).
- Cables are thick, as a thick outer case is needed to stop most electrical interference.

Fibre optic cables

Fibre optic cables are made up of many thin strips of glass, as shown in Figure 3.8. Fibre optic cables are a more modern type of cable that is used in a network.

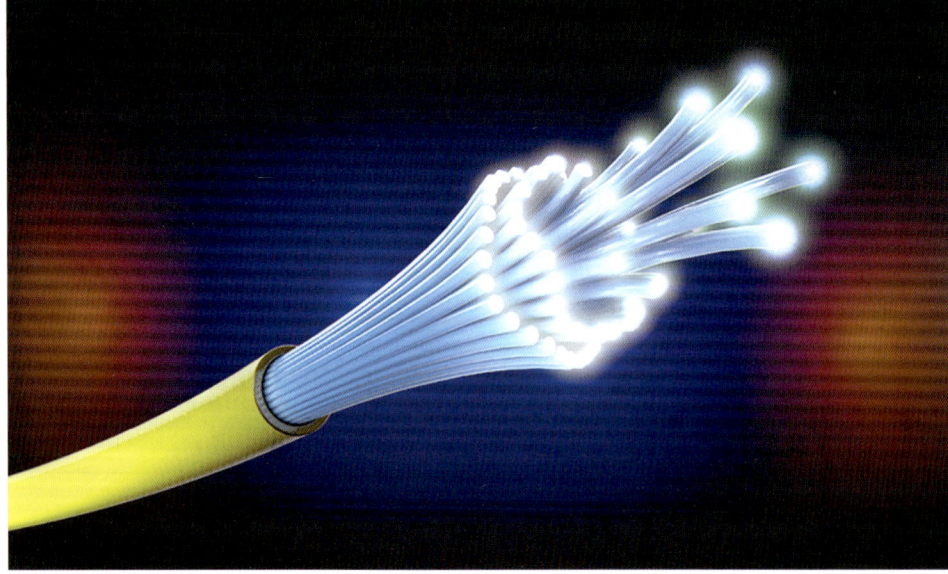

Figure 3.8: Fibre optics

3.1 Types of network

Arun has some facts for you about fibre optic cables.

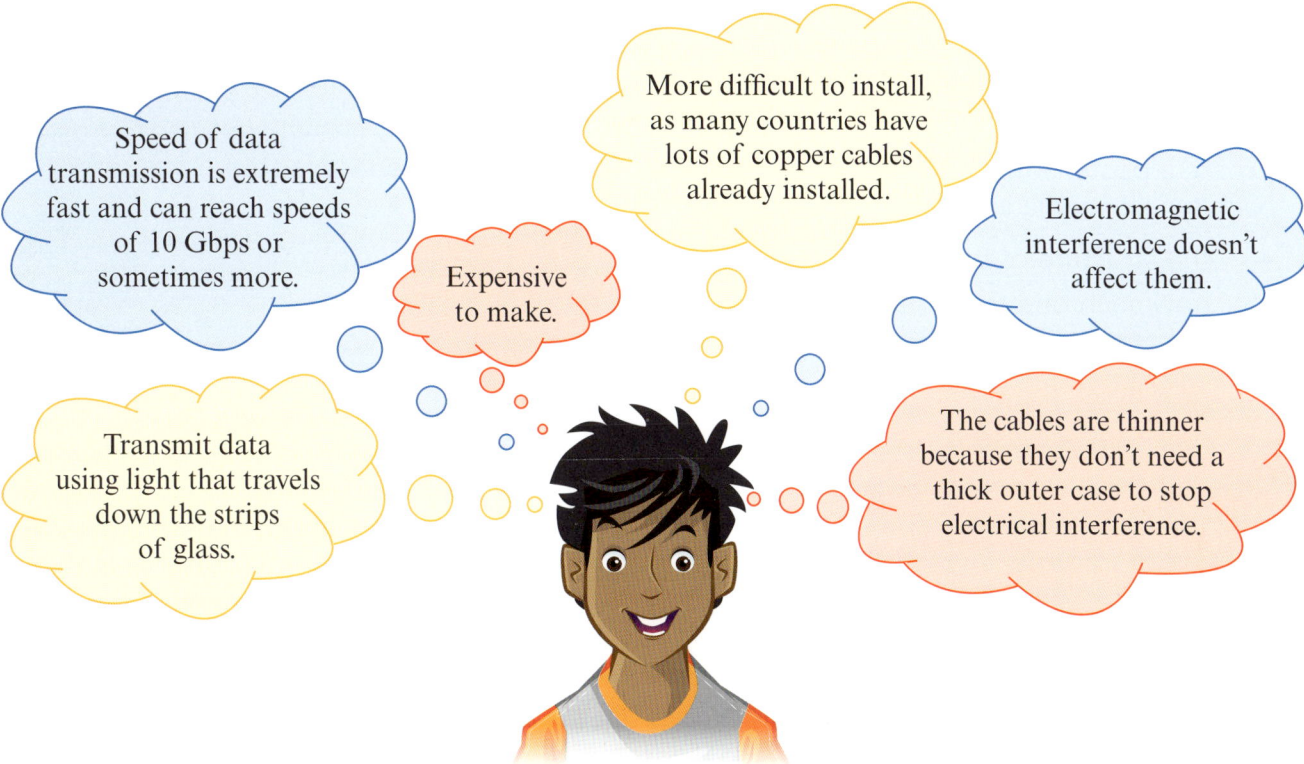

- Speed of data transmission is extremely fast and can reach speeds of 10 Gbps or sometimes more.
- More difficult to install, as many countries have lots of copper cables already installed.
- Expensive to make.
- Electromagnetic interference doesn't affect them.
- Transmit data using light that travels down the strips of glass.
- The cables are thinner because they don't need a thick outer case to stop electrical interference.

Copper cables are still installed and used in many countries. They were installed a long time ago to create telephone networks. They were then also used to transmit data across the internet. There are many different uses of copper cables. These include:

- Ethernet cables
- **HDMI (high-definition multimedia interface)** cables (which can transfer high-definition video and audio)
- (most probably) your phone charger cable.

Fibre optic cables are growing in popularity. This is mainly because of their very fast data transmission speed and the fact that they don't suffer from electromagnetic interference. Many countries have started to lay fibre optic cables underground, especially in and close to cities and towns. An increasing amount of fibre optic cable is now being used to transmit data across the internet. Some people use fibre optic cables to connect devices in their home, but they are mainly designed for long distances.

3 Networks and digital communication

Activity 3.1

You will need: a desktop computer, laptop or tablet with presentation software, a pen and paper

Create a poster with the title 'Copper versus fibre optic'. Include facts about each type of cable including:

- the structure of the cable
- how each one transmits data
- how fast they can transmit data
- how much they cost to make
- how they are used.

You could also try to include an image of each type of cable in your poster.

Peer assessment

Draw the following table on a piece of paper.

It has the title 'Copper versus fibre optic'.	
It includes information about at least one of the facts.	
It includes information about at least three of the facts.	
It includes information about all of the facts.	
What do you think the poster is missing?	

Give your poster to a partner and look at their poster.

- ☺ If you think they have done the task, draw a smiley face in the column on the right next to the task.
- ☹ If you do not think they have done the task, draw a sad face.
- Give at least one thought in the last row about what you think the poster is missing. If they have not included information about all the facts, you could tell them which information is missing.
- If they have included all the information, you could suggest one way that you think the poster could be improved. For example, adding images, changing the font, using a different colour scheme or using a different layout.

3.1 Types of network

Advantages and disadvantages of wireless and wired connections

You now know that devices in a network can be connected using a wireless or a wired connection. Why do both of these types of connection exist? Why are all devices not connected using wireless connections? Wouldn't this be better? Let's look at some advantages and disadvantages of wireless and wired connections. These are explained in Table 3.1.

Wired	Wireless
Wired connections are usually more reliable as they do not suffer from interference from objects like walls and other radio waves.	Wireless connections can suffer from interference from objects like walls and other radio waves.
The connection is usually more secure as it is hard to hack. Hacking is gaining unauthorised access to the network. The hacker would need to physically get to the network hardware and plug in a cable to their device.	The connection can be less secure, as a hacker may be able to guess or obtain the password for the connection, enabling them to connect a device to the network.
It is more difficult to connect a new device, as you need to buy a cable and find space for the device to connect to the network. Keeping wires tidy and safe in a wired network can be challenging. Adding extra wires can make this even more difficult.	It is easier to add new devices – all you need to do is enter the password for the network and request a wireless connection.
Wired connections normally have a faster data transmission speed than wireless connections.	Wireless connections normally have a slower data transmission speed than wired connections.
It is normally more expensive to set up a wired network, as you need to buy lots of cables.	It is normally cheaper to set up a wireless network, as you just need to buy a wireless access point.

Table 3.1: Advantages and disadvantages of wired and wireless connections

Questions 3.4

1. Which type of network connection normally has a faster transmission speed?
2. Which type of network connection is normally more secure?
3. Which type of network connection is normally cheaper to set up?
4. Which type of network connection is normally more reliable?

3 Networks and digital communication

Unplugged activity 3.2

Work with a partner to answer these two questions.

1. Zara has the following requirements for a network:

Our school has purchased ten computers and a printer for the library. It needs to connect them together to create a network. The computers will be spread out throughout the library. The library has two floors. The data that will be sent between the computers in the network is confidential data about students, so it needs to be kept secret.

Discuss with your partner whether the school library should use a wired or a wireless connection. What would be the advantages and disadvantages of each type of connection?

2. Marcus has the following requirements for a network:

My family has purchased two tablet devices and a laptop. We want to be able to share lots of files like photographs and watch high-definition (HD) movies using the internet. The devices will only be used within our own house.

Discuss with your partner whether Marcus's family should use a wired or a wireless connection. What would be the advantages and disadvantages of each type of connection?

> How did you come to a decision with your partner? Did you contribute equal amounts of information to the discussion? How could you work better with a partner in the future?

3.1 Types of network

> **Summary checklist**
>
> ☐ I can describe what a PAN is, including how many devices it can contain, where the devices are located and who owns the network hardware.
> ☐ I can describe what a LAN is, including how many devices it can contain, where the devices are located and who owns the network hardware.
> ☐ I can describe what a WAN is, including how many devices it can contain, where the devices are located and who owns the network hardware.
> ☐ I know the characteristics of copper cables and how these cables are used in a network.
> ☐ I know the characteristics of fibre optic cables and how these cables are used in a network.
> ☐ I can give some of the advantages and disadvantages of wired and wireless network connections.

3 Networks and digital communication

> 3.2 Data transmission and security

In this topic you will:
- learn how an echo check can be used to detect errors in data when it has been transmitted from one device to another
- understand how a firewall helps keep data secure
- understand how antivirus and antispyware help keep data secure.

Key words
antispyware
antivirus
echo check
firewall
spyware
virus

Getting started

What do you already know?
- You know why and how errors can occur in data when it is transmitted from one device to another, for example from:
  - electrical surges
  - interference from radio waves
  - crosstalk.
- You understand that it is important to keep data secure.

3.2 Data transmission and security

> **Continued**
>
> **Now try this!**
>
> Staff at your school have found that errors are sometimes appearing in data that is transmitted from one device to another in the school. The head teacher is trying to find out why this might be happening.
>
> Write an email to your head teacher that explains to them how errors can occur in data when it is transmitted from one device to another.

Error checks and security methods

Data is very important. You probably store lots of data on your computer or your mobile device, such as all your photographs and videos. You want to keep this data secure.

It is also important that the data does not contain any errors. Computers can use error checking methods to make sure that data does not contain errors. You can also use security methods to keep your data secure. You are going to learn about one error checking method and two security methods.

3 Networks and digital communication

Echo checks

You may have previously learnt how issues such as interference and crosstalk can cause errors in data when it is transmitted from one device to another. How would a computer know if errors had occurred in the data? What could be done to find out if this had happened?

The computer could check the data to see if an error had occurred. How would it know, though, if an error had occurred? What method can the computer use to find out?

One method the computer can use is called an **echo check**. An echo check is an error detection system that compares two sets of data to see if they match. These are the steps that happen in an echo check to see if the data contains errors:

1. The sender (the computer that is sending the data) sends the data to the receiver (the computer receiving the data), as shown in Figure 3.9.

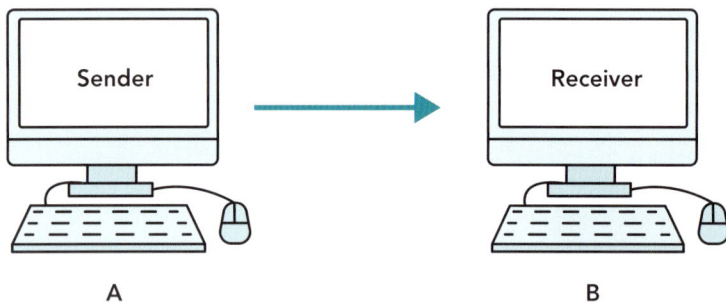

Figure 3.9: Sending data to the receiver

2. The receiver sends back a copy of the data that it has received to the sender (see Figure 3.10).

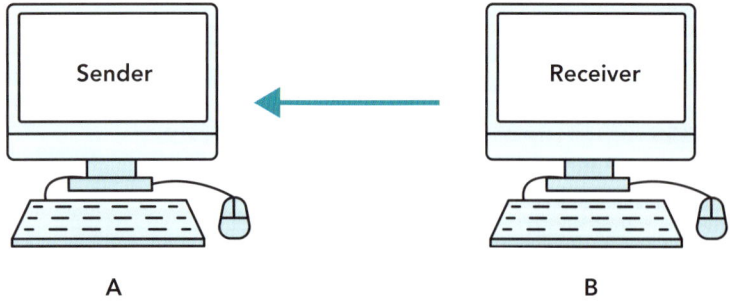

Figure 3.10: Sending data back to the original sender

3.2 Data transmission and security

3. The sender compares the copy of the data from the receiver with the original data that it sent to the receiver (see Figure 3.11).

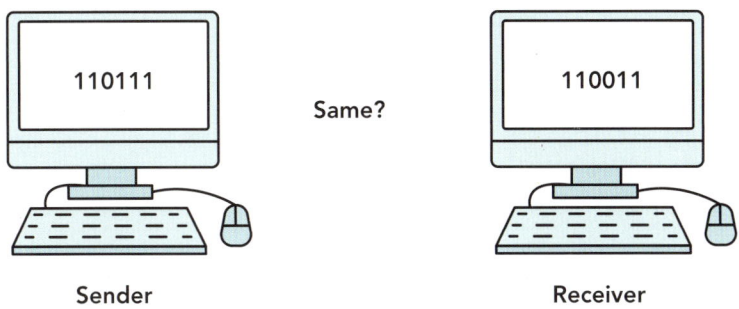

Figure 3.11: Comparing the data

4. If the original data and the copy of the data match, the sending computer knows that no errors appeared in the data (see Figure 3.12).

Figure 3.12: Data doesn't contain errors

5. If the original data and the copy of the data do not match, the sending computer knows that errors appeared in the data. The sender can send the data to the receiver again to correct the errors (see Figure 3.13).

Figure 3.13: Data contains errors

3 Networks and digital communication

> ### Activity 3.2
>
> **You will need:** a desktop computer, laptop or tablet with software to create a diagram or flowchart
>
> Create a diagram or a flowchart to show how an echo check looks for errors in data after it has been transmitted.
>
> #### Self-assessment
>
> Compare your diagram to the list of steps for an echo check here in the book. Have you included all the steps? Does your diagram clearly show how an echo check works? What have you done to make sure it is easy for another person to follow your diagram?

Firewalls

Data can be very important, so most people want to keep it as secure as possible. What would you do if someone gained access to the data that you have stored on your computer or device? How would that make you feel? What could happen if they stole your data? What problems could this cause for you?

You may have previously learnt how using encryption can help keep data secure. Another method we can use to help keep data secure is a **firewall**. A firewall can be hardware-based or software-based. This means that it can be a physical piece of hardware or a software program on a device.

I wouldn't want someone else to read my texts from my mum!

A firewall acts as a barrier for your computer. It is like a bodyguard for your computer.

The firewall has rules for the kinds of data that are allowed to enter your computer. For example, the firewall may have a list of websites that are allowed. When data is sent to your computer, it first arrives at the firewall. The firewall checks the data meets the rules, and if it does, it is allowed to enter the computer. If the data does not meet the rules, the firewall will block it and stop it from entering your computer.

3.2 Data transmission and security

The rules for the firewall show what safe data looks like. A hacker could send data to your computer to try and break into it to steal your data. The rules would show that the data does not look safe and so the firewall will stop the hacker from stealing your data. A firewall is like someone standing guard at the door to your data.

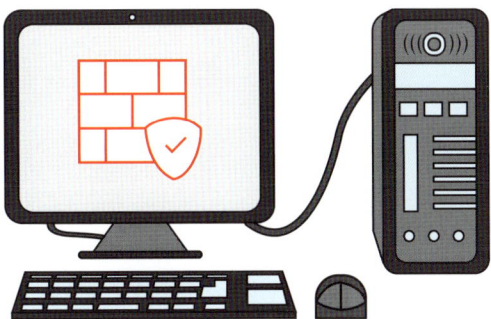

Figure 3.14: A firewall guards your data

Activity 3.3

You will need: a desktop computer, laptop or tablet with image-editing or animation software

Data Defences is a company that provides security software to keep data safe. They want you to create an advert for their new firewall software. The advert will appear on their website and other websites on the internet.

They want the advert to tell people about how brilliant their new firewall is and how it is able to keep their customers' data safe. You could create a still image as an advert or you could create an animated advert. The choice is yours!

3 Networks and digital communication

> **Continued**
>
> **Peer assessment**
>
> Work with a partner. You are going to look at each other's adverts. You are going to work together to create a feedback sandwich for each of your adverts. A feedback sandwich has three parts, like a sandwich. It has a top, a filling in the middle and a bottom (see Figure 3.15).
>
>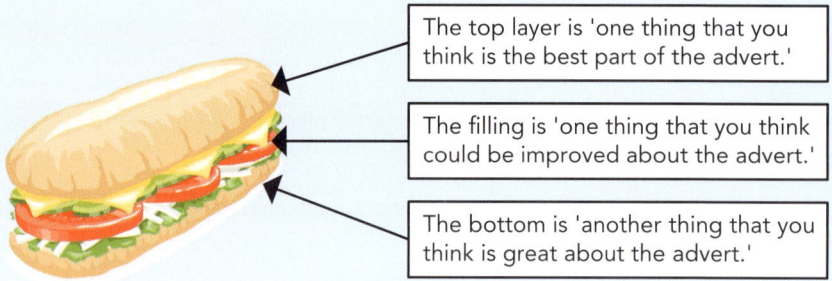
>
> The top layer is 'one thing that you think is the best part of the advert.'
>
> The filling is 'one thing that you think could be improved about the advert.'
>
> The bottom is 'another thing that you think is great about the advert.'
>
> **Figure 3.15:** The three layers of the feedback sandwich
>
> You should discuss with your partner and come to an agreement about what the three parts of the sandwich should be for each of your adverts.

Antivirus and antispyware

You probably download lots of data onto your computer or device. Most people do this on a daily basis. They download data such as emails, images and applications.

Every time data is downloaded there is a risk that it could contain a **virus** or **spyware**. A virus is a type of software that can corrupt (damage) or delete data on your computer. Spyware is a type of software that can record secret information about someone's computer use, such as which keys they press on their keyboard. The spyware then sends this information to a cybercriminal (someone who commits crime using the internet). The criminal can analyse the data to find out things like your passwords.

Figure 3.16: Smartphone with security cameras

3.2 Data transmission and security

It is important to know whether a virus or spyware has been downloaded onto your computer. You can use **antivirus** and **antispyware** to find out if this has happened. Antivirus and antispyware are both types of software and they work in the same way.

When you download a file, the antivirus will scan the file to see if it contains a virus. If the file does contain a virus, a warning message will appear on screen to tell the user that the file contains a virus. The user can then choose not to download the file. Antispyware works in the same way, but it looks for spyware instead of a virus.

Antivirus and antispyware can also be used to regularly check all the files stored on a computer to make sure that none of them contain a virus or spyware. The antivirus will scan all the files and if it finds a virus, it will either delete it or move it to a different place on the computer called a quarantine. This is a bit like a prison for data.

Figure 3.17: Computer quarantine is like a prison for data

The user can then look at the data in the quarantine and choose to delete any they do not want on their computer. When the virus is put in quarantine it can no longer corrupt or delete any data on the computer. The antispyware works in the same way – but it scans for spyware instead of a virus.

It is important to regularly scan files stored on your device to make sure they are safe and do not contain any viruses or spyware. This helps keep the data that is stored on your device much more secure.

3 Networks and digital communication

Unplugged activity 3.3

You will need: a pen and paper

Chatterbot is a new social media company that has a popular new messaging service. It allows users to leave 30-second voicemails for each other. It also allows users to upload images as attachments.

"Hi Sofia, it's Zara. Are you going to the park tomorrow?"

The staff at Chatterbot want to send an email to users warning them of the dangers of downloads that could contain a virus or spyware. They want to remind their users to make sure they are using antivirus and antispyware on their devices and to tell them about the benefits of doing this.

Work with a partner. Write a draft of the email for Chatterbot's manager to send to their customers.

Self-assessment

What have you done to make sure that the information you have included in the email is accurate and helpful for customers?

Stay safe!

It is important to scan every file that you download from the internet with antivirus software. A virus can be built into any kind of download, such as an image, a document or a video. Even if you completely trust the source of the download, you should still scan it with antivirus software to make sure it is safe. Most computers, especially ones at school, will have automatic virus scanning built in. However, if you're unsure whether the computer you are using scans automatically, it's best to check with a trusted adult.

3.2 Data transmission and security

Summary checklist

- [ ] I can describe how an echo check works to detect errors in data when it has been transmitted.
- [ ] I know the role of a firewall and how it is used to keep data safe.
- [ ] I know that antivirus and antispyware are used to scan a file to find out if it contains any viruses or spyware.

Project: Data Daily

Data Daily is a magazine that publishes lots of information about data, including network and data security.

Congratulations! You are going to be doing some work experience at *Data Daily*. You've been assigned two tasks during your work experience.

Task 1 Infographic about PAN, LAN and WAN

Your first task at *Data Daily* is to create an infographic for the magazine that shows the differences between a PAN, a LAN and a WAN. Remember to include graphics, a clear structure, titles, subtitles and lots of facts.

Task 2 Write an article about firewalls

Write a 250-word article for the magazine that will encourage readers to use a firewall and explain the benefits of doing this. You should include an image in your article. You could use the internet to find a suitable image or you could try to create one of your own.

Figure 3.18: *Data Daily* magazine

3 Networks and digital communication

Check your progress 3

1. Give one similarity between a LAN and a WAN. [1]
2. Give one similarity between a PAN and a LAN. [1]
3. Give two differences between a PAN and a WAN. [2]
4. Write the following paragraph on paper and fill in the missing words. The paragraph should describe how an echo check works.

   The _____ transmits the data to the receiver. The _____ sends a _____ of the data back to the sender. The sender _____ the copy of the data to the _____ data that was sent. If the two sets of data match, the computer knows that the data did not gain any errors. If the two data sets did not match, the data gained _____. [6]
5. Give three facts about a firewall. [3]
6. State what antivirus software will do if it finds a virus in a file on your computer. [1]

4 Computer systems

> 4.1 Computer architectures

In this topic you will:

- learn what is meant by primary memory in a computer
- understand that there are two types of primary memory – random access memory (RAM) and read-only memory (ROM)
- learn the role of RAM in a computer
- learn the role of ROM in a computer.

Key words

central processing unit (CPU)

memory

non-volatile storage

primary memory

random access memory (RAM)

read-only memory (ROM)

volatile storage

Getting started

What do you already know?

- You know that a computer has two different types of storage. These are primary memory and secondary storage.
- You know that primary memory can be used to temporarily store data and boot up a computer.

Now try this!

Write down three questions on a piece of paper that will test what information you can remember about primary memory and secondary storage. Fold the piece of paper in half.

Work with a partner.

Give the questions that you have written down to your partner. Count to three and unfold the paper you have been given. See who can answer the questions on the paper in the quickest time. Check your partner's answers to see if they are correct.

4 Computer systems

Primary memory

A computer or device will often have different types of **memory**. Memory is a piece of hardware in a computer that stores data. One type of memory that every device has is **primary memory**. Primary memory is hardware in the computer that the **central processing unit (CPU)** accesses directly. The CPU is a piece of hardware in the computer that processes all the data. The CPU is able to directly access data in the primary memory because there are wires that connect the two pieces of hardware together. The data is transmitted between the primary memory and the CPU using these wires.

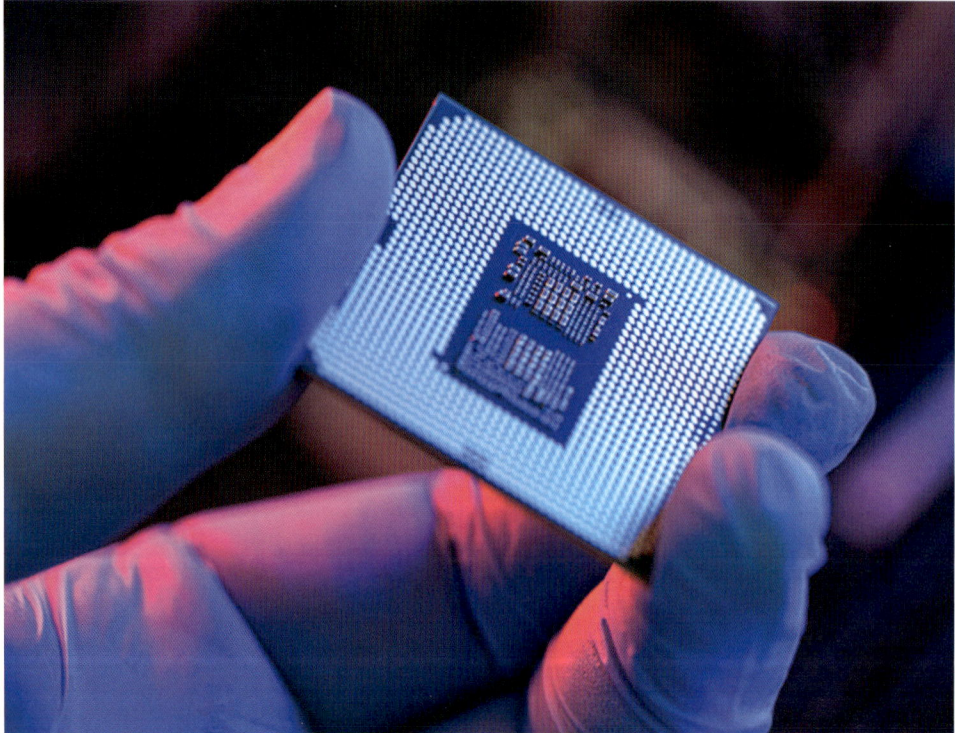

Figure 4.1: Central processing unit

Activity 4.1

You will need: a desktop computer, laptop or tablet with internet access

Use the internet to research three devices that have primary memory. Share the three devices you research with a partner.

Stay safe!

Make sure that you only use safe, trusted websites when researching information on the internet. If you are not sure if a website is safe and trusted, do not open it. Ask your teacher or another trusted adult to confirm if it is safe.

4.1 Computer architectures

There are two types of primary memory. These are **random access memory (RAM)** and **read-only memory (ROM)**.

RAM

Figure 4.2: Random access memory

RAM is a piece of hardware that stores data temporarily (for a short amount of time) while the data waits for the CPU to process it. Zara and Arun have some facts for you about the role of RAM in a computer.

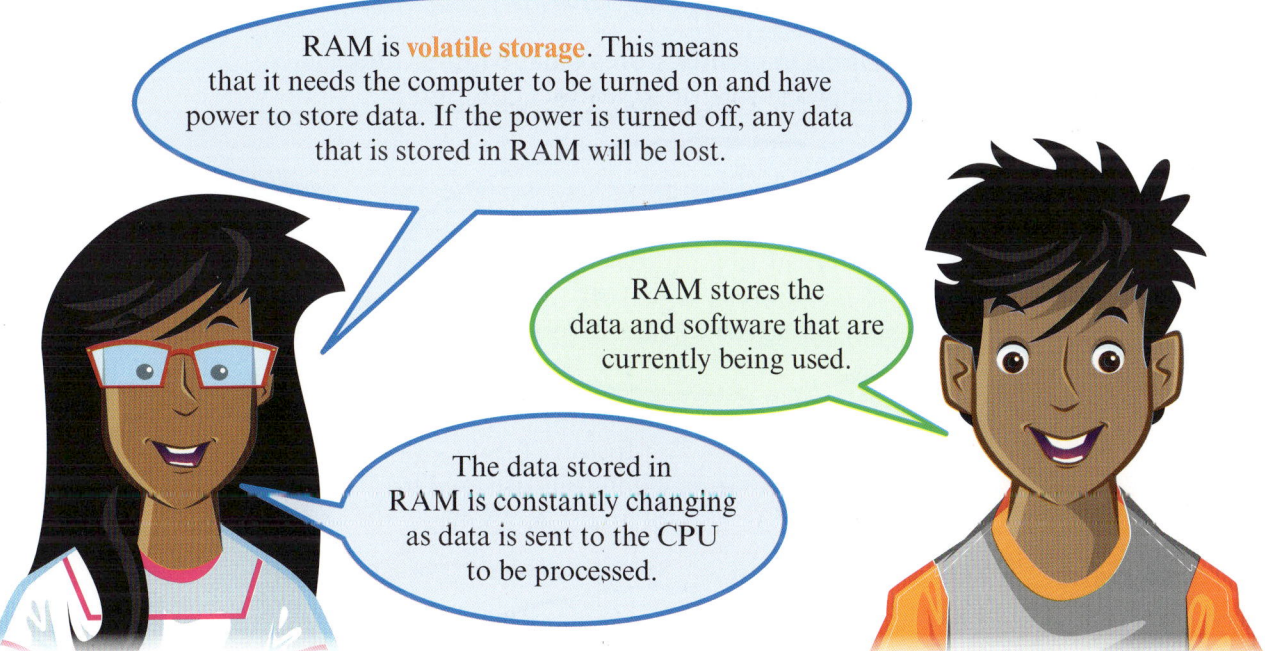

257

ROM

Figure 4.3: Read-only memory

ROM is a piece of hardware that permanently stores data. Marcus and Sofia have some facts for you about the role of ROM in a computer.

ROM is **non-volatile storage**. This means that the computer does not need to be turned on for it to be able to store data. If the power is turned off, the data stored in ROM will not be lost.

It stores the instructions that are used to boot up the computer.

The data stored in ROM does not normally change. This is because the computer needs the same instructions to boot up every time it is turned on.

4.1 Computer architectures

Unplugged activity 4.1

You will need: some coloured pens or pencils and paper

Draw a cartoon that has two characters. The first character is asking questions about primary memory and the second character is giving the answers.

For example, you might choose a duck and ram as your characters. The duck asks, 'Which type of primary memory is volatile?' and the ram answers, 'That would be RAM!'.

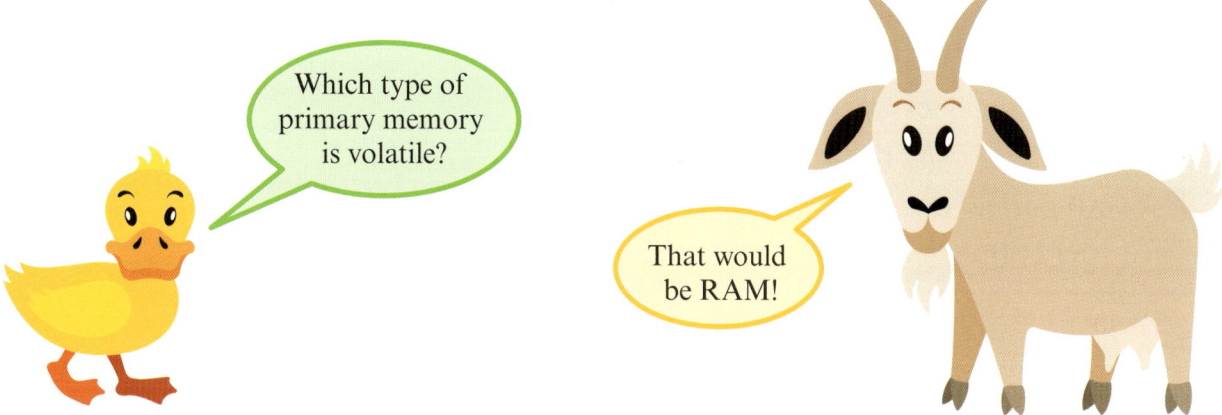

Have fun choosing characters for your cartoon! If you do not feel confident drawing a character, you could draw simple stick people and give each of them a funny hat. You should aim to include at least five questions and answers.

Self-assessment

Look at the amazing cartoon that you have created and complete the following sentences on a piece of paper:

- The best part of my cartoon is . . .
- The part of my work that I am most proud of is . . .
- The part of my cartoon that I would like to improve is . . .
- The next time I try an activity like this I will . . .

4 Computer systems

> ### Activity 4.2
>
> **You will need:** a desktop computer, laptop or tablet with software for creating a poster
>
> Create a poster that gives information about the role of primary memory in a computer. In your poster you should include:
> - three devices that contain primary memory
> - three facts about primary memory
> - an image or a diagram relating to primary memory.
>
> **Peer assessment**
>
> Work with a partner. Look at each other's posters.
> - Tell your partner one thing you really like about their poster.
> - Ask your partner one question about their poster.
> - Give your partner a helpful suggestion about their poster.

Questions 4.1

1. What are the two types of primary memory?
2. Which type of primary memory only stores data temporarily?
3. Which type of primary memory stores the instructions to boot up the computer?
4. a The data stored does not normally change in which type of primary memory?
   b Why does the data not normally change in this type of primary memory?

> **Summary checklist**
>
> ☐ I can describe what is meant by primary memory in a computer.
> ☐ I can name the two different types of primary memory.
> ☐ I understand the role of RAM in a computer.
> ☐ I understand the role of ROM in a computer.

4.2 Types of software

In this topic you will:
- learn the purpose of an operating system
- learn the purpose of a utility program.

Key words

defragmenting

interface

operating system

utility software

Getting started

What do you already know?

- You know that software performs an important role in a computer system. Without software, a user could not use the computer. There are two types of software: application software and system software.

- You know that an operating system is an example of system software.

Now try this!

Write down three facts about application software and system software. Make some true and some false. For example, you could have two true statements and a false statement, or three false statements. Make the false facts believable.

Work with a partner. Ask your partner to read your facts. Tell them to put a tick next to the fact if they think it is true or put a cross if they think the fact is false.

4 Computer systems

The purpose of an operating system

You should already know that an **operating system** is an example of system software. The purpose of an operating system is to allow you to interact with the hardware of the computer and to run applications. It simply allows you to use the computer. Examples of operating systems are Microsoft Windows and macOS. There are many more.

Unplugged activity 4.2

You will need: a pen and paper

Write down as many examples of an operating system as you can think of in 30 seconds.

Compare your list of operating systems with a partner's list. Which ones did you both get? Which ones did you miss? Did you find out about any new operating systems?

4.2 Types of software

> **Did you know?**
>
> The first computers did not have operating systems. Nobody really invented operating systems – they just gradually came to exist as the first computer users programmed the computers to complete different tasks. They then began to add a user interface, which made operating systems look more like the ones you use today.
>
>
>
> **Figure 4.4:** Computer operating system

The operating system is responsible for several different tasks that allow you to interact with the hardware.

Marcus has drawn a mind map to show you the different tasks the operating system carries out.

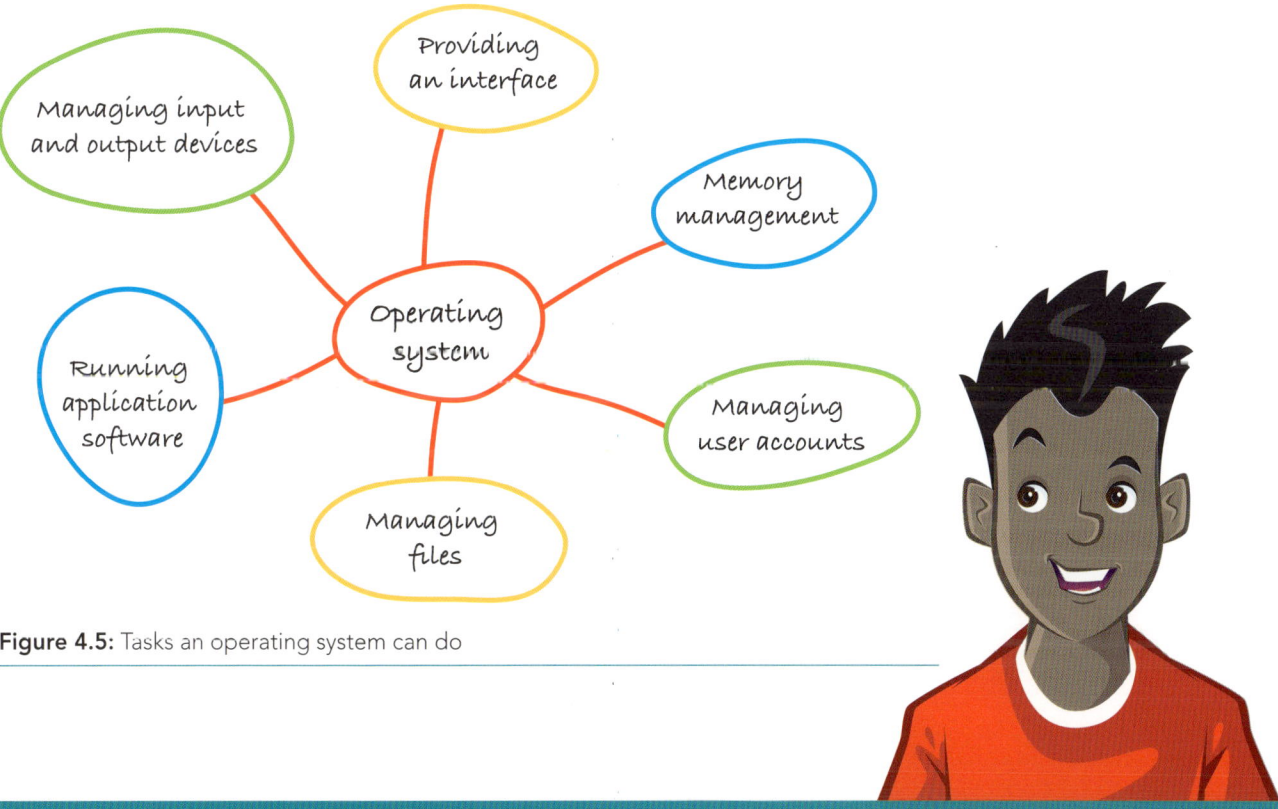

Figure 4.5: Tasks an operating system can do

Providing an interface

The operating system allows Arun to enter data into a computer and lets him see the output of that data. For example:

1. Arun clicks on the spreadsheet software icon on his desktop.
2. The software opens and Arun can see the spreadsheet.

This is possible because there is an **interface**. The interface is the method that you use to communicate with the computer. It is all the boxes, buttons, windows, icons and menus that you see, click on and type into when using a computer.

Memory management

At the start of this unit, you learnt that a computer has memory that can store data. You also learnt that data is transmitted between the memory and the CPU. The operating system is responsible for managing the movement of the data between the memory and the CPU. This is a very important job!

Managing user accounts

Zara's school has given her a user account. She logs into this account when she uses a computer at school. The operating system allows her school to set up a different account for each person in the school. The operating system is then responsible for managing these accounts by keeping the data for each user's account separate. It also helps keep the data in her account safe by allowing her to set a password for her account.

4.2 Types of software

Managing files

Marcus creates files such as documents and images using his computer. He is able to move and copy the files between folders and delete and rename the files that he creates. He is able to do this because of the operating system. The operating system manages lots of tasks relating to files, like the ones Marcus is able to do.

Running application software

Sofia uses video-editing software to create a video for her school project. This is an example of application software. The operating system allows this application software to run on the hardware of the computer so that Sofia can edit her video. Other examples of application software that the operating system allows to run on the hardware are:

- spreadsheets
- web browsers
- messaging applications
- word-processing software
- games.

4 Computer systems

Managing input and output devices

Sofia uses a microphone built into her mobile phone to leave a message on Marcus's phone. She also connects her mobile phone to a television to see a larger version of a video that she has recorded. An operating system manages the data sent to and from all the input and output devices that are connected to a computer.

As the phone is another type of computer, the phone's operating system allows Sofia to see on her television the video that she recorded. It also lets the microphone work in her phone so that she can leave the message. The operating system on Marcus's phone allows the speakers to work so he can hear what Sofia said.

Other input and output devices for a computer that are managed by the operating system include the:

- keyboard
- mouse
- monitor
- printer.

Activity 4.3

> **You will need:** a desktop computer, laptop, tablet or mobile phone with access to quiz software, or a pen and paper

Look at different features of the operating system on your computer. What do you notice about the information it gives you? What does it let you do? How do you think you would use the computer without it?

While you look at the operating system, think about what you have learnt about operating systems. Create a quiz to test a partner about operating systems. Your quiz should include at least five questions. Your questions could have simple true or false answers. If you want to challenge yourself, try creating a multiple-choice quiz that has three possible answers for each question. Be sure to make a note of the answers to the questions you have written!

Peer assessment

Discuss with a partner your thoughts about the features of an operating system. Tell them two things that you thought were really interesting about their ideas.

The purpose of utility software

You have previously learnt that system software is the software that computers use to function. One example of system software is **utility software**. Utility software has an important role for a computer: it is like the housekeeper. It helps maintain the computer and make sure that everything is working correctly.

4.2 Types of software

Utility software does this by doing tasks like cleaning and reorganising the stored data. It carries out tasks such as finding programs that have not been used in a long time and asking the user if they would like to remove them. Sometimes, when a file is stored in a computer, there isn't a space big enough to store the whole file in one place. To solve this problem, the file is split into different parts, or 'fragments', which are stored in different places. Utility software finds all the different parts of the file and puts them together by reorganising all the stored data. This is called **defragmenting**.

Figure 4.6: Utility software can reorganise data into the right order

Questions 4.2

1. What are two tasks that an operating system carries out?
2. What is the name of the part of the operating system that the user uses to communicate with the computer?
3. Which type of software is used to maintain a computer system?

> Do you find it easy to remember all of the things that an operating system can do? How do you remember them? Are there any that you don't understand? If not, how could you improve your understanding?

Summary checklist

- [ ] I can describe the purpose of an operating system, including the different tasks it carries out.
- [ ] I can describe the purpose of utility software, including examples of some tasks it carries out.

4 Computer systems

> 4.3 Data representation

In this topic you will:
- understand that binary and denary are examples of number systems
- learn how to convert a denary number into a binary number and a binary number into a denary number
- understand how ASCII is used to represent characters
- learn what compression of data is
- understand why data may need to be compressed.

Key words
ASCII
binary
character set
data compression
denary
extended ASCII
place value

Getting started

What do you already know?

- Humans usually use numbers in denary form, which uses the digits 0 to 9.
- Computers represent data in binary form, which is 1s and 0s.
- Binary numbers can be used to represent different types of data, such as numbers, characters, images and sounds.
- All data must be converted to binary to be processed by a computer.
- One example of a character set is ASCII. This set uses 7 bits (binary digits) to code each of the 128 different characters of the English language and the number characters 0 to 9.
- You know how an image is converted to binary.

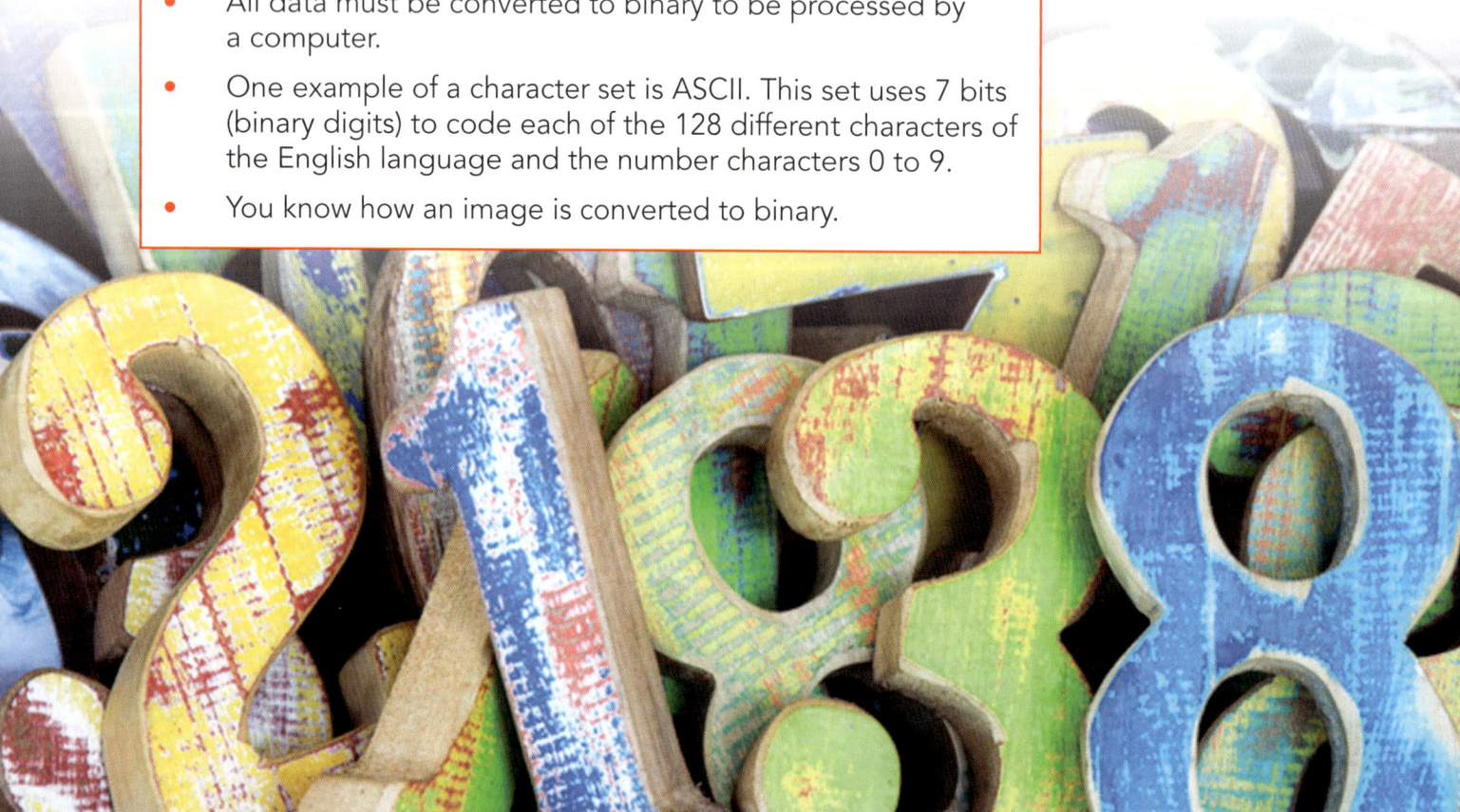

4.3 Data representation

> **Continued**
>
> **Now try this!**
>
> Copy this KWL (Know, Wonder, Learn) chart about binary and complete the first two columns. You can complete the third column when you have finished learning about binary. An example has been added to help you.
>
> | Know | Wonder | Learn |
> |---|---|---|
> | What I KNOW about binary | What I WONDER about binary | What I have LEARNT about binary |
> | I know that a computer can only process binary data. | I wonder how sound is converted to binary so that a computer can process it. | |
> | | | |
> | | | |

The binary and denary number systems

In our daily lives we use a number system called **denary**. The denary number system uses ten different digits: 0 to 9. You have previously learnt that a digit's position in a number tells you what the value of that digit is. The value of each position is called the **place value**. In the denary number system the place values are ones, tens, hundreds, thousands and so on.

For example, the denary number 4152 has 4 thousands, 1 hundred, 5 tens and 2 ones. This is easier to see if we lay out the place values and digits in a table:

Thousands	Hundreds	Tens	Ones
1000s	100s	10s	1s
4	1	5	2

← Starting here and working to the left, the place value increases by the power of 10 (you multiply by 10) each time.

Table 4.1: Place values of the denary number 4152

4 Computer systems

Computers use a number system called **binary**. The binary number system only uses two digits: 0 and 1. The place value in the binary number system doubles each time you move to the left, starting from 1. For example, the units for binary values that have 4 bits (binary digits) are 1, 2, 4 and 8.

The placement of each binary digit in a 4-bit binary sequence represents the presence or absence of a unit of that place value. For example, the binary number 1010 has one 8, zero 4s, one 2 and zero 1s.

8	4	2	1
1	0	1	0

← Starting here and working to the left, the place value increases by the power of 2 (you multiply by 2) each time.

Table 4.2: The place value of the binary digits 1010

The binary number 0001 has zero 8s, zero 4s, zero 2s and one 1:

8	4	2	1
0	0	0	1

Table 4.3: The place value of the binary digits 0001

The example below is a 4-bit binary sequence (a sequence of 4 binary digits). We can use bits with the four place values 8, 4, 2 and 1 to express different denary numbers. For example, if 8 is set to 0, 4 is set to 1, 2 is set to 1, and 1 is set to 0, this equals the denary number 6. You can check this by adding together the numbers that are set to 1: 4 + 2 = 6.

8 4 2 1	4-bit binary will always represent these denary numbers, in this order.
0 1 1 1	This binary sequence has zero 8s, one 4, one 2 and one 1, which equals 7 (4 + 2 + 1)
1 0 0 1	This binary sequence has one 8, zero 4s, zero 2s and one 1, which equals 9 (8 + 1 = 9)

Table 4.4: Two 4-bit binary sequences and how to calculate the numbers they represent

Converting a denary number to a binary number

You can follow these simple steps to convert a denary number to a binary number. We can use an example to make the steps clear.

We are going to convert the denary number 5 to a binary number.

4.3 Data representation

First, write down the binary place values. It is easy to do this in a table.

8	4	2	1

Table 4.5: The binary place values

Compare the denary number 5 to the first place value, which is 8. Is 5 greater than or equal to 8? No, it is not. This means that we *do not* need the 8 place value. So, we can write a 0 beneath it.

8	4	2	1
0			

Table 4.6: Comparing 5 to the first unit

Compare the denary number 5 to the second place value, which is 4. Is 5 greater than or equal to 4? Yes! This means that we *do* need the 4, so we write a 1 beneath it.

8	4	2	1
0	1		

Table 4.7: Comparing 4 to the second unit

We have represented 4. We need to represent 5. 5 − 4 = 1, so we have 1 left. Now compare the denary number 1 to the third place value, which is 2. Is 1 greater than or equal to 2? No, it is not. This means that we *do not* need the 2, so we write a 0 beneath it.

8	4	2	1
0	1	0	

Table 4.8: Comparing 1 to the third unit

Compare the denary number 1 to the fourth place value, which is 1. Is 1 greater than or equal to 1? It is equal to 1. This means that we *do* need the 1, so we write a 1 beneath it. We had 1 left to represent, and we have represented 1. 1 − 1 = 0, so we have no digits left to represent.

8	4	2	1
0	1	0	1

Table 4.9: Comparing 1 to the fourth unit

9 in binary is 1001, because there is one 8, zero 4s, zero 2s and one 1.

4 Computer systems

This means that the denary value 5 when it is converted to a 4-bit binary value is 0101.

Questions 4.3

1. What is the binary number for the denary number 3?
2. What is the binary number for the denary number 7?
3. What is the binary number for the denary number 12?
4. What is the largest denary number that we can represent with a 4-bit binary number?

Unplugged activity 4.3

You will need: a pen and paper

Work with a partner. Think about what you have learnt about the binary number system. You know that the first four place values are 1, 2, 4 and 8.

These are the place values for a binary number that has 4 bits. Can you and your partner work out what the place values would be for a binary number that has 8 bits?

When you have managed to work this out, try to convert the following two binary numbers to denary:

- 00110011
- 10101010

Self-assessment

How did you work out the next four place values for a binary number that has 8 bits? What did you do to check that your answers were correct?

The ASCII character set

All data must be converted to binary for a computer to be able to process it. When a computer converts text to binary, it uses a **character set**. This is a standard set of binary values, one to represent each character (letter or symbol).

4.3 Data representation

ASCII is an example of a character set. It uses 7 bits to code each of the 128 different characters of the English language and the number characters 0 to 9.

However, because other languages use many different characters, **extended ASCII** was created. The extended ASCII character set uses binary values that have 8 bits. This means that it can have 256 different characters.

You have previously learnt a bit about how text is represented in binary. You will now learn more about how text is converted to binary using ASCII.

Each character in the ASCII character set is a binary value. For example, the binary value for the letter 'A' is 01000001 (denary value 65) and the binary value for the letter 'a' is 01100001 (denary value 97).

Character	Binary code	Denary code
Uppercase letters		
A	01000001	65
B	01000010	66
C	01000011	67
D	01000100	68
E	01000101	69
F	01000110	70
Lowercase letters		
a	01100001	97
b	01100010	98
c	01100011	99
d	01100100	100
e	01100101	101
f	01100110	102

Table 4.10: ASCII codes for uppercase and lowercase letters A–F

Uppercase letters and lowercase letters have different values. This is because each character needs to have a separate value. The letters 'A' and 'a' are two different characters. As humans, we know that 'A' and 'a' are two versions of the same letter, but to a computer they are completely different symbols, so the computer needs different binary values for them so that it knows which one to display.

We can look at an example of how a simple word would be converted to binary using ASCII. The word we will convert is 'book'. We need the binary value for each character from the ASCII character set.

4 Computer systems

The binary value for 'b' is 01100010 (denary value 66).

The binary value for 'o' is 01101111 (denary value 111).

The binary value for 'k' is 01101011 (denary value 107).

This means that when the word 'book' is converted to binary using ASCII it is 01100010011011110110111101101011.

Notice how the binary value 01101111 is repeated twice (in dark blue and light blue). That is because the word 'book' contains two letter 'o's.

Activity 4.4

You will need: a desktop computer, laptop or tablet with internet access

CluedUp is a detective agency that specialises in deciphering messages. They need your help with a recent message they have been given. Are you up to the task?

Use the internet to find an ASCII table that has the characters and their matching binary values. You could use a search engine to search for this.

Each ASCII value has a matching binary value that has 8 bits. Use the ASCII table to decipher the following message:

Stay safe!

Make sure you check that web pages you visit are from a trusted source. If you do not know whether the source is safe, ask your teacher for help.

01011001 01001111 01010101

01000001 01010010 01000101

01000001 01010111 01000101 01010011 01001111 01001101 01000101 00100001

Figure 4.7: Message in binary

Peer assessment

Compare your deciphered message with a partner. Did you both get the same answer? Who managed to do it in the fastest time? Did you use any special techniques that you could share with your partner?

Data compression

As you can see from learning how text is converted to binary, a simple word is quite a long binary value. Therefore, imagine how large a file is that contains thousands of words! Your secret message in Activity 4.4 used 112 digits for three words that used 13 letters. Files that contain lots of data can often become very large and take up a lot of storage space in a computer.

Data compression can reduce the size of a file. To compress something means to reduce the size of it. Data compression is reducing the size of a file by changing the data it stores, or by changing the way it stores the same data.

Figure 4.8: Data compression is a bit like trying to fit too many clothes in a suitcase!

Have you ever tried to upload a file to an email or messaging service only to get a message saying the file is too large to upload?

Have you ever tried to save an image on your phone, but you get a message saying there is not enough storage space?

In each of these cases, you can use a data compression tool to reduce the size of the file so that it is much smaller.

Here is an example to show how data compression can reduce the size of the file. Let's look at a fun tongue twister. A tongue twister is a phrase that is difficult to say quickly and correctly. Try saying this:

red lorry, yellow lorry, red lorry, yellow lorry, red lorry, yellow lorry

Have some fun first and see how fast you can say it correctly!

4 Computer systems

Figure 4.9: Red lorry, yellow lorry!

Then, look at the different words. The computer could store the sentence as a whole in a file. However, the sentence only has three different words that are repeated. So, the computer could store each different word and the number of times it appears in the sentence. This means that the computer would store:

Word	Number of times in the phrase
red	3
yellow	3
lorry	6

Table 4.11: Storing words in memory

This doesn't look like a lot less data than the phrase written out, but imagine this phrase appears ten times in a file. The computer would still only need to store the three different words and the number of times they appear. This would be a lot less data.

But how does the computer know where to put the words?

The computer also stores the position of each word in the phrase so that it knows where to place each word when it puts the data back together. When the file is opened, the data is reconstructed to become the long phrase 'red lorry, yellow lorry . . .' again. The computer stores positions 1, 5 and 9 for the word 'red', and then the computer places this word back in positions 1, 5 and 9 when it reconstructs the phrase.

Word	Number of times in the phrase	Position in phrase
red	3	1, 5, 9
yellow	3	3, 7, 11
lorry	6	2, 4, 6, 8, 10, 12

Table 4.12: Storing 'red lorry, yellow lorry . . .' in memory

4.3 Data representation

If you need to store lots of large files on your computer, you will find that you quickly run out of storage space. If you compress each of these files to make them smaller, you will have more storage space available and will be able to store a lot more files!

Compression is also very useful if you need to send a large file to a friend. The more data you need to send, the longer the computer will take to send the file. So, if you compress the file to make it smaller, the file will be sent more quickly.

Compress files to make them smaller so you have more storage space available!

Questions 4.4

1. What is a character set?
2. Why do uppercase letters and lowercase letters have different values in the ASCII character set?
3. What is the name of the method that can be used to reduce the size of a file?

Summary checklist

- [ ] I can convert a denary number to a binary number.
- [ ] I can convert a binary number to a denary number.
- [ ] I know what is meant by a character set.
- [ ] I know how the ASCII character set is used to convert text to binary.
- [ ] I can describe what is meant by data compression.
- [ ] I know why data may need to be compressed.

4 Computer systems

> 4.4 Logic gates and truth tables

In this topic you will:
- learn how to complete a truth table for a NOT gate
- learn how to complete a truth table for an AND gate
- learn how to complete a truth table for an OR gate.

Key word

truth table

Getting started

What do you already know?

- You know that the circuits in a computer contain lots of logic gates. A logic gate is a tiny piece of hardware that uses Boolean operators to control the flow of electricity in a computer.

- You understand the role of the NOT, AND and OR logic gates. You also know the symbol for each of these logic gates.

Now try this!

Draw the symbol for each logic gate and write a description that explains the role of each logic gate.

4.4 Logic gates and truth tables

Truth tables

You have previously learnt the symbols for, and the logic of, the NOT, AND and OR logic gates, and you saw the **truth table** for each logic gate. A truth table is a great way to see all the outputs that will result from all the possible inputs into these logic gates.

The truth table for a NOT gate has two columns. The first column is for the input and the second column is for the output. There are only two columns because the NOT gate only has one input.

Do you remember the truth tables for NOT, AND and OR logic gates?

Input	Output

Table 4.13: The truth table for a NOT gate has two columns

The truth tables for the AND and OR logic gates have three columns. The first column is for the first input into the logic gate. The second column is for the second input into the logic gate. The third column is for the output that results from inputs given in column 1 and column 2. There are three columns because these logic gates have two inputs.

Input A	Input B	Output

Table 4.14: The truth tables for the other logic gates have three columns

Here is an example of a simple structure for a truth table.

Input 1	Input 2	Output

Table 4.15: An example of a simple structure for a truth table

NOT logic gate

The logic of the NOT gate is that the output is the reverse of the input to the gate. So if the input to the gate is 0, the output is 1. If the input to the gate is 1, the output is 0.

This can be shown in a truth table.

Input	Output
0	1
1	0

Table 4.16: Truth table for a NOT gate

The truth table for a NOT gate has two rows. This is because there are two different possible inputs.

AND logic gate

The logic of the AND gate is that if both of the inputs to the gate are 1, the output is 1.

This can be shown in a truth table.

Input 1	Input 2	Output
0	0	0
0	1	0
1	0	0
1	1	1

Table 4.17: Truth table for an AND gate

The truth table for an AND gate has four rows. This is because there are four different possible combinations of inputs.

OR logic gate

The logic of the OR gate is that if either or both of the inputs to the gate are 1, the output is 1.

This can be shown in a truth table.

Input 1	Input 2	Output
0	0	0
0	1	1
1	0	1
1	1	1

Table 4.18: Truth table for an OR gate

The truth table for an OR gate has four rows. This is because there are four different possible combinations of inputs.

4.4 Logic gates and truth tables

Unplugged activity 4.4

You will need: a pen and paper or a mini whiteboard and marker

Work with a partner. Copy out the truth tables for the AND, OR and NOT logic gates (Tables 4.16, 4.17 and 4.18) but do not fill in all the 0s and 1s – leave at least one gap in each row. When you have copied all the tables, swap with your partner and, without looking at the book, see if you can fill in the missing digits.

When you have both finished, compare your tables and see if they are the same. Are they correct? If not, work out where you went wrong and try the exercise again with different gaps.

When you have both completed the tables successfully, try starting with a completely blank table and filling in all the digits for each logic gate.

Activity 4.5

You will need: a desktop computer, laptop or tablet with internet access

Work with a partner.

Think about the role of logic gates in a computer system. Think of three questions about logic gates that you would like to know the answers to.

One question to get you started could be:

- How big is a logic gate?

Use the internet to find out the answers to your three questions.

Figure 4.10: Learners researching

Self-assessment

How did you keep yourself safe when using the internet to find out the answers to your questions? How did you check whether the answers you found were correct?

4 Computer systems

Questions 4.5

1. What is the purpose of a truth table?
2. Why does the truth table for the NOT gate only have two rows?

Unplugged activity 4.5

You will need: some coloured pens or pencils and paper

Create a poster about logic gates that you could display in your classroom. Your poster should include:

- the name of each logic gate
- the symbol for each logic gate
- a completed truth table for each logic gate.

Do you remember how to complete the truth tables for AND, OR and NOT gates?

Summary checklist

- [ ] I can complete a truth table for a NOT gate.
- [ ] I can complete a truth table for an AND gate.
- [ ] I can complete a truth table for an OR gate.

> 4.5 Augmented reality and AI

In this topic you will:

- learn what machine learning means
- learn what augmented reality means
- understand how augmented reality is used in different contexts
- learn how autonomous programming and AI are used in robotics.

Key words

augmented

augmented reality

autonomous programming

machine learning

sensor

Getting started

What do you already know?

- Artificial intelligence (AI) is a simulation of human intelligence within computer systems.
- AI allows a computer to take information from its surroundings and produce an output based on how it is able to process that information.
- AI is used in a range of different ways, including predictive texting, speech-to-text software, image recognition and computer games.
- Robots can work autonomously, and automation is used in industries such as health, manufacturing and advertising.

4 Computer systems

> **Continued**
>
> **Now try this!**
>
> Write down all the key terms that you can think of from what you have learnt so far about artificial intelligence. Try to list ten different terms. Here are two to get you started:
>
> - artificial intelligence
> - autonomous
>
> Make a word search that includes the terms you wrote down. You could use an online word search generator for this, or you could do it yourself by creating a grid with the words and lots of other random letters.
>
> Swap your word search with a partner and race each other to complete them.

4.5 Augmented reality and AI

Machine learning

Some AI systems use preprogrammed rules to make decisions based on data that they collect or that is input. For example, an AI character in a computer game can react to what you do as a player using some preprogrammed rules. It could be that if the player moves forwards, the AI character should move backwards. Perhaps the AI is preprogrammed to follow you, or turn to face your character. The AI character is not learning from what you do as a player – it is just reacting to what you do based on the preprogrammed rules.

Figure 4.11: A character in a video game

Some AI systems have the ability to learn. They can process the data that they receive. The system can learn from that data, and adapt its own rules as a result. This is called **machine learning**. If we give a computer lots of examples of the thing we want it to learn about, it can learn to react to the data that is input. All systems that have machine learning abilities are examples of AI.

For example, you could have a system that is able to look at pictures of animals and tell you what the animal is. You can train the AI system to do this by giving it lots of pictures of animals and telling it which pictures are cats, which pictures are pandas and so on. The AI system will start to learn how to tell if something is a cat from looking at all of the images of cats you give it. Eventually, you will be able to show the AI system a picture of a cat and it will be able to tell you that it is a cat.

4 Computer systems

Figure 4.12: A person taking a picture of a cat

In this example, when you first start showing the AI system the pictures, it will not know what the picture is, as it does not have enough data and rules stored to be able to make an accurate decision. Over time, as you show the system more and more pictures, it collects data from the pictures and learns all the different features of a cat, such as:

- whiskers
- pointy ears
- fur
- a tail
- two eyes.

Figure 4.13: These cats are different, but AI would be able to identify that they are all cats

4.5 Augmented reality and AI

The system stores this data. When it is shown a picture and asked, 'What is this?', the system looks at its rules and asks:

- Does this have whiskers?
- Does this have pointy ears?
- Does this have fur?
- Does this have a tail?
- Does this have two eyes?

If the answer is 'yes' to all these questions, the AI system will answer, 'This is a cat'.

If the answer is 'no' to any of the questions, it will say, 'This is not a cat'.

But what if it was a cat with no tail? We would need to show the AI system pictures of cats without tails. The system will then learn that this is also a cat, and that not all cats have tails. This is how AI systems learn and adapt to become smarter, just like you can!

> **Activity 4.6**
>
> **You will need:** a desktop computer, laptop or tablet with internet access
>
> You are going to contribute to machine learning and see it in action!
>
> Quick, Draw! is an online game where you draw an image, and the AI must guess what it is. For example, you may be asked to draw a book. The AI will then guess what you have drawn. When lots of people draw a book, the AI will start to recognise the features of a book drawn by a human and will learn what to look for!
>
> You are going to play this game. In doing so, you will help the AI to learn and see how it reacts to human input first-hand.
>
> The site will ask you to draw six things in total, and you will have 20 seconds for each drawing.
>
> 1. Open the Quick, Draw! website. Your teacher will give you the web address.
> 2. Press 'Let's Draw!'.
> 3. Follow the instructions on the screen.

Did you know?

There is a test that can be used to see whether a computer is able to think like a human being. It is called the Turing Test because a famous mathematician and scientist called Alan Turing developed it. The test involves asking the computer questions to see if it is able to give responses that can fool a human into thinking they are human responses.

Figure 4.14: Alan Turing

4 Computer systems

Questions 4.6

1. What does it mean when a machine has the ability to learn?
2. Do all AI systems have machine learning?
3. Are all machines that have machine learning abilities an example of AI?

Augmented reality

You may have heard the word **augmented** before. But what does it mean and how does it relate to reality? To augment something means to make it better, bigger or more effective by adding things to it. In computer games, you can collect tokens or buy special features that will augment an item such as a shield to make it more effective. You can also augment characters in video games. If you have played Pokémon, you may have done things like augmenting your Charmander by giving it a fire stone to evolve it into a Charmeleon, and then a Charizard. Or, you might have used a thunder stone to evolve your Pikachu into a Raichu!

Figure 4.15: The world's largest Pikachu sculpture in Shanghai – it is 10 metres tall!

What else can we augment? You can augment your money box by adding more money to it! Anything that we can add something to to make it better, larger or more effective can be augmented.

4.5 Augmented reality and AI

We can even augment language! For example, we can add lots of descriptive words into our conversation to make our language more effective.

For example:

A rabbit is eating the grass.

Could become:

The fluffy white rabbit is sitting in the warm sunshine, happily nibbling the sweet green grass.

How does augmentation relate to reality? **Augmented reality** (AR) is when you look at a real place or object through a device, such as your phone, and see computer-generated additions to that reality. In augmented reality, the computer places information or items over the top of an image of the real world.

For example, if you look at a street in a city through your mobile phone's camera, augmented reality can display information over the top of the image to show where there are useful things, like a café or public transport. Augmented reality can also be used for a heads-up display in a car. This is a display that appears across the windscreen of a car that gives the driver lots of information about the environment outside the car.

Figure 4.16: An augmented reality heads-up display in a car

4   Computer systems

Augmented reality in entertainment

Pokémon GO is a mobile game in which you can 'catch' creatures called Pokémon that are roaming around you. You catch the Pokémon by throwing a ball at it, and if you are successful you can train the Pokémon like a pet! Pokémon GO's AR mode allows you to see 3D models of Pokémon that are available to catch in your real environment. When you look at your phone's screen, you will see Pokémon integrated into your surroundings – you have augmented reality!

Figure 4.17: Eevee, a Pokémon, in the street

There are many more games like Pokémon GO that let you see 3D models of virtual characters or objects in front of you. Do you play any of these games?

Another way we might use AR in entertainment is fun filters. If you have ever used a filter on your phone to make you into a cat or give you cute bear ears when talking to your friend, this is all done using augmented reality.

4.5 Augmented reality and AI

Figure 4.18: Augmented reality can make chatting with friends even more fun!

AR in entertainment is still being developed. Although there are many apps which include AR, some future possibilities include:

- controlling app or website menus using AR glasses
- real-time subtitles when watching a show or movie
- virtual attractions such as museums or galleries
- visiting places you want to travel to, but are very far away from!

Augmented reality in retail

Shops have now started to use augmented reality to help improve the shopping experience for customers. Some shops now have an AR mirror. This is a mirror that can show you what you would look like in certain clothes without needing to try them on. You just scan the code for a product and the mirror will show you what you would look like wearing that product.

This technology also works well for internet shopping. In some online stores, you can use the camera on your phone like an AR mirror to try on clothes virtually. AR can also allow customers to virtually try different hairstyles, make-up or glasses. Some furniture shops also offer an AR service that lets you see what a large piece of furniture might look like in your house before buying it!

Figure 4.19: Someone using an AR mirror to see how different hairstyles would look

You can also use AR to see the value of some objects. AI identifies the object and then augments reality by adding a price tag, and sometimes a link to buy it, near the object. This can help people to identify where to buy something they like, or to see whether something is within their price range.

Augmented reality in education

Augmented reality can be a really useful tool in education. Imagine learning about the human body while actually seeing what happens inside it. You can use augmented reality for this! AR can place information over the top of a real human body to show where all the different muscles and organs are, and how blood flows around the body. This is better than an image in a book, as you can see it moving in 3D and understand exactly where everything is in a real body. You don't even need a real body to augment – you could make a computer-generated image of a human body appear in front of you.

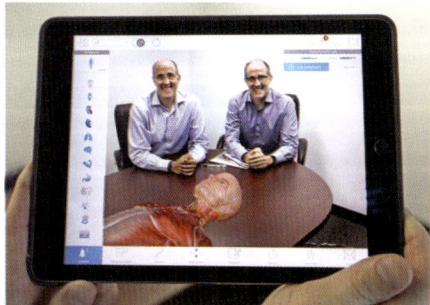

Figure 4.20: Augmented reality showing a computer-generated human body

4.5 Augmented reality and AI

Augmented reality can also be really useful for learning about history. Imagine you are learning about some really interesting ancient Egyptian artefacts (objects that people made). Instead of just reading about them in a textbook, you could use AR to make a computer-generated 3D image of the artefacts appear in front of you. You would be able to see the objects from all different angles and look really closely at all the details. You could even see what is inside an ancient Egyptian coffin!

AR can also let you see 3D models of dinosaurs (even the really big ones), while providing interesting facts about their behaviour.

Google Expeditions lets you see exciting historical events such as the moon landing or volcano eruptions. Imagine how much more memorable that would be than just seeing pictures in a book!

Unplugged activity 4.6

You will need: a pen and paper

Imagine that you are doing work experience at Quizzical, an online quiz company that has lots of different quizzes for their users to enjoy. They want you to create a quiz that will test users' knowledge about machine learning and augmented reality.

They have given you a list of the answers to the questions they want in the quiz, but they want you to write the questions. Each of the items in this list is a quiz answer, so you need to write a question for each one:

- artificial intelligence
- autonomous
- machine learning
- augmentation
- augmented reality.

Peer assessment

Test your questions on a friend. Did they get the correct answers? Did they find any of your questions unclear? Which question do they think is your best one?

AI and autonomous programming in robotics

You already know that AI is a simulation of human intelligence using a computer system. But what is **autonomous programming**? This is when a computer system captures data from its environment and, based on this data, finds a solution and makes decisions to produce an output, all without direct human control.

The system captures the data using **sensors**. A sensor is a type of input device that takes readings from the environment around it. An example of a sensor is a temperature sensor, which measures and records the temperature of the surroundings.

Figure 4.21: A phone showing the temperature of a room

Sensors take readings without any human interaction. In autonomous programming, the computer system captures the data and makes decisions without any human interaction. For example, an air conditioning system would receive readings from a temperature sensor and decide whether warmer or cooler air is needed based on the temperature reading. Some autonomous systems also use AI.

4.5 Augmented reality and AI

AI and autonomous programming in robotics are used in car factories. The robots are built with sensors that allow them to capture the data they need for their task, and the robots make decisions based on this data. For example, a robot that sprays cars with coloured paint will have sensors to make sure that:

- the factory is the correct temperature for spraying the paint
- the robot is the correct distance from the car to spray the paint evenly
- the car is in the correct place for the robot to be able to spray the paint onto it.

The robot will require no human interaction for it to spray the car. It will keep capturing data and making the decisions that are necessary to correctly spray the car. The robot could also have AI. This means that the robot can learn from the data its sensors capture, and make smarter decisions in future based on what it learns.

Figure 4.22: Robots spray painting a car

4 Computer systems

Another example of the use of AI and autonomous programming in robotics is in space exploration. The new Mars rover uses autonomous programming and AI to navigate its way around the planet Mars. It uses sensors to find out where obstacles are and it uses AI to learn how to move around the obstacles more efficiently.

> ### Did you know?
>
> NASA has sent five robots called rovers to Mars. The names of the five rovers are Sojourner, Spirit, Opportunity, Curiosity and Perseverance. When this book was written, the most recent rover to be sent to Mars was Perseverance. It landed on Mars in February 2021.
>
>
>
> **Figure 4.23:** An artist's impression of a rover on Mars

4.5 Augmented reality and AI

Unplugged activity 4.7

You will need: paper and some coloured pens or pencils

Work with a partner to design your own robot!

You and your partner should think about what task or tasks your robot will perform. You should also think about how it will use autonomous programming and AI to complete these tasks.

Create a poster to tell people about your robot and what it will do. Make sure you draw a picture of your robot too!

Self-assessment

Look at the brilliant poster that you and your partner have created and write an ending to these sentences on a separate piece of paper.

- The part of our poster that I am most proud of is . . .
- I think the best thing I added is . . .
- I think the best thing my partner added is . . .
- I think my partner and I communicated best when . . .

Which task helped you learn the most in this chapter? What do you think was most helpful about this task for your learning?

Summary checklist

☐ I can explain what machine learning is.
☐ I can explain what augmented reality is.
☐ I know how augmented reality is used in different contexts.
☐ I can explain what autonomous programming means.
☐ I know how autonomous programming and AI are used in robotics.

4 Computer systems

Project: Technology work placement

There is an online company that creates lots of courses about technology and computer science. They produce lots of learning resources to teach students. Zara has a work experience placement with this online company. Zara wants to make sure the resources are fun for learners, so she has decided to ask the users what they would like.

Zara has been asked to produce three resources for the website, and she has asked you to help. Based on the results of her user questionnaire, Zara would like to produce the following things.

Task 1 Infographic about RAM and ROM

Zara would like an infographic that will help learners understand the differences between RAM and ROM in a computer.

Task 2 Video about operating software

Zara would like a short video to describe the role of an operating system. It should include the different tasks an operating system does. Zara doesn't want any people to feature in the video, so you will need to be creative with how you provide the information.

Task 3 Game about AI, machine learning and augmented reality

Zara would like a game that students can play online to learn about AI, machine learning and augmented reality. For example, you could create something simple like a card matching game with key words on one set of cards and the meaning of the words on another set of cards. The purpose of the game is to match each word with its definition. If you have a different idea, you could create a different type of game. The choice is yours!

4.5 Augmented reality and AI

Check your progress 4

1. Give one similarity between RAM and ROM. [1]
2. Give one difference between RAM and ROM. [1]
3. Describe the main role of an operating system. [1]
4. Give three tasks that an operating system does. [3]
5. a State what a character set is. [1]
   b Give an example of a character set. [1]
6. Give the name of the logic gate that has the following truth table:

Input 1	Input 2	Output
0	0	0
0	1	0
1	0	0
1	1	1

[1]

7. Explain the difference between a standard AI system and an AI system with machine learning abilities. [2]

› Glossary

Antispyware: software that scans files on a computer for spyware and removes it if it finds any — 251

Antivirus: software that scans files on a computer for viruses and removes them if it finds any — 251

Arithmetic operators: symbols we use to perform mathematical calculations, such as +, −, * and / — 22

ASCII: an example of a character set that uses 7 bits to code each of the 128 different characters of the English language and the number characters 0 to 9 — 273

Assignment: storing data in a variable by assigning (giving) a value to it — 21

Augmented: made better, bigger or more effective by having things added to it — 288

Augmented reality: an image of the real world with computer-generated information or objects added over the top — 289

Autonomous programming: when a computer system captures data from its environment, finds a solution based on this data and makes decisions to produce an output, all without direct human control — 294

Binary: a number system that uses only the numbers 1 and 0; the language computers use to store all data — 270

Boolean: relating to a system of logic that uses only two values: true and false, or 0 and 1 — 50

Boolean data type: a standard data type in programming – this kind of data only has two possible values: true and false (or 0 and 1) — 108

Boundary test data: data that is on the edge of being accepted; for example, if a number has to be 1 or more, then 1 is boundary test data — 167

Brackets: the symbols (and) that we can put around code; when used in a calculation, the code inside the brackets is executed first — 55

Call: the command in an algorithm that executes a sub-routine — 128

Casting: changing data from one data type to another, for example, casting the string `'123'` to the integer `123` — 122

Central processing unit (CPU): a piece of hardware in a computer that processes all the data by receiving input, executing instructions and producing an output — 256

Character set: a list of text characters (letters, symbols and digits) and the binary code that represents each character — 272

Concatenation: in programming, joining two strings together to make one string, for example "Foot" + "ball" = "Football" — 18

Condition: a comparison test that gives a true or false result; a situation that must be true in order for something to happen — 29

Conditional statement: (also known as a selection statement or branching statement) a section of code that tells a program to execute different actions depending on whether a condition is true or false; we use a conditional statement when an algorithm needs to make a decision — 30

Constant: a named space in memory used to store data; similar to a variable but can only store data that remains the same throughout the course of a program — 113

Construct: the main tools used when writing programs; constructs include sequence (the order statements run in), selection (checking a condition and running different code if it is true or false) and iteration (repeating loops of code) — 15

Copper cable: a type of cable made up of lots of thin strips of copper metal surrounded by a thick plastic outer case — 237

Data compression: reducing the size of a file by changing how much data is represented, or the way in which the data is represented — 275

Declaration: a line of code that declares a variable or constant (tells a program we want a variable or constant, and what name and value we want it to have) — 116

Declare: to tell a program we want a constant or variable by writing a statement that says what name and value we want the constant or variable to have — 116

Decomposing: splitting a problem into smaller sub-problems; breaking something down into different parts — 152

Decomposition: the process of splitting a problem into smaller sub-problems that are easier to solve — 152

Defragmenting: a function of utility software; the action of reorganising all the stored data on a computer's storage drive so that pieces of the same file are stored together in one place — 267

Denary: the number system mainly used by humans, with ten different values (0 to 9) used in different combinations to represent all possible numbers — 269

Echo check: an error detection system after data transmission that compares the sent data with the received data to make sure they match — 246

ELSEIF statement: a conditional statement in programming that starts with an IF statement, then runs one or more ELSEIF statements until a condition is true; an optional ELSE can run if all the conditions are false — 37

Extended ASCII: a character set that uses 8-bit binary values, so it can code 256 different characters — 273

Feature: one aspect of something, such as a piece of information that is output or an option a system presents to a user — 201

Fibre optic cable: a modern type of cable that is made up of lots of thin strips of glass used to create high-speed internet connections — 238

Field: a collection of the data about one aspect of every record (row) in a database, such as date of birth; a column in a database table — 216

Firewall: a type of hardware or software that is used to check data coming into your computer and block any data that does not meet the rules of the firewall — 248

Flag: the name given to a (usually) Boolean variable – the flag stores whether an event has happened, or if a condition is true or not — 110

Format: the structure of an item of data — 217

Function: a sub-routine that has an identifier and can be called from another program – it returns a value to the program that called it — 128

Goal seek: a tool in spreadsheet software that tells you what certain values in the spreadsheet need to be in order to achieve a goal that you set — 208

Group ID: an identification number that groups micro:bits into sets of devices that can transmit and receive each other's data, but cannot receive data from other groups — 178

High-definition multimedia interface (HDMI): HDMI can send uncompressed digital signals from a video and/or sound source to a screen; HDMI cables can transfer high-definition video and audio — 239

High-level programming language: a programming language such as Python that uses words from natural human language and helps human programmers communicate easily with computers — 11

Identifier: the name we give to a variable or a sub-routine — 17

IF ELSE statement: a conditional statement in programming that starts with an IF statement, then runs an ELSE statement if the condition is false; there can only be one ELSE and this is always the last part of the statement — 78

IF statement: a conditional statement in programming that checks a condition and runs the code within the IF statement if the condition is true; if the condition is false the code within the IF statement does not run; an IF statement can have multiple ELSEIFs and an ELSE — 30

Import: to tell a program to fetch and use code from a pre-existing program library — 135

Indent: to start writing text or code further to the right on a page by using the tab key or space bar, depending on the programming language — 73

Indentation: the act of starting a line of text or code further to the right on a page; in languages like Python, this shows (and controls) which lines of code are part of conditional statements — 30

Input: giving a computer data from a user and adding this data into a program, for example, by typing a word — 13

Interface: the aspect of an operating system that enables a user to communicate with a computer — 264

Internet service provider (ISP): a company that provides an internet connection to houses and organisations — 234

Invalid test data: data that a program should not accept, but that might produce a message, for example, 'That is not a valid option' — 167

Iteration: repetition of a process or cycle — 160

Iterative: repeating; when the same cycle or set of processes is done multiple times — 160

Iterative development: a method of developing a program one part at a time by repeating cycles of development, testing, amending and improving until the program is complete — 160

Key feature: an aspect of something (such as a system) that is particularly important or interesting — 201

Language independent: not reliant on someone knowing a particular programming language; pseudocode is language independent because anyone who knows any programming language can understand it — 14

Linear: in a straight line, or moving from one item in a row or list to the next — 64

Linear search: a searching algorithm that looks at each item of data in order to see if it is the one it is looking for; if it isn't, it checks the next item until it finds the data it is looking for or runs out of items to check — 64

Local area network (LAN): a network made up of devices in the same building or group of buildings, such as an office or school — 231

Machine learning: when a system learns by processing data that it receives and adapting its own rules as a result so that it makes different decisions in future — 285

Memory: a piece of hardware in a computer that stores data — 256

Model: a computer file or program that represents a real-life system or process where data is changed to see what happens — 199

Network: a group of connected computers or devices that can transmit data to each other — 231

Network hardware: physical equipment such as cables, switches and routers that are needed to create a network — 232

Non-volatile storage: computer memory that will not lose its data if its power source is turned off — 258

Normal test data: data that a program should accept — 167

Null: unknown or missing — 219

Operating system: software that allows the user to interact with the hardware of the computer — 262

Output: data that a computer provides to the user, for example, by displaying words on a screen — 13

Parameter: a value that a main program sends to a function when it calls it, which the function uses when it executes — 132

Personal area network (PAN): a small network made up of a few devices that are very close together, often connected wirelessly — 231

Place value: the value of a digit (how much it is worth), which we know from its position in a number; the place value of the 4 in the number 345 (three hundred and forty-five) is 40 — 269

Precedence: priority in the order in which calculations are performed; the calculation with the highest precedence is done first — 55

Predict: to say what you think will happen based on what you can see; with a program, this is stating what output will result from certain inputs without actually running the program — 162

Primary key: a field in a database that gives each record a unique entry to identify it — 218

Primary memory: a type of memory that the CPU (the computer's central processing unit) accesses directly — 256

Procedure: a sub-routine that has an identifier and can be called from another program but which does not return a value to the program that called it — 132

Program library: a collection of useful pre-written sub-routines that we can import and use in our programs — 133

Pseudocode: code-like language that we can use to design a program without having to worry about the exact order and spelling of words and statements; it is somewhere between normal written English and a high-level programming language — 11

Purpose: the reason why something exists – what is it for? — 213

Radio waves: a type of electromagnetic radiation that we use to transmit data wirelessly — 175

Random access memory (RAM): a piece of hardware that stores data temporarily (for a short amount of time) while the data waits for the CPU to process it; it stores the data that is currently in use, and the data is lost when the power is switched off — 257

Random number: a number a computer generates by choosing in an unpredictable way — 144

Read only memory (ROM): a piece of hardware that permanently stores data, such as the instructions to boot up the computer; the data is not lost when the power is switched off — 257

Record: the set of data about a single object in a database, made up of one data item from each field (column); a row in a database table — 216

Return: to send back; the action of a function when it sends a value back to the program that called it — 128

Searching algorithm: an algorithm designed to look for a specific item in a set of data by following a particular method — 61

Selection statement: (also known as a conditional statement or branching statement) a section of code that tells a program to execute different actions depending on whether a condition is true or false; we use a selection statement when an algorithm needs to make a decision — 72

Sensor: a type of input device that automatically takes readings from the environment around it 294

Simulator: a type of computer model that provides a realistic copy of how a real-life system or scenario works 199

Spyware: a type of software that can record secret information about someone's computer use, such as which keys they press on their keyboard, and then send this information to a cybercriminal 250

String: the data type for one or more characters that are treated as text; strings must be placed inside double quotation marks, for example: `"Hello"` 15

Sub-problems: individual problems that result from breaking a large problem into its parts; we can solve the smaller, easier sub-problems separately and then combine the results to solve the original larger problem 152

Syntax: the arrangement of words and phrases in a sentence, and the structure of statements in a programming language, which must obey strict rules 11

Test plan: a formal structure that identifies how a program will be tested, which usually includes the type of test data we will use, the data we will enter, the element we will test and the result we expect 168

Truth table: a table that shows all the outputs that result from all the possible inputs into a logic gate 279

Utility software: software that maintains a computer system and makes sure it is working properly 266

Validation: rules for the data that a user enters into a field 217

Variable: a named location in memory that can store one item of data; when writing programs we can store data in a variable and then use and change the data in the variable during the program 11

Variable declarations: statements that tell a program we need a variable 11

Virus: a piece of software that can corrupt (damage) or delete data in your computer 250

Volatile storage: computer memory that loses its data if its power source is turned off 257

What-if analysis: changing values in a spreadsheet to see what effect the changes have on other values in the spreadsheet 205

Wide area network (WAN): a network where the connected devices are spread over a large area; this could be across a town or city, in several cities or even several countries 231

Wired transmission: a physical connection between two devices; data is sent from one device to another through a wire, such as a copper cable 175

Wireless transmission: a connection between two devices that uses radio waves, not wires, to transmit data; types of wireless connection include Bluetooth Wireless Technology and wi-fi 175

Wizard: a tool in some software that gives the user step-by-step instructions on how to complete a task as they are doing it 221

> Acknowledgements

The authors and publishers acknowledge the following sources of copyright material and are grateful for the permissions granted. While every effort has been made, it has not always been possible to identify the sources of all the material used, or to trace all copyright holders. If any omissions are brought to our notice, we will be happy to include the appropriate acknowledgements on reprinting.

Thanks to the following for permission to reproduce images:

Cover vladystock/GI *Inside* **Unit 1** Fatcamera/GI; Luis Alvarez/GI; Solstock/GI; ATHVisions/GI; SDI Productions/GI; MR.Cole_Photographer/GI; Alvarez/GI; Frankramspott/GI; Skynesher/GI; Klaus Vedfelt/GI; Maryna Terletska/GI; Richard Newstead/GI; Sergey Shulgin/GI; Filo/GI; Coffeeandmilk/GI; Cris Cantón/GI; fotograzia/GI; Jesper Klausen/GI; Mattjeacock/GI; MoMo Productions/GI; Leoimage/GI; Maartje Van Caspel/GI; Westend61/GI; Youst/GI; Alpamayophoto/GI; Sean Gladwell/GI; Dimitri Otis/GI; Johner Images/GI; Lisegagne/GI; Bubaone/GI; Maxiphoto/GI; Artpartner-images/GI; Robert Daly/GI; Peter Dazeley/GI; Yuichiro Chino/GI; Jonathandowney/GI; Michael Regan-The FA/GI; Bortonia/GI; Jonathan Kitchen/GI; Johner Images/GI; Richard Drury/GI; Ilona Nagy/GI; Dougal Waters/GI; -Victor-/GI; David Madison/GI; Vgajic/GI; Dorisj/GI; FotografiaBasica/GI; Flavio Coelho/GI; Imaginima/GI; Yuichiro Chino/GI; SolStock/GI; Catherine Delahaye/GI; PhotographerOlympus/GI; Photo 12/GI; Simon Potter/GI; Skynesher/GI; Amtitus/GI; Izusek/GI; Cavan Images/GI; Nora Carol Photography/GI; PhotoAttractive/GI; Mikkelwilliam/GI; Ivary/GI; Jordi Salas/GI; Jasmin Merdan/GI; Yuichiro Chino/GI; mattjeacock/GI; SDI Productions/GI; JakeOlimb/GI; Marc Mcdermott/GI; Boris SV/GI; We Are/GI; **Unit 2** MR.Cole Photographer/GI; Karl Hendon/GI; DiMaggio/Kalish/GI; Thomas_EyeDesign/GI; Wikimedia Commons: This photograph was made at Freeman Field, Seymour, Indiana. TSgt James R. Schneid is shown at the controls of this early flight simulator. 1943; Easy Company/GI; JuFagundes/GI; Gustavo Ramirez/GI; ArtMarie/GI; Ridvan Celik/GI; Apos Tophy/GI; Kali9/GI; DNY59/GI; Jonathan Knowles/GI; Marianne Purdie/GI; Iuliia Bondar/GI; FatCamera/GI; **Unit 3** Tim Robberts/GI; Vm/GI; Skynesher/GI; FG Trade/GI; Yuichiro Chino/GI; Michael Phillips/GI; Katsumi Murouchi/GI; Christoph Burgstedt/GI; Shulz/GI; Alengo/GI; Bortonia/GI; Jeffrey Coolidge/GI; Filo/GI; Andriy Onufriyenko/GI; Zf L/GI; **Unit 4** Richard Newstead/GI; Mailsonpignata/GI; Mkos83/GI; Jose A. Bernat Bacete/GI; AlonzoDesign/GI; Andresr/GI; RLT Images/GI; Grant Faint/GI; Catherine Falls Commercial/GI; Peter Dazeley/GI; Grafissimo/GI; Olaser/GI; Pasieka/GI; Morsa Images/GI; MirageC/GI; Oscar Wong/GI; Gremlin/GI; Kilito Chan/GI; GK Hart/Vikki Hart/GI; Pictures from History/GI; Future Publishing/GI; Coneyl Jay/GI; Bloomberg/GI; Artur Debat/GI; Metamorworks/GI; David L. Ryan/The Boston Globe via GI; Sciepro/GI; Oscar Wong/GI; Monty Rakusen/GI; Stocktrek Images/GI; Ivcandy/GI; Olemedia/GI; Kate_sept2004/GI; TEK Image/GI

Key GI = Getty Images

Python program Copyright © 2001-2023 Python Software Foundation

Illustrations and photos showing the BBC Micro:bit are created and used with permission from the Micro:bit Educational Foundation

Screenshots from Microsoft Excel and Microsoft Access are used with permission from Microsoft